STUART WALES
1603-1714

W. S. K. THOMAS

GOMER PRESS
1988

First Impression—1988

ISBN 0 86383 439 6

© W. S. K. Thomas

Printed by J. D. Lewis and Sons Ltd
Gomer Press, Llandysul

I Audrey
Clayton a Julia

CONTENTS

PREFACE

This volume is devoted to a period which, rather surprisingly, has not captured the public imagination to quite the same extent as the Tudor period. Yet the fabric is rich and varied and more than deserving of a close and careful study. The book is mainly targeted at sixth-form pupils who will shortly be grappling with the complexities of new Advanced Level Syllabuses, though I sincerely hope that a much wider audience will find within its covers something of value and interest.

Anyone who makes forays into this century is immediately made acutely aware of the immeasurable debt of gratitude that is owed to a host of researchers and particularly to the great pioneering efforts of scholars such as Sir Frederick Rees, Professor A. H. Dodd, Professor William Rees and Professor Glanmor Williams to mention only a few. It is with much pleasure that I record my gratitude to them all.

I record my very considerable indebtedness to Emeritus Professor Glanmor Williams with particular satisfaction. He read the book in typescript and was continually called upon to exhibit the patience of Job and the wisdom of Solomon. His shrewd and perceptive observations and comments enabled me to avoid some, at least, of the pitfalls strewn so liberally along the way. For the errors that remain I hold myself entirely responsible.

I also wish to acknowledge the contributions made by colleagues of mine at Brecon: Mrs D. Widnall for typing the first copy; Mr Denzil Hackford for certain of the maps; and Mr A. Whiley, Mr S. Foulkes and Mr G. Powell for reading the proof sheets with such meticulous care. The staff at Brecon Public Library also proved most courteous and helpful, and Mr Christopher Price, the Deputy Area Librarian, has a particular claim on my acknowledgements.

Powys County Council is also most deserving of my gratitude for its active promotion of the publication of the volume, and in particular I should like to thank most sincerely the Director of Education, Mr Robert Bevan, and the Principal Adviser, Mr Denzil Hackford, for their interest and encouragement.

My thanks are also extended to my wife, son and daughter for their tolerance in allowing me to entertain the Stuarts under the family roof so soon after the departure of the Tudors.

Finally, a most sincere thank you to my publishers, Gomer Press, for undertaking the publication of the manuscript and for such kindly consideration throughout.

Dr W. S. K. Thomas
November 1988

ILLUSTRATIONS

MAPS

INTRODUCTION

A stroll through seventeenth-century pastures can prove stimulating, exciting and revealing since the age bore witness to so many interesting, even fascinating, developments. In the popular imagination the era may lack the pulsating dynamism of the Tudor age, yet in the political, religious, social and economic fields, developments took place which cannot fail to rivet attention, and richly reward the diligence of the researcher. The century cannot, and should not, be studied in isolation since developments from the previous age now reached fruition, and the period also provided a seed-bed for the crops harvested in such abundance in both the religious and economic fields in the eighteenth and nineteenth centuries. Thus, in the century under review, individual Welshmen in government, church, law, business and banking and military enterprises on both land and sea reaped the full benefits of the Union of 1536/43. Wales had now truly entered into the main stream of English politics. On the other hand, the slow development of Puritan Nonconformity during the course of the century, and the technological advances in industry, certainly paved the way for the great religious awakening associated with Methodism, and the ever-quickening tempo of the pulse of that economic development we call the Industrial Revolution.

The briefest sojourn in the century soon helps to dispel the popular fallacy that the Welsh were largely indifferent to the great issues involved in the constitutional struggle between Crown and Parliament. The leaders of the political nation were well informed on what was at stake, and despite their adoption of a largely pro-royalist line, they were not uncritical of certain aspects of royal policy, particularly in the realms of finance, monopolies, the King's prerogative powers, and foreign policy. The Welsh Members of Parliament most ready to attack the royal prerogative were Puritan in sympathy, though Puritanism, in the early-Stuart period, had made little headway in Wales. Indeed, it can be averred that there was very little in the way of determined Puritan opposition to the Established Church before the outbreak of the Civil War despite the distrust of Protestants in Wales, as elsewhere, of the religious policies of both James I and Charles I, a feeling which, at times, even bordered on the hysterical. By the summer of 1642 the die was cast. Only the clash of arms could now decide the issue and the Welsh, despite their earlier opposition, were not prepared to become instruments in the overthrow of the monarchy. Consequently, they drew sword for the King, and the 'Welsh Interest', built up in Tudor and early-Stuart days, was destroyed as a political force. The raising of the royal standard at Nottingham was to mark the end of an era in Welsh politics.

Though Wales was Royalist, and this loyalty undoubtedly constituted an element of strength for Charles I, there was a nucleus of parliamentary families within every shire in Wales whose allegiance was invariably dictated by religious, and commercial and business, considerations. However, the moderately enthusiastic response to the royal cause soon waned. It was replaced by a note of sour resentment as battles took a heavy toll of able-bodied men, areas of a largely unspoilt countryside were ravaged by ill-disciplined marauding armies, the financial demands of an increasingly hard pressed King became more burdensome, and English professional soldiers took over from local amateurs as captains in battle. On 22 August 1485 there had been ushered in a period of growing prosperity for the peninsula west of the Severn and the Dee; on 22 August 1642 the Principality entered upon a period when it was to pay dearly in material terms for attempting to uphold the dignity of the sovereign and the integrity of his throne.

The defeat and execution of the King led inevitably to the establishment of the Commonwealth and the victorious Parliamentarians, flushed with success, and alarmed at the slow spread of the Puritan gospel in Wales, launched a determined campaign to puritanise the country. The Commissioners appointed under the terms of the Propagation Act 1650 attempted to tackle the problem of the 'famine of the Word' mainly through the continued use of itinerant ministers. In many instances these were unfitted for the task, and they became objects of ridicule and derision. Despite the efforts made by the Puritan authorities, the new system instituted under the Progagation Act was, on the whole, a failure and resulted in the country being plunged into a state of religious chaos, with some churches falling into ruin, and services in others being conducted very irregularly. However, the attempt to make Wales Puritan was not confined to thunderous sermons from the pulpit delivered by impassioned and dedicated preachers. Education, as the handmaiden of religion, was also harnessed to the service of the state, and some sixty schools were established in the chief market towns with the avowed aim of removing 'ignorance and prophaneness'. The Triers who, in 1654, replaced the Commissioners, brought the system of itinerants to an end, but the continued paucity of suitable candidates for the ministry resulted in this body being shipwrecked on the same rock.

However, these eleven years created the conditions conducive to the expansion of the sects, though the radicalism and aggressive propaganda of the Fifth Monarchists and Quakers seriously disturbed the authorities and led to a vigorous and sustained persecution of the devotees of the Inner Light.

Though the Puritan Revolution largely failed in Wales, it cannot be denied that it had led to a certain regeneration of spiritual life and this, in turn, was reflected in changes in the pattern of social behaviour. Furthermore, despite the difficulties, Puritan nonconformity was enabled to take a deeper hold on the country and many dark places, according to Puritan propagandists, experienced for the first time the light of the Gospel.

Successive experiments at governing the country without a King, and without a House of Lords, proved abortive, though at local level there was an element of stability since the day-by-day conduct of business was vested in County Committees. The balance of power within the localities was significantly changed since the old, well-established families, largely royalist in sympathy, withdrew from public life; and new men, drawn from the lower echelons of society, who had hitherto remained outside the narrow circle of governing families, replaced them on committees and also in the traditional offices of Sheriffs, Justices of the Peace, Coroners, Bailiffs and Constables. Thes changes were also evidenced in the boroughs, possibly to a greater extent than the counties, because small corporations could be more easily manuipulated, and here again power passed into the hands of parliamentary supporters.

Attempts were made by the Puritan authorities to broaden the base of local government by including representatives of the older families on committees, and changes in the political climate were reflected consequently in the ever-changing composition of these local bodies. However, the true Cavalier never accepted the Puritan regime, tainted as it was by the blood of a martyr King. The hostility of the Welsh generally was further deepened by changes in the pattern of land ownership, the rapacity and corruption of sequestrators, the imposition of military rule, the incidence of high taxation, the enforcement of the narrow Puritan moral code and finally the destruction of the old order of things in the Church. It was not surprising that the restoration of monarchy in 1660 should have been greeted in Wales with genuine jubilation and relief.

The year 1660 witnessed not only the restoration of monarchy; it also ushered in a period of draconian persecution of the nonconformists under the cloak of the Clarendon Code. The fact that nonconformity survived the white-hot intensity of the Cavaliers' lust for revenge for their trials and tribulations during the Puritan ascendancy is striking testimony indeed to the raw courage, strength of conviction and hardiness of those adherents who remained true and steadfast. However, the floggings and beatings, the fines and periods behind bars, were to prove too great a burden for many among them, and these sought to create new lives for themselves in another world. They emigrated in large numbers to America and colonised considerable areas of that vast continent. Even more merciless was the persecution of the Catholics, and despite the favour of the royal brothers Charles II and James II, their numbers were to be seriously diminished.

Closely identified with this hounding of the dissenters was an intolerant Anglican Church since bishops, as well as a king, were restored in 1660. Despite its manifold imperfections, there were within the Restoration Church lay as well as clerical elements that were wide-awake, scholarly and reforming. In the reign of Anne there is evidence even of a regeneration in church life, and this national institution was undoubtedly held in great affection by the mass of the Welsh people. But clerical zeal was not confined to the home front. The foreign mission also attracted their attention, and Anglican missionaries were particularly active in America and the West Indies. Though discord and dissension were keynotes in post-Restoration religious history, politically the country provided a spectacle of stability, and this situation stemmed very largely from a natural dread of the renewal of civil strife and the dominance of the great landowners. These Leviathans monopolised both the county and borough representation in Parliament, and local politics were controlled by those smaller squires who moved within their orbit. Loyalty to Crown and Church became a cornerstone of people's political beliefs. This allegiance was sufficiently strong to enable the country to weather the squalls of disquiet and discontent occasioned by the religious policies of Charles II and James II and the overthrow, albeit without bloodshed, of yet another Stuart. But the 'Glorious Revolution' of 1688 still proved a watershed; the special relationship with the Crown was destroyed; the magic had departed, and the feeling of loss was reflected in the fact that many a Welsh squire continued to toast in his cups the health of the King 'across the water'.

These often dramatic developments in state and church have to be considered in the context of a Principality whose population could hardly have exceeded 350,000; where life expectancy was only too short, and the few years spent here on earth by man could be rather brutish, though in the latter half of the century philanthropists, both lay and clerical, attempted a 'reformation' of manners through the establishment of charity schools and the dissemination of religious literature. In spite of a certain degree of mobility, this was a largely static society and people, living in widely-scattered and closely-knit communities, were innately conservative and clung tenaciously to traditional beliefs and practices. This society was also stratified, and it was generally held that man's position in the hierarchical structure was divinely ordained. However, the whole social scene was straddled by the gentry living in considerable style and comfort in their sumptuous manor houses dotted all over the landscape, and this was a political and social dominance that was to last for a further two hundred years.

The economic base of this society was provided by agriculture and here the emphasis was very much on the rearing of cattle and sheep. However, the incomes of farmers, particularly in mid and

North Wales, were supplemented from the spinning and weaving of very coarse white cloth and over this widely-scattered cottage industry, the Shrewsbury Drapers had imposed effective control. Despite the setbacks caused by the turmoil of the Civil Wars, technological advance and increased demand had led to significant developments taking place in industries like coal, iron, lead and copper and in this expansion native landowners as well as English entrepreneurs had a hand.

Chapter 1

THE EARLY STUARTS

The Second Brutus

'I came not as a usurper but as a
rightfull Kinge discended out of the
loines of the Kinges of this lande'.
(James I, 1608)

On 24 March 1603 the aged Queen Elizabeth died peacefully
in her sleep at Richmond Palace. A long reign, spanning nearly
forty-five years, had come to an end. Robert Cecil, the Queen's
chief minister, and others had already been in secret correspond-
ence with James VI of Scotland, and these machinations were
intended to ensure a peaceful transfer of the Crown from the
Tudor to the Stuart line. Throughout the land the proclamation
of James as King was greeted with relief and, by most, with rejoicing, and in Wales the loyalty of the Welsh to the Tudors was
now transferred to the Stuart Crown. Sir William Maurice of
Clenennau, member of Parliament for Caernarvonshire, and
regarded by the bard Richard Owen as 'penn plaid brytaniaid',[1]
exhorted his colleagues sitting on the benches of the House of
Commons to salute the new monarch as King of Great Britain.
In Wales, the Bye Plot of 1603, which was an attempt by some
Catholics to seize the King, and compel him to fulfil his promise
of granting toleration to the recusants, won little support since
only a handful of Catholics in the south-east became actively involved. When, a little later, in 1604/5, Catholic conspirators
attempted to blow up the King and the Houses of Parliament in
what became known as the Gunpowder Plot, there were still no
answering echoes from Wales. Even Welsh Catholic exiles
abroad, doubtless hoping for his conversion, favoured the
succession of James, the one notable exception being Hugh
Owen who was deeply committed to the idea of a Spanish
crusade to overthrow a heretical King and who threw in his lot
also with Guy Fawkes. James, however, was careful to cultivate

[1] 'Leader of the British party'.

1

King James I

the Welsh and he was well pleased with their 'loyalty, faith and obedience'. He had just cause to remember with gratitude that the second Earl of Essex,[2] who was possessed of vast estates in Wales and, consequently, of influence there, had espoused his right to the throne and through his agent and right-hand man, Sir Gelly Meyrick,[3] had tried to whip up support among his clientele in mid and South Wales. Though Sir Gelly Meyrick perished with Essex on the scaffold in 1601, James I, in 1606, restored his son and daughter in both blood and name.

The execution of Essex, together with the death of the second Earl of Pembroke in 1601, was to bring to an effective end the period of the dominant influence of the great hereditary peers in Welsh life since the next generation of rich peers were to be entirely non-resident. Their influence in Wales had sprung from an intricate web of relationships with the gentry who had regarded them as their patrons. They were an essential part of a social pyramid at the apex of which had stood Queen Elizabeth, whose position the alien James could never hope to occupy. Their passing, consequently, is generally held to mark the dividing line between the Tudor and the Stuart age since the links between the gentry and the great houses were now finally broken.

James, in his desire to consolidate among the Welsh the good opinion found of himself, in 1624 swept away the last vestiges of the old penal legislation of Henry IV. Earlier, in 1618, his desire not to offend resulted in his turning a deaf ear to proposals submitted to him by the Surveyor of Crown Lands in South Wales to colonise certain waste lands there with Englishmen, after the Irish fashion. Most important of all, aspiring Welsh squires soon discovered that they were still welcome at Court and that royal favour could lead to fame and fortune. This was demonstrated by the meteoric rise of John Williams of Conway, descended from the ancient houses of Cochwillan and Penrhyn on his

[2] Robert Devereux (1567-1601), 2nd Earl of Essex, and 3rd Viscount Hereford, was the great-grandson of Walter Devereux, Lord Ferrers, whose quarrel with Rhys ap Griffith, grandson of Sir Rhys ap Thomas, culminated in the revolt of Rhys at Carmarthen in 1529.
[3] He was the eldest son of Rowland Meyrick, Bishop of Bangor, and Catherine, daughter of Owen Barrett of Gelliswic, Pembrokeshire. His devotion to Essex was proverbial.

father's side, and from the house of Wynn of Gwydir on his mother's side. Educated at Ruthin grammar school and St. John's College, Cambridge, he became Dean of Westminster in 1620, and Bishop of Lincoln and Lord Keeper of the Great Seal in the following year. His position of authority enabled him to ensure that many a fat plum fell into the laps of his kinsmen. With the death of James, his fortunes declined since he incurred the enmity of both Charles's favourite, Buckingham, and his Archbishop of Canterbury, Laud. He was deprived of the Great Seal and in 1637 heavily fined, suspended from his ecclesiastical functions and finally imprisoned. The Long Parliament secured his release and Charles, at far too late a date to disperse the gathering dark clouds of civil strife, finally sought his advice. He became Archbishop of York in 1641, a year before the outbreak of hostilities, a tragedy which he might possibly have been able to avert.

But John Williams was unique only in the degree of eminence that he attained. Other ambitious Welshmen sought and found success and riches in other walks of life. The Church certainly provided a well-trodden path for preferment, but there were other avenues for advancement as well. These were to be found in the practice of the law, in martial prowess on land and sea, in the employment of entrepreneurial acumen in the business and banking worlds and in the exercise of administrative skills in the realms of government. For the Welsh, the fruits of the union between the two countries were ripe for the picking, the harvest was varied and abundant, and for the more adventurous and fortunate among them it was an opportunity that was not missed.

So the Welsh in 1603 rejoiced in the succession of James just as they had rejoiced at the landing of Henry of Richmond near Dale in Milford Haven in August 1485. But while Henry VII had been welcomed as the 'son of prophecy', as the promised saviour who would deliver the Welsh from their 'miserable servitudes', James was greeted with enthusiasm because he was the one most likely to guarantee the solid achievements gained during the preceding century and which ironically stemmed, to some extent, from the union of the two countries; he was the one most likely to safeguard the new order of things and doubtless, in their minds also, he was the best guarantor of still more favours to come. There were, of course, other strands to be found in this loyalty, not least among which was the inescapable fact that James, after all, was the great-great grandson of the victor of Bosworth field and that Elizabeth had tacitly acknowledged him as her successor. Furthermore, since there were plenty of Spanish pretenders around, his succession was the one most likely to ensure that the transition from one dynasty to another would be effected without bloodshed, and the horrors of civil strife, as exemplified in the Wales of the fifteenth century, were evident to others apart from Sir John Wynn of Gwydir. Wales now entered fully into the orbit of British politics and so it was with some poetic justice that William Herbert,[4] lord of Glamorgan, hailed the new King as the second Brutus—'ein hail Frutus'.

Although the Welsh embraced the Scottish unicorn in 1603, it is still as erroneous to speak of the largely indifferent attitude of the leaders of Welsh society to the great constitutional and ecclesiastical issues of the day during the period 1603-1642 as it is to speak of the 'blind loyalty' of the Welsh to the throne. Welsh opinion, and certainly that of the political nation, on the matters at stake during the period was informed, and though the gentry on the whole adopted a pro-royalist line, this did not imply that they were uncritical of royal policy. The constitutional struggle between Crown and Parliament was not clear-cut or simple and, consequently, loyalty to the throne and criticism of royal policy were not incompatible. During Elizabeth's reign there had emerged in Parliament what has been described as a 'Welsh Interest'. The Welsh gentry were becoming politically conscious. They eagerly sought seats in the House of Commons since this was a tangible demonstration of the dominant position that they occupied in local society. Their attendance in the House became more regular, they sat on committees, and particularly on those dealing with specific Welsh issues, and in general, within the House, they expressed themselves freely and vigorously. These were good House of Commons' men and it

---

[4] High in favour with both James I and Charles I, William Herbert, 3rd Earl of Pembroke, was appointed to various offices of importance by both monarchs. According to Clarendon, his affability was such that he was 'the most universally belov'd and esteem'd of any man of that age'. Vicar Rhys Prichard called him *colofn y deyrnas* ('the pillar of the realm'). He died on the 10 April 1630 of apoplexy after a 'full and chearful Supper'.

was not unexpected, therefore, that they should have been critical of the attempts by James I and Charles I to exercise the royal prerogative. However, they could not be described as radical and few of them subscribed to the view that the House of Commons should be the supreme body in the Constitution. Charles Price of Pilleth in Radnorshire was probably reflecting the standpoint of most of the Welsh members when he described Parliament as the body and the King as the head and added that 'if any blow be given to the body the head will feale it, and if there be any violation of the previledge of this house it will concerne the whole Kingdome'. It was not until the eve of the Civil War that the issues over which King and Parliament were at variance were presented as a straightforward choice. When these issues were finally defined, when the crunch eventually came, most of the Welsh gentry declared for the King.

The political issues which caused rumbles of discontent in the ranks of the Welsh gentry were pre-eminently those that related to finance, the grant of monopolies, such instruments of the King's prerogative as the Council in Wales and the Marches, and finally foreign policy.

Since Wales, economically, despite the improvements effected under the Tudors, was still a comparatively backward country, dependent on a not-too-prosperous pastoral economy, it was very natural that the Welsh should have resisted the attempts made by the early Stuarts to exploit the country financially. Even the collection of the parliamentary subsidy was resisted. In 1626 the Welsh counties were very reluctant to meet the royal request for a subsidy, though Carmarthen and Radnor did pay up in 1627. Monmouthshire and Pembrokeshire, after angry county meetings, refused point blank to pay, the former on the ground that the subsidy had not been approved by Parliament and the latter on the ground of their 'extraordinary burdens'. When James attempted to apply the royal right of purveyance there were howls of protest from Wales, and particularly from the chief cattle-raising counties, those of Anglesey, Flint, Denbigh, Brecknock and Glamorgan. Purveyance, a feudal survival, was the practice by which the King could stock his larder from provisions provided by his subjects when he and his court went on progress. Despite the fact that James never visited Wales, his purveyors still made compulsory purchase of Welsh cattle at prices fixed by themselves, and their activities certainly exercised a debilitating effect on this vital Welsh trade. A parliamentary committee was established to enquire into the abuse, and the members of Parliament for Denbigh, Brecknock and Monmouth were co-opted on to it. However, the King promised to review the situation and thereupon the matter was dropped.

Another expedient adopted by the early Stuarts, and particularly Charles I, to raise money was forced loans and benevolences. There was much opposition to the benevolence of 1622 which was required to assist Frederick, Elector Palatine,[5] James's son-in-law, and the forced loan of 1626 was largely a failure in Wales. Breconshire contributed only £105, Flint excused itself on the ground that it was a poor county, while Glamorgan complained of the attacks by pirates in the Bristol Channel. When in 1629 Charles I decided to rule without Parliament, his main financial device for raising money in the absence of parliamentary grants was ship money. Originally an occasional levy on coastal towns in lieu of providing a ship for the King's service, in 1635 it was extended to embrace inland towns and counties. In 1635 the total contribution which Wales had to make amounted to £9000, and each county was allocated a specific sum. Glamorgan's share was £1449, Brecknock £933 and for a much smaller county like Radnor the amount was £490. It is significant that not one of the Welsh counties was to object to this impost on the ground of principle, possibly because visible benefits accrued from its payment, since improvements were made to the navy, and attempts were made to rid the shipping lanes of marauders and particularly the Barbary pirates. These very desirable objectives undoubtedly had the effect of influencing Welsh attitudes. Nevertheless, there were loud protests against the amount of the exactions. While Glamorgan in 1635 paid promptly, the town of Pembroke aired its grievances in no uncertain manner. Still, on the whole, in 1635 the collection of ship money in Wales was effected quite smoothly; there would appear to have been no village

[5] James had married his daughter, Elizabeth, to the Elector Palatine, a leading German Protestant, in 1613. In 1618 Frederick was invited by Czech Protestants to accept the Crown of Bohemia. His acceptance plunged Germany into the Thirty Years War, 1618-1648.

Hampdens[6] to challenge the King's right. However, the prospect of ship money becoming an annual exaction, and the fifth successive levy in 1638 had made this demonstrably clear, resulted in protests in Wales gaining in volume and vehemence. Doubtless, the opposition displayed by such a person as the very successful lawyer, David Jenkins of Hensol in Glamorgan, typified the general mood. When in 1637 news of Hampden's trial reached Wales considerable interest was understandably aroused. In 1635 two counties only had defaulted; in 1639 all the counties in Wales were guilty of this to a greater or lesser extent. The sixth and final levy in 1640 happened to co-incide with the King's demand for soldiers from Wales to fight against the Scottish Covenanters, Breconshire's contribution being one hundred soldiers to meet the King at York. Welsh reaction to these twin burdens was predictably strong and the elections for the Long Parliament, which met on the 3 November 1640, resulted in the return from Wales of the most critical body of members to have sat there hitherto.

Closely linked with finance as a bone of contention between the early Stuarts and their Parliaments was the grant or sale of monopolies, often to royal favourites. Even during Elizabeth's reign, monopolies had aroused opposition and in the Parliaments of 1571, 1597 and 1601 members had denounced the system. In the later Parliaments of James the issue was to crop up again, and two monopolies in particular were to cause a stir. One was the monopoly of the sale of Welsh cloth held by the Shrewsbury Drapers' Company, and the other was the monopoly of the sale of Welsh butter in the hands of a syndicate of English speculators. After a protracted struggle Welsh members, powerfully supported by London merchants who championed the cause of freedom of trade, succeeded in having both monopolies quashed, although in the event the victory was to prove an empty one.

Instruments of the King's prerogative also came under attack and the early decades of the seventeenth century bore witness to a sustained attack on the Council in Wales and the Marches. Even

---

[6] This was John Hampden, a Buckinghamshire squire, who was imprisoned for refusing to pay ship money. The case was tried in the Court of Exchequer in 1637 where the judges, by a narrow majority of two (seven voices to five), decided in favour of the Crown.

in the sixteenth century the Council had never been completely immune from criticism since its wide powers had overlapped the jurisdictions of such courts as Quarter Sessions, Great Sessions, Assizes, Common Pleas, King's Bench and the ecclesiastical courts. Furthermore, during Elizabeth's reign Bristol (1562) and Cheshire (1569) had succeeded in freeing themselves from the control of the Council, while the attempts by Worcester and Gloucester to gain similar exemptions had failed. During the last decade of the century an attack on a much broader front had been launched on the jurisdiction of the Council. This was the attempt to extend the powers of King's Bench and Common Pleas, to transfer the civil jurisdiction of Great Sessions in Wales to Westminster, and to abolish the Council's authority over the four neighbouring English shires of Gloucester, Worcester, Shropshire and Hereford. The principal agents of this onslaught were the Westminster lawyers and the English border gentry. The Westminster lawyers attacked the Council because its authority threatened their incomes derived in the main from legal fees; the English border gentry were critical because of the increasing incidence of fines imposed upon them, and also because the Council, by its very presence, through its supervisory role, challenged their local dominance and all this at a time when for social and commercial reasons they were averting their faces from Wales and looking more and more towards London.

However, though much of the opposition was motivated by self-interest, and this applied to some of the leading families at Court as well as to the Westminster lawyers and border gentry, the Council itself was also partly responsible because in many of its practices it was not blameless. Officials were guilty of pluralism and absenteeism and, furthermore, there had been a substantial increase in their number; other officials were corrupt and mainly interested in the multiplication of fees, and it was for this reason that so much encouragement was given to malicious suits, and so much latitude granted to disreputable informers. Quarrels among the judges only served further to undermine the authority and prestige of the Council.

The increase in the Council's activities in the 1630s was followed by renewed attacks on its authority when the Long Parliament met in 1640, and in 1641, 'divided by jealousies and enfeebled by fear', its jurisdiction came virtually to an end.[7] Well might the Chief Justice of Chester, Sir Thomas Milward, remark that 'they did but attend a dying body'.

Just as attacks on the Council of Wales impinged on the royal prerogative, so also did the Commons' insistence on having a say in the conduct of foreign affairs. James I, very sensibly, had brought the long and profitless struggle with Spain to an end in 1604, a peace which provided little satisfaction to many Welsh members of Parliament steeped in the Elizabethan tradition of hostility toward Spain, with the dreaded *dynion duon* ('black men'). Furthermore, the menace of that Iberian kingdom was still very much of a reality in the minds of Welshmen since memories of impending invasion, or threats of invasion, on the highly vulnerable coasts of Wales were still fresh in people's minds, and the flying visit of Hugh Owen of Gwaenynog, a recent convert to Catholicism, to his home, which greatly emboldened local recusants, was not calculated to allay fears about the vulnerability of Anglesey's defences. To the committed Protestants among the Welsh members, a policy of friendship with Spain threatened the Protestant supremacy at home. However, this policy of *détente* with Spain came to an end in 1624 after the fiasco of the secret visit of Charles and Buckingham to the Spanish Court to enable the Prince to woo the Infanta in person,[8] and among those who accompanied them, and were thus in a position to relay information at first hand back to their kinsmen in Wales, were such representatives of the *plastai* as Sir Richard Wynn of Gwydir and Lord Vaughan, the future Earl of Carbery. The fact that the heir to the throne and his favourite returned home bent on war with Spain warmed the hearts of

---

[7] It was the outbreak of the Civil War that finally brought its sittings to an end.

[8] The fears of the Vicar Prichard concerning a possible union of England and Spain cemented by a marriage alliance were reflected in these four lines of verse:

> 'Duw'n ddiffynno rhag bradwriaeth,
> Cadwed Crist ef rhag Pabyddiaeth,
> A rhag pawb sydd yn amcanu
> Drwg neu sbeit i Brins y Cymry'.

[God protect him (i.e. Charles) from treason, and Christ protect him from Popery, and from everyone who plans wrong or spite against the Prince of Wales.]

most, but at the same time it sent shivers through less warlike breasts, and Bishop John Williams was to lose favour with both Charles and Buckingham because of his outspoken criticism of their bellicose intentions. Welsh members, and particularly Sir Robert Mansel[9] of Margam in Glamorgan, the Vice-Admiral and member of the Council of War, soon became increasingly disenchanted with Buckingham's conduct of the war with Spain, a mismanagement which culminated in the disastrous Cadiz expedition. Indeed it was because of this criticism that Mansel was removed from the commission of the peace. Furthermore, the mishandling of the negotiations with France, which in 1627 led to the outbreak of hostilities with that country, thus reviving the Tudor nightmare of a Franco-Spanish-Papal alliance against England, together with the débacle of the ill-fated expedition to relieve the hard-pressed Huguenots at La Rochelle, resulted in more condemnation being heaped on the head of the unfortunate royal favourite.

These developments led to the sounding of alarums all over Wales with attention being focused on the inadequacies of coastal defences, the activities of papists within—these were regarded as a kind of fifth column—and their potential allies, the despised Irish, without. In South Wales Sir James Perrot brought again to the attention of the government his concern about the maritime needs of Wales in general and of Milford Haven in particular, while in Flintshire equal concern was shown about the activities of pilgrims at St Winifred's Well. Though Wales was little troubled by such vexatious questions as the arbitrary imprisonment of those who resisted the King's demands, or the billeting of soldiers on civilians, matters which greatly vexed Southern England at this time, Welsh members still supported the Petition of Right 1628, Charles Jones the lawyer member for Beaumaris even helping in its framing. But after this date Welsh enthusiasm for opposition visibly waned. Opposition had now gone far enough. The constitutional safeguards which they required had been provided. Buckingham, the favourite they held responsible for all the wrongs committed in the King's name, had fallen at Portsmouth to the

[9] The son of Sir Edward Mansel he was the 'only valiant man whom King James ever loved'.

assassin's blade; John Williams, happily back in favour, and the Earl of Pembroke, also now restored to grace, and who throughout had strongly influenced the views of the Welsh members, were no longer to be found in the ranks of the King's critics. When in 1629 the Speaker was held forcibly in the Chair, and the Three Resolutions of Sir John Eliot were passed, and the doctrine of the sovereignty of Parliament showed itself unmistakably, Welsh members would appear not to have joined in this final act of defiance before the dissolution.

Religion also helped to exacerbate feelings between Crown and Parliament. Broadly speaking, it is undoubtedly true to say that the members of Parliament most ready and willing to attack the royal prerogative were Puritan in sympathy. In Elizabethan and early Stuart Wales Puritanism had made very little headway, Puritan influences being confined mainly to South Pembrokeshire, port towns on the south coast like Swansea and Cardiff, border towns like Wrexham, and Monmouthshire. John Penry, though regarded by many as the first Welsh Puritan, spent most of his adult life outside Wales and his influence was felt more in England than in his native country. When the Book of Sports was re-issued in 1633, and ordered to be read from the pulpits, this constituted a real challenge to the Puritan clergy. However, in Wales, very few were evicted. [10] By and large, therefore, it can be claimed that there was very little in the way of determined Puritan opposition to the Established Church in the Principality before the outbreak of the Civil War.

However, Protestants everywhere were very distrustful of the religious policies of the early Stuarts. Substance was given to their suspicions when, in his desire to grant toleration to the Catholics, James suspended the penal laws. His son, Charles, further fuelled these suspicions by marrying a Catholic princess, Henrietta Maria of France, and then by favouring the Arminianism of Archbishop Laud. [11] The depth of passion

[10] Infra, p. 61.

[11] Laud was Bishop of St David's in 1621, of London in 1628 and appointed Archbishop of Canterbury in 1633. He was extremely pious and narrow in outlook and emphasised the virtues of order, uniformity and discipline. At Oxford he had grown to detest Puritanism and at that University he successfully stamped it out. Having disciplined Oxford he thought he could do the same to England using such instruments as the Court of High Commission, Star

aroused by these developments can only be appreciated when it is borne in mind that very few at this time believed in religious toleration, and that this century was also one of the most religious ages in British history. Indeed, it is quite possible that the constitutional debate might never have ended in armed conflict without the influence of, and the bitterness engendered by, religious differences in such an age. It can be appreciated, then, how much more volatile the situation became after 1605 when Catholic extremists attempted to blow up both King and Parliament. But the cry of 'no popery' reverberated around Wales as well and feelings bordered on the hysterical when rumours were spread abroad of secret preparations being made at Raglan and Powis castles for an armed uprising, with the 'Welsh Popish Army' to be officered by local recusants, and ready to make common cause with a popish invading force. This myth was promoted both by the special exemption which Charles granted to the Catholic Earl of Worcester and his son enabling them to carry arms, and by the wide and mysterious powers which the Earl was empowered to exercise in the South Wales counties. What added greater urgency to the situation was that these activities at home were taking place against a European background of Protestants fighting for their very existence in Germany in the Thirty Years War (1618-1648), a conflict regarded by Protestants as a struggle between the forces of good and evil, between Geneva and Rome, between Christ and anti-Christ. The fear of papists in Wales was admirably reflected in a Monmouthshire petition of May 1642 when it was said: 'We in Wales of all others, and in Monmouthshire above the rest, cannot but be most sensible and suspicious of our own imminent destruction, as being compassed about with Papists, more in number, and stronger in power, Arms, Horse and Ammunition than any other Country (as we conceive) in the Kingdom besides'.

Tolerance of Catholics and the High Anglicanism of Laud could not fail, therefore, to arouse passions. But there were

Chamber, Episcopal Visitation, the censorship of the press, the suppression of lecturers and substituting the catechism for the sermon. He placed considerable emphasis on ritual and repudiated the Calvinist doctrine of Predestination as being too harsh. In the final analysis it can be said that he set out to give the Church a good spring cleaning.

Raglan Castle
Home of the Somerset family, Earls of Worcester

other, and possibly more immediate, aspects of the religious policy of the early Stuarts that were also calculated to cause offence. The attempts to recover for the Crown the patronage of livings, and to limit the freedom of action of bishops in granting leases of Church property, although undertaken in an effort to raise standards within the Church, still alienated many in Wales. The activities of the Court of High Commission, and the increasing interference of clerics in lay matters, were other matters that caused considerable resentment. Finally much was made of the neglect of preaching, with the result that 'sum churches in Wales have not had a sermon in them this 9 yeares, scarse prayers'.

In Wales, therefore, before the outbreak of the Civil War, there was a charged atmosphere of genuine fear and suspicion of recusants, Spaniards and Irish and a keen awareness of the vulnerability of the long Welsh coastlines. Furthermore, government policy had served to undermine, to some extent, the prestige and standing of the Court. The Welsh members who assembled in the Short Parliament (it sat for only three weeks) in April 1640, a Parliament finally summoned by Charles after eleven years of personal government to drive out the Scots who had occupied Newcastle in the north, were in critical mood. They were still in opposition when the King, in an attempt to pay off the Scots, summoned the Long Parliament in November 1641. Events were now rapidly building up to a climax. As the parliamentary opposition became more and more extreme, and as it became increasingly clear that this opposition was now directed against the King himself, the Welsh members began to draw back from the brink. When the Bill of Attainder was passed against Strafford[12] in 1641, this action represented a decisive challenge to the royal prerogative. Though the bill was passed by 204 votes to 59, many of the Welsh members were to be found among those who opposed it and were subjected to hoots of derision by the London mob. The Irish rebellion of November 1641 when hundreds, possibly thousands, of English Protestants were killed, caused great panic in England and Wales, arousing fears of an Irish Catholic invading force landing at either Pembroke in the south or Anglesey and Llŷn in the north. An army had to be raised to reconquer Ireland and Parliament was determined to seize control of the military machine since ultimate power within the state hinged on this one factor. When Parliament, consequently, tried to enforce its Militia Ordinance in the Welsh counties, it met with little success since one county after another declared against it. There was a general awareness now that the army to be raised was not to be used against the Irish, but rather

[12] This was Sir Thomas Wentworth, 1st Earl of Strafford (1593-1641). As member of Parliament for Yorkshire he had been an active member of the House of Commons and had resisted Charles's attempts to raise money by unconstitutional means. He had been imprisoned for refusing to pay the forced loan of 1627, and even the Petition of Right 1628 had secured his support. However, he was taken into royal favour and as a result the Presidency of the Council in the North became his. In 1629 he was made a Privy Councillor, and in 1632 Lord-Deputy of Ireland. In these official capacities he displayed fine administrative vigour and a ruthless disregard and intolerance of opposition. To his methods he applied the name 'Thorough'. His great friendship with Laud sprang from a common aversion to Puritanism and both attempted to elevate the prerogative and its courts above Parliament and the Common Law. To Charles, in his hour of need, he offered the use of the Catholic army that he had raised in Ireland against both Scottish and English rebels, and as a result of this advice was popularly dubbed 'Black Tom the Tyrant'. During the first Session of the Long Parliament he was impeached, but when it became apparent that this procedure would fail, a Bill of Attainder was passed against him by the Commons. Dread of mob violence led to Charles assenting to the Bill and on 12 May he was executed on Tower Hill.

against the King. It would appear that Welsh members had no
share at all in the Grand Remonstrance of November 1641 which
was passed by a majority of eleven votes only (159-148). The last
and faintest chance of accommodation between the King and the
Parliamentary opposition disappeared with the passing of the
Nineteen Propositions in July 1642 which would have left
Charles, in his own words, 'but the sign, the picture, the outside
of a King'. Only the sword could now decide the issue and the
Welsh, though they had opposed the Court, were not prepared to
be instruments in the overthrow of the Crown. It was not unexpected, therefore, that in August 1642 only seven of the Welsh
members, and this number was soon reduced to five, remained
loyal to Parliament.

The unfurling of the royal standard at Nottingham on 22
August 1642 marked the end of an era in Welsh politics, an era
which had started with the Act of Union 1536/43, for the outbreak of hostilities meant that the 'Welsh Interest' in Parliament, built up under the Tudors and early Stuarts, had finally
disappeared as a political force.

Chapter 2

BY THE SWORD DIVIDED

THE BACKGROUND IN ENGLAND
On 22 August 1642 King Charles I raised his standard at Nottingham. The first Civil War had begun. Richard Baxter, the eminent Puritan divine, classified the supporters of King and Parliament in the war in the following way: 'A very great part of the Knights and gentlemen of England, and also most of the poorest of the people, whom the others called the rabble, did follow the gentry and were for the King. On the Parliament's side were the smaller part of the gentry in most of the counties, and the greatest part of the tradesmen and freeholders and the middle sort of men, especially in those Corporations and counties which depend on clothing and such manufactures'. This economic factor was one of the most important considerations which determined the loyalties of both persons and corporations. In the period 1540-1640 the great rise in prices, consequent to some extent upon the growth in population and also on the influx of gold and silver bullion from the New World, had resulted in the Crown, which was dependent for much of its revenue on fixed rents, becoming impoverished. On the other hand it had given a great stimulus to industrial activity which had taken place outside the old corporate boroughs, and thus outside the controlling influence of the guilds. Most of the capital for these industrial developments had come from the merchants in the towns, but a great deal had come from the landowners. During this period also there had been a revolution in the use of land. As a result of the price revolution rents had risen, enclosures had taken place, while capitalistic methods had been applied to land exploitation. The people who stood to benefit most from the changed economic climate, and from the unparalleled opportunities presented by these one hundred years, had been the prosperous gentry and merchant groups. For these, therefore, constraints on the freedom of economic development, such as were imposed by the granting of monopoly rights and the farming of customs, formed no part of their philosophy. The older

17

aristocracy, on the other hand, the heirs of ancient wealth, dispersed rights and large responsibilities, had found it increasingly difficult in many cases to match the growing prosperity of some of the gentry largely because of their inability to adjust an extravagant mode of living to a decreasing revenue. The balance of social forces on which the stability of a constitution depends was upset. The early Stuarts had failed to appreciate that a modification of the constitution, to correspond with the new conditions, was necessary. In this failure may be found one of the main causes of the Civil War.

However, while according to Professor Tawney[1] the gentry had risen as a class at the expense of the aristocracy and on the profits of agriculture, Professor Trevor-Roper,[2] on the other hand, argues that it was only a section of the gentry—that connected with the Court, and with trade, and those who held office —which flourished. The other gentry, whom he describes as the 'mere' gentry, found themselves in difficulties. Hard hit by the price revolution, slow to redeem their losses by 'good husbandry', and heavily taxed, the mere gentry felt themselves to be a depressed, declining class and grumbling, consoled-or armed-themselves with religious dissent. According to this thesis the Civil War represented a struggle between the 'Ins' and the 'Outs', between the 'Haves' and 'Have nots'. Some little piggies went to Court and had roast beef; and some little piggies stayed at home and had none. In other words what was witnessed in 1642 was the revolt of the country house radicals.

This cleavage between Court and Country represented more than a matter of access to economic privilege. As Justices of the Peace, the gentry enjoyed great power and prestige in their own localities. The attempts by the early Stuart Kings and their ministers to manage local government from Whitehall only served to exasperate the natural leaders of town and country. In this sense, the Civil War was also the revolt of the decentralisers.

But however powerful the economic, social and political factors were in helping to bring about conflict, the influence of religion must not be underestimated. Indeed, if the fabric of dispute had not been interwoven with the threads of religious

[1] H. R. Tawney, 'The Rise of the Gentry', *Econ. His. Rev.*, IX, 1941.
[2] H. R. Trevor-Roper, 'The Gentry 1540-1640', *Econ. His. Rev.*, 1953.

dissent and discord, in an age which did not believe in religious toleration, conflict might never have ensued. The Stuarts had tried to use the Established Church to bolster the cause of monarchy and this had made the Church of England vulnerable to attack both from those who wanted to supersede it, and from those who wanted to strengthen the Protestant element within it by ridding the Church of all semblances of Catholic survivals, the 'dregs of popery'. The claims which were made by the Church on its own behalf, and on behalf of the Crown, had become increasingly extravagant, and this development had made it impossible for the clergy and laity within the Church to propose changes in a Protestant direction. In the consequent inability of the Church to embrace the growing forces of religious dissent may be found another very important cause of the Civil War.

Though the early Stuart monarchy, unlike the walls of Jericho, was never overthrown solely by trumpet blasts, it is doubtful whether the English Revolution could have taken place without the influence of ideas. Puritanism obviously provided a *corpus* of ideas since one could brave the King of England if one was obeying the orders of the King of Kings and it is as well to remember that in the seventeenth century the Geneva Bible, with its highly political marginal notes, was something of a revolutionist's handbook. But there were other strands of thought which undermined men's beliefs and respect for established institutions, and these were provided by developments in the fields of science, history and law associated mainly with Francis Bacon, Sir Walter Raleigh and Sir Edward Coke. While these were not original thinkers, they certainly helped to create a climate of opinion which made revolution both possible and probable.

CAVALIER OR ROUNDHEAD

Many factors determined the attitude of Wales towards the struggle. Compared with England the country was economically backward and the towns, while not inconsiderable in number, were small in size. This situation meant that the 'middle sort of men' had but few representatives in the country. Again the gentry, and a few only of these were in a position to get involved in the struggle between the 'Ins' and 'Outs', were loyal to the

Crown. Their tenants, as was to be expected in such a closely-knit society, were loyal to them. The gentry had been extremely loyal to the Tudors partly because the Tudors were Welsh and consequently there existed a strong sentimental attachment to the Crown. But there was far more to it than that. The gentry were loyal also from gratitude for favours already granted, and through a lively expectation of more favours to come. This attachment they had, in 1603, transferred to the Stuarts but Professor Dodd has shown that in the process of transfer it had undergone an important change. No longer did it attach itself merely to persons (but for this it could hardly have survived the neglect and misrule of Charles); rather it embraced the whole complex of institutions through which the monarch acted-Parliament, the law, the church establishment. Support for an arbitrary despotism, therefore, was no part of their creed, but any sympathies which they may have felt for the parliamentary cause were soon swept away by the growing violence of the opposition, and above all by its attack on the Church. Another factor which may help to explain the attitude of Wales is to be found in the language in which the parliamentary appeals were made. Of all the hundreds of pamphlets that appeared in the years before and after the outbreak of the Civil Wars, not one tried to explain the parliamentary standpoint in Welsh.[3] The bards, ballad-mongers and clergy, on the other hand, who were, at this time, the main agents for the dissemination of news-and propaganda-in Wales, were unswervingly loyal to the Crown and the episcopate. Again it must be remembered that as far as Wales was concerned Puritanism had not as yet made any great appeal. Its influence was very largely limited to South Pembroke, South Wales ports like Swansea and Cardiff, and areas near the English border like Wrexham and Monmouth.

Most parts of Wales, then, were royalist in sympathy. Only in those limited areas which had commercial contacts with London or Bristol, or which had felt the influence of border Puritanism, did parliamentary supporters gain the upper hand. The nucleus of parliamentary strength in South Wales lay in the towns of Pembroke, Tenby and Haverfordwest whose English-speaking

[3] It has been calculated that between 1640-1661 more than 22,000 sermons, speeches, pamphlets and journals were published in England.

populace, and close connections with London and Bristol, had always tended to make them less immune to radical influences than most of Wales. At Wrexham, in Denbighshire, Puritanism had early taken root and here, also, the influence of the Myddeltons of Chirk was of marked significance. The two brothers, Thomas and Hugh, had made their fortunes in London. Thomas, having started his business career as a grocer's apprentice, rose to become a founder member of the East India Company, a banker and money lender and eventually, in 1613, Lord Mayor of the City. His younger brother Hugh was apprenticed to a goldsmith and so successful was he in his chosen profession that he amassed a very considerable fortune. In 1617 he secured a lease on the lead mines of the Society of Mines Royal in Cardiganshire for £400 a year, and the venture was to prove a great financial success.[4] However, he is possibly best remembered for his New River Scheme, which aimed at providing London with an adequate supply of fresh water.

Of the great magnates who sided with Parliament two exercised considerable sway in South and West Wales and their influence, or the pressure that they were able to exert, may well have helped to determine the allegiance of South Pembroke. These were the Earls of Pembroke and Essex. The fourth Earl of Pembroke, who was a great landowner in Glamorgan and owned Cardiff castle, opposed the King from personal pique; Essex, on the other hand, unlike the unstable Pembroke who was described by an acquaintance as one 'of a very quick apprehension, a sharp understanding, very crafty withal and of a discerning spirit, but extremely cholerick by nature', was a man of principle and his devotion to the parliamentary cause was such that he was made commander-in-chief of the parliamentary forces.[5]

But within every county there were pockets of parliamentary supporters, usually smaller gentry or yeomen, or representatives of the trading classes. It was a question of balance, and in Wales the scales, in most cases, were tilted heavily in favour of the Crown. Denbigh had its parliamentary supporters in those very successful London businessmen, Thomas and Hugh Myddel-

---

[4] Infra, pp. 172-3.
[5] This was Robert Devereux (1591-1646), 3rd Earl of Essex. Apart from a brief spell in 1613 spent at Lamphey, he is not known to have resided on the Welsh estates of the family.

Sir Hugh Myddelton (1560-1631)

ton; in Breconshire the parliamentary cause was upheld by Colonel Jenkin Jones of Llanddeti, Sir William Lewis of Llangorse[6] and Henry Watkins of Caebalfa. In Glamorgan the disaffected included figures like Philip Jones of Llangyfelach, whose original freehold was assessed at between £17 and £20, and Rowland Dawkin of Kilvrough (Cilfrwch) in Gower. Among the parliamentary stalwarts in Pembrokeshire were John Poyer, a prosperous merchant who traded with the Puritan stronghold of Bristol, Rowland Laugharne, who had served in the household of the Earl of Essex, and Rice Powell who, having served a military apprenticeship in Ireland, became one of Laugharne's lieutentants in the first Civil War.

Together with laymen there were Puritan divines who saw in the war a religious crusade against an oppressive and intolerant Church. In their ranks were to be found ministers of the stature of Vavasor Powell, Walter Cradock and Morgan Llwyd. These were all border Puritans, since Walter Cradock and Morgan Llwyd were associated with the Wrexham area, while Vavasor Powell, who hailed from Knucklas in Radnorshire, and had come under the influence of Walter Cradock at Brampton Bryan, a few miles away in Herefordshire, spent most of his time at Clun. The outbreak of the Civil War saw these Puritan divines, apart from Morgan Llwyd, who fought with the parliamentary forces in both Civil Wars, fleeing in haste to safer and more congenial quarters in Bristol and London. Their goods having been seized by Royalists, Parliament established a Committee of Plundered Ministers to look after the welfare of these refugees.

But there were others who were motivated to draw sword for Parliament for reasons that were completely unconnected with loyalty to the House of Commons, or belief in the justice or legality of their cause. These were the gentry who saw in the wars a chance for pursuing, at county level, their own personal feuds, for settling old scores; here also was an opportunity for recovering lost family property or adding to existing acres. There were also the swordsmen eager for glory and reward; and there were the members of the smaller landowning families who sought to

---

[6] His grandfather had made a fortune as a mercer in Brecon and, on two occasions, he had been Sheriff of the county.

take advantage of the turmoil to advance their own interests. As the war progressed many defected to Parliament as an expression of their dissatisfaction at the way royalist commanders, and particularly Rupert and Gerard, conducted themselves in the field, or as an indication of their disquietude and dismay at the employment of Catholic Irish in the King's armies.

Just as the adherents of Parliament were impelled by a variety of motives, so also were the followers of the King. Despite their criticism of court policy, the Welsh gentry still saw in Charles a descendant of the noble Brutus, who would be a shield and buckler against the darts of those who would destroy what they genuinely believed in. For many, the sovereign represented the best guarantee that the fabric of society would not be rent apart, that family would not be pitted against family, that the servant would not emerge triumphant over the master, that the social order from which they had gained so much would not be overthrown. Staunch Anglicans saw in their King the head of their Church, of whose order of service they approved, and whose Prayer Book they held in real affection. Again, a substantial number among them had received a legal training at the Inns of Court, and with them a cardinal tenet was the upholding of the rule of law, which alone could provide and ordered framework for society. There were also those who felt that the whole affair had been started by Parliament and that right was consequently on the King's side. And on the lips of most ardent royalists were the words from the First Book of Samuel: 'for who can stretch forth his hand against the Lord's anointed, and be guiltless'?[7]

These are the considerations that dictated the allegiance of Charles's principal supporters in Wales, and pride of place among these must be accorded to the Catholic Earl of Worcester, advanced in years, and living in regal style in his much-extended and greatly beautified castle at Raglan. Reputedly the wealthiest man in England, he fortified and garrisoned this great house at his own expense. His son, Lord Herbert, became the King's Lieutenant-General in South Wales and it was through him, acting as intermediary, that the Earl provided Charles with financial aid amounting altogether to some £900,000. Without assistance on such a munificent scale, it is doubtful whether

---

[7] First Book of Samuel, Chapter 16, V. 9.

Charles could have put an army in the field at all in 1642. As reward for these services the Earl was created Marquis of Worcester, with promises of the Garter and the dukedom of Somerset, while his son was given the title of Earl of Glamorgan.

But while the Earl of Worcester was championing the King's cause in South Wales, a notable figure on the royalist side in the north, at least until 1645, was Archbishop John Williams. A sermon which he preached before James I in 1611 having secured for him royal favour, preferment came rapidly his way. However, the death of James I in 1625 brought about a sudden change for the worse in his fortunes since he incurred the enmity of both Buckingham and Laud, and it was not until 1640 that he was reconciled to Charles. In May 1642 he followed the King to Yorkshire, but in the same year he returned to North Wales on hearing that the younger Hotham was marching against his episcopal palace. There he acted as the linchpin between English and Welsh royalists on the one hand and Ormonde, the commander of the King's forces in Ireland, on the other and, at his own expense, repaired and fortified Conway castle. In 1645 he defected from the royalist side—even to the extent of actively assisting the Roundheads to occupy Conway castle—an act of apostasy that he was later to regret.

Lesser luminaries on the King's side were represented by such persons as Sir John Owen of Clenennau, 'gŵr a nerthai'r Goron',[8] an impoverished squire but a capable and courageous commander, and one of the staunchest of the royalist supporters in Wales; Sir Roger Mostyn, who generously expended £60,000 on the King's cause; William Salusbury of Rug and Bachymbyd, popularly and affectionately known as 'Hen Hosanau Gleision',[9] who declared that he 'desired not to live longer than I approve myself true to my King and country'; Sir Edward Stradling of St Donat's, who raised a regiment of foot, a

---

[8] 'A man who strengthened the Crown'. He was seriously wounded at the siege of Bristol in July 1643. According to a letter which he wrote to his wife from his sickbed, a ball had entered the right hand side of his nose and exited under his left ear with the result that he almost choked on his own blood. From this account, and considering the trajectory, it seems more than likely that the ball had been fired by a defender on the town wall. Despite the severity of the injury he was to make a complete recovery.

[9] 'Old Blue Stockings'.

Sir John Owen of Clenennau

thousand strong, to serve the King; and Sir Nicholas Kemeys of Cefn Mabli, who is reputed to have raised a regiment of horse at his own expense and to have made weapons from his own private armoury available for the King's forces. The influence of men such as these was to prove of paramount importance in determining the allegiance of the shires wherein they dwelt, in these cases of Caernarvon, Flint, Denbigh, Glamorgan and Monmouth.

But there were others who were not to display the same degree of loyalty to the King, who showed little evidence of the chivalrous abandon of the true Cavalier who would gladly choose ruin and exile rather than desert his prince. Their support for the royal cause was lukewarm to say the least, even to the extent, in the case of many, of wishing to remain aloof from it all. When persuasion failed, they had to be cajoled or even bullied to help. This attitude sprang occasionally from an ignorance of the issues involved, but more usually from an awareness of the devastation and impoverishment of the country which would follow in the wake of armed conflict, for the destructive capacity of armies had been demonstrated in the Thirty Years War in Germany. [10] This accounts for the defections, the ambivalence, the reluctance to serve outside their own localities. Well might James Howell, the royalist propagandist, make an impassioned plea to his Maker to 'amend the times, and compose those woful divisions which menace nothing but public ruin'. [11]

As the war progressed, and as professionals and strangers, high-handed in their conduct, came inevitably to replace local amateurs as captains of royalist armies, and as the demands on the Welsh populace increased, a new note of resentment is heard. Though Prince Charles at Raglan might be given assurances of continued Welsh loyalty by Sir Hugh Vaughan, a more realistic appraisal was provided by another royalist officer, Captain Thomas Dabridgecourt in a letter addressed to Prince Rupert from St. Pierre, near Chepstow: 'if your Highness shall be pleased to command me to the Turk, or Jew, or Gentile, I will go on my bare feet to serve you, but from the Welsh, good Lord deliver me . . . And I shall beseech you to send me no more into this country . . . without a strong party to compel them . . . They value neither Sir John Winter, his warrants, nor mine, nor any. Some say they will not come; the rest come not and say nothing'.

---

[10] It would appear that the war had left Berlin nothing better than the centre of a desert. Not unexpectedly, therefore, it was at this time that the word 'plunder', current in Germany, was introduced into the English language.

[11] He was the second son of Thomas Howell, curate of Llangamarch Wells in Breconshire and later rector of Cynwil and Aber-nant in Carmarthenshire. From Hereford Free School he proceeded to Jesus College, Oxford which he entered in 1610. His fluency in languages led to both James I and Charles I using him on diplomatic missions. In 1627 he entered Parliament as M.P. for Richmond, Yorkshire. His support for the royalist cause led to his imprisonment in the Fleet from 1643 to 1651.

Even corporate towns like Swansea which had openly declared for the King, and which were prepared to expend money on repairing the defensive works of their castles, [12] and thus assume once again their medieval status as garrison towns, a role which they had discarded after the Act of Union, showed an alarming readiness to throw open the town gates at the first approach of the enemy. At Brecon the inhabitants even destroyed the castle and the walls of the town to obviate the danger of siege and the necessity of maintaining a garrison. This attitude can be accounted for on the ground that the townspeople were more intent on the physical preservation of their boroughs than in defending the Majesty of the King. They were merchants, traders, shopkeepers and craftsmen and what they desired above all else was peace and stability to enable them to pursue their commercial and business activities unimpeded. To them the town was the means of creating their wealth and a symbol of their prosperity. Its destruction, on the other hand, would have spelt disaster, economic and otherwise. Hence their unwillingness to play the role of a Basing House. [13]

In view of the lukewarmness displayed by Corporations as well as individuals, one should not, perhaps, over-emphasise the differences between the adherents of King and Parliament because the lines of demarcation between them were often rather blurred. After all, it was with deep misgivings and instinctive reluctance that men had embarked on what the parliamentary general Waller, writing to the royalist Hopton, called 'this war without an enemy'. It was never a war between geographical areas or rival classes, and the absence for many of clear-cut issues is aptly illustrated in Glamorgan in the conduct of Rowland

[12] The items in the Common Attorneys' Accounts for Swansea relating to the repair of a turret in the castle are of some interest:

paid to the maysons for worck about the turret in the Castle	00-03-06
paid to 3 men to attend the maysons	00-02-04
paid for 8 bushells of lyme	00-03-04
paid for carring the said lime	00-00-04
paid for carring of water	00-00-04
paid for the Vane	00-05-08
paid for 6 li and a ½ of lead	00-01-00

[13] The Catholic defenders of Basing House in Hampshire were prepared to die to the last man rather than surrender to the Roundheads. The house was taken after a bloody assault on 14 October 1645.

Dawkin and Bussy Mansel for the former, before joining the parliamentary forces, had compounded for his delinquency to the royalist Commissioners of Array, while the latter had long been a royalist stalwart before finally going over to the parliamentary side.

Welsh loyalty was of very great importance to Charles. Strategically Wales was important because the Principality provided the King with easy access to Ireland, from where he expected support in men, materials and money. Wales in royalist hands also provided a useful counterpoise to London and the counties of the south-east where lay the main strength of the parliamentary party. Furthermore, in the country west of the Severn and the Dee, the King could expect to find a safe retreat when he was hard pressed in England.

In addition to her strategic value Wales was a fruitful recruiting ground for soldiers, and particularly of infantry, the levying of whom was the responsibility of Commissioners of Array. According to Arthur Trevor, the country was the 'nursery of the King's infantry' and, theoretically, all able-bodied males between sixteen and sixty were liable for service though there were some reserved occupations. Despite the fact that one knows tantalisingly little about these Welsh levies, it is known that they took part in some of the major engagements of the Civil War. They were present at Edgehill, where the first shots of the Civil War were fired on 23 October 1642; they formed part of the forces that laid siege to Bristol and Gloucester in 1643 and in June 1645 at the battle of Naseby they were decimated in number, and many taken prisoner and later paraded through the streets of London, when the King was crushingly and decisively defeated. It would appear that for the most part the Welsh levies were poorly armed, badly trained and conspicuously lacking in will. When in August 1643 Bussy Mansel, Walter Thomas and William Thomas were ordered by the Commissioners of Array to raise in the three hundreds of Swansea, Llangyfelach and Neath, sixty, twenty and forty able men respectively and to despatch them to Cardiff, William Thomas immediately wrote to Sir Anthony Mansel protesting against the order. In his answer he indicated that it would impose a great hardship on the hundred of Swansea since 'their Whole Band is already in Service and are longe Continued vnder your Comaund in y^e

Garisen'. He desired that Llangyfelach should be spared as well. Delay in despatching the forces resulted in the Commissioners writing to the 'Westerne Gentlemen' urging them to greater expedition. Forty fit men only, however, could be raised from Swansea and these, with the twenty from Llangyfelach, were delivered over into the hands of the High Constables. The shortfall in the Swansea numbers was accounted for on the ground that 'these partes are soe Gleaned of all spare people wth those seu'all occacions of late that the Husbanmen wilbee hardly able to manadge their tilladge, And therby not only a scarcity of Grayne will ensue butt alsoe an Inabilitye to mantayne any necessary Chardge that shalbe Imposed vpon them'.

From the same reply it becomes clear that these men were poorly armed: 'Wee receaued xii billstaues from m^r William Gybbes wch are Caried by some of these men more armes Wee Could not gett together Vpon soe short Somons Neyther doe wee Conceaue that the Contrey will affoorde any worth the sheweinge in the feild'. This corroborates the evidence provided by a contemporary on the equipment of the Welsh contingents at Edgehill. 'Arms', he remarked, 'were the great deficiency, and the men stood up in the same garments in which they left their native fields; and with scythes, pitchforks, and even sickles in their hands, they cheerfully took the field and literally like reapers descended to that harvest of death'. Armed in this fashion it is hardly to be wondered at that Welsh casualties should have been heavy[14] and that this factor, in the long run, should have had the effect of undermining morale.

Such was the royalists' shortage of arms that they had to borrow from the armouries of private individuals and attempt to import arms from abroad. For this latter purpose, harbours in

---

[14] The following lines of verse reflect the rejoicing of London wits at the news of the discomfiture of the Welsh levies:

> 'In Kineton Green
> Poor Taffy was seen,
> O Taffy, O Taffy:
> Taffy her stood
> To her knees in blood
> O do not laugh ye;
> But her was Led on
> With false commission
> To her unknown . . .'

Pikeman and Musketeer

South Wales, not too far removed from France, obviously offered many advantages, even though the ships involved in the trafficking had to run the gauntlet of the parliamentary blockade organised from Milford Haven. It would appear that in Glamorgan the garrison town of Swansea was the port used for this purpose and on 24 July 1643 the Commissioners of Array for the County made an agreement with two Frenchmen, Hammon le Baut and Francois le Milbeau, whereby they were to procure and deliver at Swansea the following munitions:

'200 hundered Barrelles of Powder whearof 2 p'tes must bee muskett Powder and the third Cannon at 18d p' pownd, the one wth the other/
1000pownd of Match at 6d p' pound and 500 li Muskettes and Bandelieres of the best at 18s Muskett & bandelieres/'

Once the powder and arms had been safely delivered these munitions were to be divided among the trained bands of the ten hundreds of Glamorgan after due trial of the muskets to ensure that they were serviceable.

Important strategically, a recruiting ground for infantry, and a point of entry for arms purchased abroad, Wales was also a milch cow for Charles in his desperate search for money to prosecute the war. Indeed, it was because he could not raise the essential finances in sufficient quantities that he was ultimately defeated. The richer royalists in Wales had been extremely generous with their gifts and loans of money to the Crown. Thomas Bushell, who had succeeded Sir Hugh Myddelton as the lessee of the Cardiganshire lead and silver mines, had even helped to clothe the royalist armies. But the King's need for money was continuous, and so all available means for raising ready cash had to be exploited. Undoubtedly, the principal device employed by Charles was the county levy and on 18 October 1643 Glamorgan was assessed at £1000 and each of the hundreds within the county had to make a contribution towards this sum according to its means. Another common expedient was the sequestration of the estates and possessions of delinquents, an indication that the enemy, as far as was possible, was to be made to pay for the war.

Chapter 3

THE PURITAN INVASION

Charles I raised his standard at Nottingham on 22 August 1642. By coincidence or by design this was the very day and month on which an ancestor of his, Henry Tudor, had unfurled the Red Dragon on Bosworth Field when the Yorkist Richard III had been defeated and slain. However, it is quite possible that Charles viewed the prospect of conflict with Parliament with a far greater degree of confidence than the Earl of Richmond had displayed so many years earlier in 1485, even though Richmond, like Charles, had felt that he could count on Welsh support. Certainly Charles did not envisage a lengthy campaign. A speedy ending was required since the King's financial resources were not such as to permit of a protracted struggle. After all, his Queen, Henrietta Maria, had been despatched in haste to France to pawn the royal jewels in an attempt to replenish the royal coffers, and it was only the generosity of the Catholic Earl of Worcester, with his seat at Raglan Castle, that had enabled him to raise an army at all in 1642. Speed, while the initiative still lay with the King, was obviously the keynote of success. London, the greatest city in the land, and the heart of the disaffection, had to be taken immediately, and his avowed enemies either put to the sword or to flight. Charles must have appreciated the magnitude of the task that he had set himself, since he would be opposed by the trained bands of the most populous and wealthy city in England. The King's forces had to be augmented, and it was for this purpose that Charles left Nottingham on 13 September for Shrewsbury[1] where he was joined by contingents of Welsh infantry recruited by the loyal Welsh gentry in their capacity as Commissioners of Array. These forces were led by Sir Edward Stradling of St Donat's and William Herbert of Cogan Pill, the Member of Parliament for Cardiff, and a distant relative of the Earl of Pembroke, who had elected to draw his sword for Parliament.

[1] According to Clarendon the decision was taken so that the King would be 'near the borders of Wales, where the power of the Parliament had been least prevalent, and where some regiments of foot were levying for his service'.

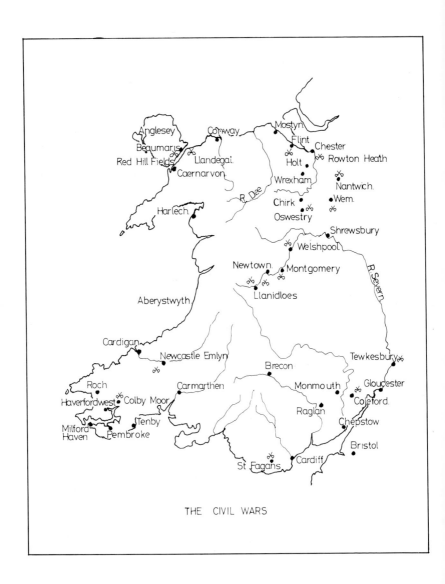

Anglesey
Conway
Mostyn
Beaumaris
Flint
Chester
Red Hill Fields
Llandegai.
Rowton Heath
Caernarvon.
Holt
Harlech.
Wrexham
Nantwich.
Chirk
Wem.
Oswestry
R. Dee
Shrewsbury
Welshpool
Newtown.
Montgomery
Aberystwyth
Llanidloes
R. Severn
Cardigan
Newcastle Emlyn
Tewkesbury
Brecon
Roch
Carmarthen
Monmouth
Gloucester
Haverfordwest
Colby Moor
Coleford.
Tenby
Raglan
Chepstow
Milford
Pembroke
Haven
St Fagans
Cardiff
Bristol

THE CIVIL WARS

While at his headquarters at Shrewsbury, the King decided to establish a second base at Chester and he, and his son, Prince Charles, were enthusiastically received by the inhabitants when they visited the town. On the return journey to Shrewsbury, Charles visited Wrexham and loyalists from Flintshire and Denbighshire pledged their unswerving loyalty to him. At Wrexham he was joined by his nephew, Prince Rupert[2] who, during the course of the Civil War, was to display considerable skill and daring as a cavalry leader. Prince Charles meanwhile, a mere stripling of ten years, was despatched to Raglan to act as a focal point for support for the royalist cause in South Wales.

The King now appointed William Seymour, Marquis of Hertford, Lieutenant-General of the western counties and for the whole of South Wales. His reception in the south-west, which he had hoped to hold for the King, was so hostile, however, that he and his men, some five hundred in number, were compelled to flee from Minehead to Cardiff in coal boats. On his arrival at Cardiff on 3 October, where he was welcomed with open arms by William Herbert of Grey Friars, he easily captured Cardiff castle, which was owned by the Earl of Pembroke, and he then proceeded to raise a royalist army.

Meanwhile Charles, with the complaints of the outraged citizens at the behaviour of his troops still ringing in his ears, left Shrewsbury on 12 October to begin his march on London. His army had swollen to sixteen thousand troops and in its ranks were substantial numbers of Welshmen from both North and South Wales. This royalist force now moved south by way of Bridgenorth, Wolverhampton and Kenilworth but between Kineton and Edgcott, on 23 October, it was intercepted by the parliamentary army under the command of the Earl of Essex. At Edgehill an indecisive battle was fought; but Welsh losses in the engagement were heavy. Among the officers killed was William Herbert of Cogan Pill, and among those taken prisoner Sir

---

[2] The 3rd son of Elizabeth, Queen of Bohemia, and Frederick, Elector Palatine, he was born in Prague in 1619. The experience that he had gained in foreign wars was put to good use by his uncle, Charles I, in the first Civil War when he was General of the Horse. Though a dashing and successful cavalry leader, his main weakness was a certain lack of restraint which led him to chase the opposing cavalry out of sight rather than reform and attack the parliamentary centre.

Edward Stradling of St Donat's. The sadly mauled royalist army, however, its confidence badly shaken, was able to continue on its march to London. The King passed through Oxford and at Brentford, the Welsh levies under the leadership of Prince Rupert, atoned for their ineffectual display at Edgehill by valiantly storming the enemy barricades. Nevertheless, despite this success, Charles was never allowed to take the Capital because, at Turnham Green, his progress was effectively barred by the London trained bands. The King then had no alternative but to return to Oxford, which he made his headquarters for the remainder of the war.

While these events were taking place in England, in South Wales the Marquis of Hertford, actively supported by the Worcester family, had succeeded in raising another royalist army, estimated to have been seven thousand strong, though the Pembrokeshire gentry, who had been summoned to meet Hertford at Carmarthen, excused themselves. On 4 November 'with colours flying and drums beating', he left Cardiff at the head of his army to reinforce the King at Oxford. However, the Earl of Stanford, who was the parliamentary Governor of Hereford, which had been occupied by a force sent from Worcester by Essex, overtook him at Tewkesbury and inflicted heavy casualties on the Welsh troops. According to a parliamentary observer, while Hertford's own men fought bravely, the Welsh played an inglorious part. Wild, ragged and inexperienced, they 'betook themselves to a shameful flight'. Despite this reverse Hertford was able to regroup his forces and, in the absence of Stanford, reoccupied Hereford. Later, just before Christmas, with a force of some two thousand men, he was able to join the King at Oxford.

The year 1642 must have ended on a very disappointing note for Charles. His armies had neither suffered any major reverses nor managed to achieve any spectacular successes, but London remained still the distant, impregnable citadel. In the far north and west of the Principality, well away from the major war zones, there were only faint echoes of the struggle in progress. In a town as far removed from the battle areas as Swansea in south-west Wales, the first and only indication of impending trouble is to be found in the Common Attorneys' Accounts when £12-19-1 was spent 'on makinge of ye newe Magazan in ye lower towne hall'. Since most of the able-bodied men were either performing gar-

rison duty or had been recruited to fight the King's battles in the
field, women and young girls had to be employed to help with the
work. The references to their contribution are as follows:

'To woemen for carriage of lyme & Water 0-3-0
To ye maides for attendinge ye Fier 0-1-0
To a woeman to white lyme ye Rome .... 0-0-3'

Despite the setbacks in 1642, at the commencement of 1643
the initiative still lay with the King, and a three-pronged attack
on London was now planned. One army was to attack from
Yorkshire; another was to move along the Thames valley; while
a third was to advance from the south-west. The success of this
strategy was dependent on the ability of the royalists to take the
great parliamentary strongholds of Hull, Bristol and Gloucester,
and Plymouth. The reduction of these cities was a *sine qua non* of
any advance on London, since as long as they were in parliamentary hands royalist forces could not advance beyond them
for fear of being attacked from the rear. Their supply lines could
be cut and the means of retreat blocked. Success at Bristol and
Gloucester, on the other hand, would provide the King with
positive advantages where Wales was concerned, since it would
guarantee him complete control of the marches from Bristol to
Chester, and permit free movement of troops and supplies from
Wales for the war effort in England. Hull, though besieged,
proved far too difficult a nut to crack since it could be supplied by
sea, and the fleet, apart from a few ships, had gone over to the
parliamentary side. The defection of the navy was one of the
major factors accounting for the ultimate triumph of Parliament
in the war. The ghost of Raleigh did indeed pursue the House of
Stuart to the scaffold.

Since Bristol and Gloucester were of such strategic importance, the royalists now made a determined effort to take these
strongpoints. Lord Herbert of Raglan who had been made Lieutenant-General in South Wales and Monmouth by Charles, who
thus defied anti-Catholic prejudice, promised that he would
raise an army at his own expense to capture Gloucester. In February 1643, with fifteen hundred foot and five hundred horse he
moved towards his objective. At Coleford, in a minor skirmish,
Colonel Lawley, who was in command of the foot, was killed and
there was no one of experience to replace him. The royalists

successfully reached Highnam, on the outskirts of Gloucester and there, in entrenched positions, they waited for the King's forces from Oxford to join them so that a combined assault could be made on the city. The parliamentarians, in the meantime, were not inactive and they despatched Sir William Waller with cavalry and dragoons to the aid of Gloucester. Waller managed to cross the Severn in broad daylight without being detected by the Welsh, who were taken so completely by surprise that they surrendered with no resistance being offered. The 'mushroom army' had disappeared and Edward Hyde, Earl of Clarendon, was of the opinion that 'if the money which was laid out in raising, arming and paying that body of men, which never advanced the King's service in the least degree, had been brought into the King's receipt at Oxford, I am persuaded the war might have been ended the next summer'. Flushed with success, Waller now pushed into south-east Wales and occupied Newnham, Ross-on-Wye, Monmouth and Chepstow, but news of the advance of a royalist force led to a hurried withdrawal to the safe haven of Gloucester. Within a fortnight, however, he was outside the walls of Hereford and, after a short siege, the city fell.

Rupert now made a determined assault on Bristol and he pressed home the attack with such vigour that the port fell on 26 July. Loss of life on the royalist side was heavy and it was in this engagement that Sir John Owen of Clenennau received his severe neck wound. [3]

The King himself now decided to attempt to take Gloucester and, for this purpose, Lord Herbert of Raglan used his immense financial resources to raise yet another force of four thousand foot and eight hundred horse to assist him. The importance of Gloucester, however, was fully appreciated by the parliamentarians, and the London trained bands, led by Essex, marched down the Great West road to its relief. To avoid being caught between the relieving force and the besieged, Charles withdrew and the city was saved. This was not a moment too soon since Lieutenant-Colonel Massey, who had been placed in charge of the defences, was down to the last three barrels of gunpowder. The relief of Gloucester was not only Essex's greatest military achievement, it was also a turning point in the fortunes of Par-

[3] Supra, p. 25*n*.

liament. Psychologically, it provided the parliamentarians with a much needed boost; it compensated for the loss of Bristol, and it also meant that South Wales, the wealthiest and most densely populated part of the Principality, was effectively isolated. On the return journey to London, Essex was intercepted at Newbury by the Cavaliers. The battle, as at Edgehill, was bloody but indecisive. The trained bands, however, were able to resume their march to London, while Charles returned to Oxford.

In August Richard Vaughan, the Earl of Carbery, who was the royalist commander in West Wales, decided to advance from his base in Carmarthenshire and occupy the parliamentary strongholds in Pembrokeshire. At Tenby and Haverfordwest he was enthusiastically welcomed, and castles and houses in the area were garrisoned by his troops. Pembroke alone, with its castle, defied him and the reduction of these twin bastions was to be a prime concern of the royalists in the early months of 1644.

Meanwhile, in north-east Wales the course of the war was not proceeding so favourably for the King. The parliamentary commander, the Puritan Sir Thomas Myddelton of Chirk, together with Sir William Brereton, having garrisoned Beeston, Nantwich and Wem, embarked in November upon the conquest of North Wales. Wrexham declared for Parliament and the castles of Hawarden, Flint, Mostyn, Mold and Holywell fell in

The 1st Marquis of Worcester

General Sir Thomas Myddelton

rapid succession. It appeared as if the whole of North Wales was at the mercy of the parliamentary forces. However, the situation was retrieved by the landing at Chester, Mostyn and Anglesey— where they were welcomed by Archbishop John Williams and Thomas Bulkeley—of reinforcements from Ireland, and the timely arrival of these troops, ill-armed and ill-clad though many were, and especially the Irish, compelled the Roundheads to abandon their conquests and retreat to Nantwich. It was the turn of Nantwich now to be besieged by the forces newly arrived from Ireland under the command of Lord Byron. The garrison, however, put up a stubborn resistance before finally being relieved by Fairfax in January 1644.

These troops from Ireland had been made available as a result of developments in the early autumn of 1643. The military situation in England had reached deadlock and Parliament, in a desperate attempt to break the stalemate, had signed the Solemn League and Covenant with the Scots in September 1643. In return for Scottish military aid, Parliament agreed to introduce Presbyterianism. Charles, not to be outdone, turned to Ireland and in the same month concluded a truce with the Irish rebels, which released troops for service in England.

1644 opened auspiciously for Parliament in south-west Wales. Carbery, intent on taking the last parliamentary stronghold in the area, Pembroke, had built a fort at the entrance of the Haven to prevent the town from being relieved from the sea, and in this objective he was also assisted by ships despatched from Bristol. Unfortunately for the royalists, the whole plan was foiled by the quite fortuitous arrival at the Haven of the parliamentary fleet under the command of Richard Swanley. These ships had been patrolling off the south-east coast of Ireland and had been driven to seek shelter in the Haven by a violent winter storm. The fort built by the royalists at Pill was taken after a combined land and sea assault, and Rowland Laugharne, the young and energetic parliamentary commander at Pembroke, was quick to take advantage of this success by advancing on Haverfordwest, which fell without a single shot being fired. With the assistance of the fleet he then proceeded to occupy Tenby. The fall of Carew to Poyer, the Mayor of Pembroke, meant that the whole of Pembrokeshire was in Roundhead hands. Laugharne now advanced on Carmarthen which quickly capitulated. The direction of the attack was then switched to Glamorgan and Robert Moulton, on board the frigate *Lion* at Milford, summoned Swansea to surrender, an invitation which was declined in the strongest terms. [4] Cardiff, however, did not display the same resolution, and the town was taken. With the King now in danger of losing control over the whole of South Wales, Carbery was replaced by Sir Charles Gerard, a very able but ruthless professional soldier. At the head of a troop of horse he landed at the Black Rock, near Chepstow in Monmouthshire, and advanced to meet Laugharne. Cardiff was retaken, and so was Kidwelly. He then proceeded to reoccupy Carmarthen, Cardigan and Newcastle Emlyn, together with the castles at Laugharne and Roch. On 22 August, after inflicting a severe defeat on Laugharne, he took Haverfordwest. Pembroke was now besieged, but owing to the ill fortune which beset the King's forces in England—Charles was defeated by Cromwell at Marston Moor in July which meant that the north of England was lost to the royalists—Gerard was recalled with his work unfinished.

But however satisfying these successes in south-west Wales were for the royalists, in England the military situation was deteriorating rapidly for the King. In January 1644 a Scottish army crossed the border and the impact of this force evidenced itself on 2 July 1644 when the combined armies of Scotland, Yorkshire and the Eastern Association met the King at Marston Moor in the largest single engagement of the whole war. The royalists were overwhelmingly defeated and a crucial factor in this victory, apart from the strong Scottish presence, was the fine discipline displayed by the cavalry of the Association, led with supreme skill by a Huntingdonshire squire by the name of Oliver Cromwell. [5]

The parliamentary success in relieving Nantwich was followed by a spectacular campaign in north-east Wales. Despite

[4] The answer was so sharp that it is attributed to the hand of the famous David Jenkins of Hensol, 'The Judge of the Mountains'.

[5] Cromwell was an outstanding military leader. He had commanded a troop of horse at Edgehill and was quick to perceive what the Roundhead forces lacked. He informed his cousin and good friend John Hampden that 'our troops are most of them old serving-men, tapsters, and such kind of fellows. Do you think that they will ever be able to encounter gentlemen that have honour and courage and resolution in them?' He wanted men who 'know what they are fighting for, and love what they know'.

Myddelton's bitter complaints that his men were melting away for lack of pay, he succeeded in raising the siege of Oswestry and followed this up by capturing Welshpool. Newtown was next to fall and then on 18 September there took place at Montgomery the greatest battle of the first Civil War on Welsh soil. The field was hotly disputed for an hour but the parliamentary triumph was complete. Four hundred royalists were slain and fourteen hundred taken prisoner. Myddelton then turned north to occupy Ruthin before returning to mid-Wales to capture Abbey Cwm Hir on 5 December. Myddelton, therefore, by the end of the year, had succeeded in effectively destroying the King's power in North Wales and in separating, in strategic terms, north from south.

In the early months of 1645 Parliament riveted its control even more firmly over the north-east, since Brereton laid siege to Chester, Beeston and Hawarden, and desperate royalist attempts to relieve these towns were only partially successful. The King having now completely lost the initiative in the north, was in the new year to lose it in the south as well. The recall of Gerard had enabled Laugharne in the winter of 1644 to recover his losses in south-west Wales and the towns and castles at both Laugharne and Cardigan were to fall into his hands. These setbacks led to Gerard returning to South Wales in the spring of 1645. He marched south from Chester, ravaging the countryside as he went, and at Llanidloes met and defeated Sir John Price, the parliamentary Governor of Newtown. Later, at Oswestry, Myddelton was to suffer a similar fate at his hands. Living off the countryside, his soldiery plundered to such an extent that a contemporary was provoked to write: 'The barbarous and cruel enemy drive away our cattle, rifle our houses to the bare walls. All provisions of victuals, where they come, carried away or destroyed. Divers villages and country towns, being neither garrisons nor any annoyance to the enemy, burnt to the ground. The standing corn they burn and destroy. All sexes and degrees are stripped naked by the enemy-aged and unarmed. Persons inhumanely murdered in cold blood, and others half hanged, and afterwards stigmatised, and their flesh burnt off their bodies to the bare bones, and yet suffered in great torture to live'.[6] On 23

[6] In 1644-45, as the King became increasingly short of money, so the

Charles I Dictating Dispatches to Sir E. Walker
A contemporary painting

April he inflicted a crushing defeat on Laugharne at Newcastle Emlyn, a victory which was proclaimed at Swansea and, presumably, elsewhere in Wales by the tolling of bells, and the royalists then occupied Haverfordwest, Cardigan, Picton and Carew. Once more Laugharne was compelled to withdraw to the relative safety of Pembroke and Tenby, those 'crows nests', as one royalist observer caustically described them.

Yet again fate intervened since Gerard was once more summoned to make his blade available for Charles in another theatre of the war. The Roundhead defeat at Lostwithiel in September 1644, and the indecisive second battle of Newbury in October, had strengthened the demand for the removal of officers like the Presbyterian Earl of Manchester who were only half-hearted in their prosecution of the war. The Self-Denying Ordinance of April 1645 deprived all peers and Members of Parliament of their commands though the right of reappointment was reserved. Parliament was now free to appoint Sir Thomas

plundering of the countryside by his troops, in both England and Wales, increased proportionately.

Fairfax as Captain-General of the New Model Army, while
Cromwell was made his Lieutenant and put in command of the
horse. The consequence of this reorganisation was immediate
and dramatic, because in June 1645, at Naseby, in the last major
battle of the first Civil War, Charles suffered another resounding
defeat. One thousand royalists lay dead on the battlefield while a
further five thousand were taken prisoner.

With Gerard away, Laugharne decisively defeated the local
royalist commanders, Stradling and Egerton, at Colby Moor,
outside Haverfordwest, on 1 August taking four field guns, five
barrels of gunpowder and eight hundred arms. With Pembroke
now firmly under his control, he occupied Carmarthen in
October, and then, advancing through Glamorgan, reached
Brecon by November and by the end of the year was laying siege
to Aberystwyth. In April 1646 the town fell to Colonel Rice
Powell, one of Laugharne's lieutenants.

After the defeat at Naseby, Charles fled to Hereford and from
there to Raglan, which he made his temporary headquarters.
But his attempts to raise another army in South Wales met with
little success despite the assurances of support given by the Commissioners of Array for the South Wales counties at Abergavenny when 'they promised mountains'. Too much Welsh blood
had been spilt to so little avail; there was deep resentment at the
employment of English officers like Gerard and Byron and at the
rape of the countryside by their ill-fed and unpaid troops. Feelings ran so high that a 'Peace Army' was formed in Glamorgan
to protect the county from further spoliation. At St Fagan's, on
29 July, the 'Peaceable Army' presented its terms to Charles.
The shire was to be rid of papists, the English garrison at Cardiff
was to be removed and the Governor, Sir Timothy Tyrell, replaced by Sir Richard Bassett of Beaupré and the charges
imposed upon them by Gerard were to be remitted. On the
following day, at Cardiff, Charles agreed to these terms and he
further accepted the need to deprive Gerard of his command in
South Wales. In return for these concessions an army of one
thousand men was to be raised for the King but Charles, despair-
ing of the situation, on 5 August left for Brecon.

The Roundhead success at Colby Moor in August, and the fall
of Bristol, the second city in the land, on 10 September, saw the
Glamorgan leaders entering into negotiations with Laugharne,

who despatched to them by sea the arms which had been captured at Colby. The Puritan Edward Pritchard of Llancaeach now replaced Sir Richard Bassett as Governor of Cardiff, while Philip Jones of Llangyfelach, a staunch parliamentarian, was made Governor of the other garrison town of Glamorgan, Swansea. Bussy Mansel of Briton Ferry, previously a royalist stalwart in the Swansea area, was appointed commander-in-chief of all forces within the County. The counties of Carmarthen, Cardigan, Brecon and Radnor now followed the lead given by Glamorgan by declaring for Parliament. The King had lost control of South Wales.

There was a flutter of hope in February 1646 when the sheriff, Colonel Edward Carne, declared in favour of the King and, marching on Cardiff, summoned Pritchard to surrender the castle. The reasons for the rising are not far to seek and may be found in the intervention of outsiders, in the raising of the county contribution from £67 to £162 a week, in the fact that while baronets, knights and gentlemen were passed over, men of no social status were nominated to places on the county committee, and finally in the control which sectaries, the Independents and Baptists in particular, had gained over affairs. It was said that 'schismatics of several kinds are of greatest trust with some in chiefest places of government in this county, whereby our souls and lives our liberties and estates must be at their desire'. Sir Charles Kemeys with royalist forces from Monmouthshire now converged on Cardiff where he was joined by the besiegers led by Carne, but this force was defeated by Laugharne, and Carne was taken prisoner. This defeat signalled the end of the first Civil War in South Wales and on 19 August, rather symbolically, after withstanding a vigorous siege, conducted by Fairfax himself, Raglan capitulated, an event which Parliament commemorated with a day of thanksgiving.

Unlike the brief spasm of royalist activity in Glamorgan in 1646, there were no hopeful signs for the King in the north. In September 1645, from the town walls of Chester, Charles had witnessed the defeat of his forces at Rowton Heath. Chester itself managed to hold out for a little longer but Byron, having secured honourable terms, finally surrendered the town to Brereton on 3 February 1646. There now only remained the mopping-up of the last pockets of royalist resistance and Mytton, assisted by Colonel Philip Jones, was entrusted with the task. He moved west and, one by one, the royalist strongholds of Ruthin, Holt, Denbigh, Flint, Caernarvon, Beaumaris and Conway were reduced. On 15 March 1647 Harlech capitulated, the last of the King's fortresses in England and Wales to do so. The first Civil War was finally over.

THE SECOND CIVIL WAR

Parliament having won the war had now to win the peace. In the country as a whole there was a general atmosphere of unease and the triumph of their cause brought to a head the latent dissensions in the ranks of Puritans and Parliament. The royalists, though defeated, were not supine and the King's agents were busily fostering trouble in the localities and taking advantage of the groundswell of sympathy for Charles. Meanwhile the King, though a prisoner, endeavoured to recover through duplicity and intrigue what he had lost on the field of battle. By playing off his opponents, the Scots, the New Model Army and Parliament, the one against the other, he hoped to come into his own again and thus recover what he genuinely believed to be legitimately his. It was a dangerous path to follow and one that was eventually to lead to the scaffold. Suspicions as to Charles's intentions were further deepened by his clandestine attempts to obtain help from Irish Catholics. In the shires there were complaints about the heavy financial burdens that had to be borne, and the activities of the county committees came under fire as well, particularly their tolerance of the new sects. This was exemplified in the Vale of Glamorgan where, in 1647, the gentry gave vent to their feelings in a mass demonstration. Furthermore, the Cromwellian armies were a seedbed of radical, even revolutionary, ideas[7] and the discontent in their ranks was further fomented by such considerations as arrears of pay, and the decision taken by Fairfax to reduce the burden of military expenditure by disbanding forces which were regarded as supernumerary. Among those affected by this decision were men who had served with Laugharne, and doubts about his loyalties had led to his being summoned to London by Parliament to answer charges of conspiring with the King's agents. John Poyer, a violent, impulsive and boastful

[7] Vide 'Putney Debates' in *Puritanism and Liberty*, Ed. A. S. P. Woodhouse, London, 1950.

man, was now replaced as Governor of Pembroke castle by a Colonel Fleming, but when the parliamentary commissioner arrived in Pembroke in 1648 to carry out the disbanding, Poyer decided to defy him and, withdrawing his men inside the castle, fired on that part of the town where Fleming's men were billeted. These shots heralded the outbreak of the second Civil War, and it was ironic that this war should have started in what had formerly been a bastion of the parliamentary cause in Wales.

Another dissident, Rice Powell, now threw in his lot with Poyer and marched to join him at Pembroke. Fleming meantime had sent for reinforcements, but on arrival this force was defeated by Poyer and Powell, who then gained control of the town as well as the castle. Following this battle Fleming was fortunate in that he was provided with refuge on board a parliamentary vessel.

Encouraged by events in Pembroke, the royalists decided to join in, and the rebels declared for the King. Horton was despatched to Wales by Fairfax to suppress the rebellion. From Hereford, by way of Brecon and Neath, he marched to Swansea, where he was joined by Fleming. There was considerable skirmishing with Powell during the course of which Fleming accidentally shot himself and died. Horton's supplies running low, he was forced to return to Brecon.

Powell now went on the offensive and entering Glamorgan by the coastal road, he quickly took Swansea[8] and Neath, and proceeded to negotiate with the royalists of the Vale of Glamorgan and the Governor of Cardiff castle. To prevent the possibility of Cardiff falling, Horton hurriedly left Brecon and marching south intercepted Powell's forces at Llandaff. Meanwhile Laugharne had left London and joined Powell, thereby breaking an undertaking which he had entered into not to leave the City until the charges against him had been heard. Horton refused Laugharne's invitation to withdraw, and both sides became

[8] In a charge brought against Philip Jones in 1650 it was declared that 'Coll. Rice Powell in Feby last, with a brace of pockett pistols singly forced the said Jones his centinells from their standinge at Swansea, he being then personally in the garrison, and not making the least resistance, but permitted the said Col. Powell to place sentinels of his own there when he first appeared against the Parliament, and soe immediately Jones quit the towne and fled to Herefordth (sic) Haverfordwest'.

Pembroke Castle

Roundhead

Cavalier

locked in conflict at St. Fagan's on 8 May 1648. This engagement was to prove the largest battle of either Civil War in Wales. Though Horton was considerably outnumbered—he had only three thousand men as opposed to Laugharne's eight thousand —he had seasoned veterans at his command and, after a battle which lasted for some two hours, he inflicted a crushing defeat on his adversary taking over three thousand prisoners.

After this reverse, Laugharne and Powell retreated to South Pembroke, Powell installing himself at Tenby while Laugharne and Poyer took refuge in Pembroke. Cromwell himself now, obviously disturbed by developments in West Wales, decided to take a hand. By way of Cardiff and Swansea[9] he reached Pembroke, where he laid siege to the castle. The taking of Tenby he entrusted to Horton and on 31 May the town surrendered. At Pembroke, Cromwell was confronted with a task of the first magnitude, for the walls were strong, and the garrison was prepared to offer stern resistance. Furthermore, he lacked heavy siege guns and his supplies soon ran low. Cromwell, however, was not a military leader to be deterred by difficulties. He had the guns brought by sea from Gloucester and, after a siege lasting forty eight days, Laugharne and Poyer surrendered on 11 July.

Laugharne, Powell and Poyer were now condemned to death, but Fairfax decided that one only should die. Lots were drawn and it was in this manner that fate decreed that Poyer should be the one to atone for all three 'sinning against so much light'. On 25 April, 1649, courageous to the very end, he was shot at Covent Garden.

But the order for the disbandment of supernumerary troops applied to North as well as South Wales, and as in the south it led to unrest among the soldiers. There were local grievances to complicate matters further, since the gentry resented not only the heavy impositions laid upon them, but also the loss of status which they had suffered within their own counties. To them, as to the gentry in Glamorgan, it appeared as if the whole world had been turned topsy-turvy:

[9] A grateful Parliament had conferred on Cromwell all the estates of the Marquis of Worcester in Gloucestershire, Monmouthshire and Glamorganshire. It was in this manner that Cromwell's lively interest in the town began. This interest was exemplified by his conduct while at Swansea for he gave £10 'to bee sett out att interest for the benefitte and advantage of ye said poore'.

'Rhoddi'r pen yn lle'r gloren
A rhoi'r gynffon ar y talcen'[10]

The first indication of approaching trouble occurred in Anglesey, when quarrels broke out over the appointment of a Deputy-Governor for the island. Major-General Thomas Mytton was refused admission into Beaumaris castle and, discomfited, he retired to Caernarvon castle where he proceeded to strengthen the garrison. Meanwhile, Sir John Owen of Clenennau had been stirring up trouble in Caernarvonshire and he was joined by forces from the neighbouring counties as well as from South Wales. Twistleton, the very active parliamentary Governor of Denbigh castle, in an effort to prevent royalist reinforcements from reaching Caernarvonshire, rode with a small detachment of eighty horse into Merioneth and at Barmouth surprised a royalist force and compelled it to surrender. Mytton now sent an urgent message to Twistleton to come immediately to his aid and the latter, gathering what forces he could from Denbigh, Conway and Chester, marched to the relief of Caernarvon. However, at Aber, he was intercepted by the royalists, but in the ensuing battle at Llandegai he inflicted upon them a crushing reverse. Sir John Owen was wounded and taken prisoner and transported to Denbigh castle where the royalists made a determined but unsuccessful attempt to rescue him by seizing the castle in a night attack. From Denbigh he was taken to London and condemned to death, but owing to the intercession of General Ireton, Cromwell's son-in-law, his life was spared and he lived to see the restoration of monarchy in 1660.

.   The 'invasion' of England by the Duke of Hamilton with ten thousand Scots was a source of great encouragement to the royalists who began to gather from far and wide in Anglesey, though Archbishop John Williams counselled his fellow countrymen to make peace. Byron landed on the island to take charge of the revolt there, but he failed to enlist the support of Richard Bulkeley and the other local gentry, and so he withdrew to the Isle of Man. Bulkeley, who had been selected as leader, proved a vain and incompetent commander.[11] He failed to prevent

[10] Placing the head where the tail should be, and the tail where the head should be'.

[11] He was to be killed in a duel with Richard Cheadle, a Major in the parliamentary army, on Lavand Sands on 19 February, 1650.

Mytton from crossing the Menai Straits, and at the battle of Red Hill Fields he was completely routed. For its contumacy the island was fined £7000. The fine for the South Wales counties for their part in the second Civil War had been fixed at £20,500.

The second Civil War convinced the army generals, including Oliver Cromwell, that Charles Stuart, 'that man of blood', had to be brought to trial as a traitor. London was occupied and in December 1648 about one hundred members, regarded as lukewarm in their attitudes, were excluded from the House of Commons by Captain Pride. Among those purged were some fifteen Welsh members, including Sir Thomas Myddelton, Simon Thelwall, Sir John Price and Sir Hugh Owen. Two Welshmen only, Colonel John Jones of Maesygarnedd, and

Archbishop John Williams

The Banqueting House, Whitehall

Thomas Wogan, member for the Cardigan boroughs, were to sit on the High Court of Justice and to sign the King's death warrant. On 30 January, 1649, outside the Banqueting Hall, Whitehall, on a cold and frosty day, Charles I was beheaded. Far away in North Wales, at Gloddaeth, an elderly Archbishop fainted on hearing the news; but John Williams would not have been alone in his grief and horror at the execution of the King. His feelings would have been shared by the greater part of the Welsh gentry and people, for to them this was a foul deed which seemed to signal the end of an era.

The Effects of the Wars on Wales

The Civil Wars in Wales were not characterised by savagery nor did they leave a trail of devastation across the land. There was little of the carnage or material damage which are associated with the Thirty Years War in Germany. Large areas of the countryside were almost completely unaffected by the campaigning, and the towns hardly suffered at all. In these areas the normal tenor of life would hardly have been disturbed. It is doubtless true that, as at Swansea, successive demands for able-bodied men to fight the King's battles led to some neglect of tillage, but there is no evidence that this neglect led to shortages of any description. The towns, apart from those which had suffered from the sustained pounding of siege guns, did not display the scars of war since their burgesses were far more intent on the physical preservation of their boroughs than defending the royal prerogative. The approach of an enemy was invariably greeted not with a martial show of defiance, but rather with the white flag of submission. In some instances the citizens themselves destroyed the town walls to demonstrate tangibly their peaceful intentions. Castles did not fare as well since some had their towers and walls breached by gunfire while others, when the hostilities had ended, were quite deliberately destroyed so that they could never again be of any military value. Those which ceased to be used as residences suffered from neglect and pillage and were only too soon to provide the ingredients for romance. Here and there, the landscape was dotted with burnt-down manor houses, barns and hayricks, and even with damaged or desecrated churches. It was Myddelton's troopers that melted down the organ pipes of Wrexham church to make shot for their guns. But the extent of the damage must not be exaggerated, and the wounds inflicted by man on a countryside are quickly healed.

Far more traumatic for the Welsh than physical damage in this 'unnatural' war, was the death and suffering as a result of battle, and the legacy of sorrow left in so many aching breasts. Contingent after contingent of Welsh foot soldiers, ill-armed and ill-trained, had marched off to fight, and many had found a bloody and unmarked grave. Those that survived were often wounded or maimed for life. It was at the siege of Bristol that Sir John Owen was shot through the neck and very nearly died. When Mytton laid siege to Beaumaris castle, Vavasor Powell, the notable Puritan preacher, received wounds to his head, his side and his hand with the result that he lost the use of two of his fingers. Occasionally, though it was unusual, there were acts of great brutality, as at Naseby when the victorious parliamentarians attacked wives and camp followers of royalists, killing about a hundred and slitting the noses of others. The sum total of human suffering and grief was great and this helped to strengthen and foster the belief that the old régime, after all, had been preferable to the new.

Great as was the anguish of the heart, there were lamentations also over loss of income, since there was a general dislocation of trade and both the drovers and the clothiers suffered from the disturbances. The cattle drove was a primary source of revenue since it was a means of bringing into Wales the coin that was in such great demand and in such short supply. According to Archbishop John Williams the drovers were to Wales what the galleons had been to Spain, 'bringing hither that little gold and silver we have'. Indeed, it was by this means that Welsh tenant farmers were enabled to pay their rents. The concern of the Welsh was reflected in a petition which the gentry of North Wales presented to Charles in 1643 requesting safe conduct for their herds. The sale of Welsh cloth to the Shrewsbury drapers was also disrupted, particularly after the fall of the town to the parliamentarians, with the result that the clothiers suffered considerable financial losses. It was with some justification then that

Market Hall, Shrewsbury.

Sieffre Dafydd ab Ifan complained of rampaging armies trampling the Welsh vineyard.

But trade by sea was also dislocated since markets were closed, ships had to be convoyed and taxation on coal cargoes became a recognised source of revenue of some value. In July 1643 the Commissioners of Array for Glamorgan prohibited trade between the county and those parts of England in rebellion against the King. From Milford the parliamentary fleet kept a very close surveillance on shipping bound for Welsh ports, and Robert Moulton, when he called upon Swansea to surrender to Parliament in 1644, declared that if the town failed to comply with the request, he would 'endeavour to keep you without trade till your forced obedience bring you to the mercy of him that tendereth you grace and favour'. That the parliamentary blockade of the South Wales ports was not without effect is demonstrated by a report in 1645 that the parliamentary ships had taken 'many of Swansey boates, and some from Cardiff'.

However, the closing of markets and the need to convoy vessels were not the only factors that disrupted the export trade of Wales. Equally important, possibly, was the heavy taxation on exports and particularly coal. In 1644 the foreign exporter paid 13s.2d. export tax on each Newcastle chaldron (then 52 cwts) and the English trader 11s.6d. per chaldron on coal shipped abroad. Unfortunately, it is not possible to assess the extent of the decline in coal exports consequent on the imposition of this tax, since Port Book data for this, as for the Commonwealth period, are not available; but one can assume that it must have been considerable.

The victory of the parliamentary armies and the parliamentary fleet was no less a victory for the Puritan ministers. Many of those who had fled from Wales early in the Civil Wars lost no opportunity of returning again along with the parliamentary forces, and since Puritanism now basked in the sunshine of official recognition, it could reasonably be expected to grow and flourish. On 27 July 1646 Ambrose Mostyn who, in 1642, at the request of the parishioners, had been nominated by Parliament to minister at Pennard, near Swansea, but who, on the outbreak of the Civil War, had been constrained to flee to safer quarters, was appointed by the Committee of Plundered Ministers to officiate at Swansea. For a stipend of £50, 'he was required to preach and officiate as well in ye parish church of Swansea, as in ye parishes and places thereto adjacent'. It would appear that he was not there for long because on 20 July 1648, he, Morgan Llwyd and Vavasor Powell were named as 'Itinerant Ministers for North Wales'. During his short stay in the Swansea area, it is quite possible that he became instrumental in establishing the first gathered church there.

Socially, though the royalists were defeated, they were by no means entirely eliminated from public life. On the other hand, the new men among the parliamentarians, hailing from humbler stock, and the trimmers had come to the top, and most of them were to remain there even after the Restoration. The balance of social forces within Wales had been radically changed and the more so as the majority of the older families had backed the wrong horse.

Chapter 4

MILITARY OVERLORDSHIP, 1649-1660

RELIGION AND EDUCATION

Wales, which had been royalist throughout the period of the Civil Wars, soon occupied the attention of the new Commonwealth which was confronted with challenges at home and abroad. Wales constituted both a threat and a challenge; a threat since, after all, the second Civil War had started there and the red-hot embers of royalism could be fanned into life very easily again. A challenge because if the revolutionary authorities in London were to win any measure of general support in Wales, then something had to be done about the slow progress of Puritanism there. This faith, after all, had inspired opposition to Charles I, and Puritan fervour had been a potent force impelling the soldiers of the New Model Army from victory to victory on the field of battle. But the Puritan plant had never flourished in Welsh soil, partly because it was not an indigenous growth—like Protestantism it was introduced into Wales along the trade routes from such Puritan strongholds as Bristol, Gloucester, Chester and London—and partly because the environment was not wholly propitious for its development even though the Church in Wales, like its counterpart in England, was sadly in need of reform and the Puritans were among its fiercest critics.

Royal policy and the greed of laymen had contributed to the impoverishing of the Church in the sixteenth century for lands, tithes and rights of advowson had been transferred to the gentry. As a result of this poverty, and the unscrupulousness of lay impropriators, the stipends paid to the clerics were abysmally low, and they were compelled to become pluralists and consequently guilty of absenteeism. The unattractiveness of livings in Wales resulted in the best among the clergy being attracted to fatter benefices in England. The position was exacerbated by bishops, eager to supplement their incomes, holding livings *in commendam*, and leasing out Church property such as rectories and glebelands. Furthermore, and especially in the eyes of the Puritans, the Church suffered from the fact that Catholic

survivals in worship abounded, that many of the clergy were
English, and that there was a serious lack of preaching of the
Word in Welsh. These were the clerics dubbed by John Penry as
'dumb ministers'. Indeed, there were parishes where not a single
sermon had been preached in a whole year. The Puritan element
within the Church had attempted to improve matters in this respect by buying up the impropriated tithes of various parishes,
and using the revenue to pay the salaries of preachers, more particularly in the towns. Among the twelve authors of this scheme,
which was put into operation in 1625, were John White, descended from a family of Tenby merchants, and Rowland Heylin
who, together with Sir Thomas Myddelton, was responsible for
financing the publication of the first portable edition of the
Welsh Bible in 1630. [1] The largest purchase made was that of the
living of Presteigne in Radnorshire, but the government soon
intervened and the funds were confiscated by order of the Court
of Exchequer. Again, many of the lower clergy were ignorant
and superstitious, and neglected such essential pastoral duties as
christenings, visiting the sick and bereaved, and even the burial
of the dead. In their private lives there were scandals and irregularities, and it was not uncommon for clergymen to be involved in
drunken brawls or even to keep ale-houses. Though a popular
edition of the Bible had appeared in 1630, there were still insufficient copies. Vavasor Powell, in 1646, speaking with a fair
degree of hyperbole, declared that there was 'not one (Bible) in
five hundred families'. This generally unsatisfactory condition
of the Church culminated inevitably in spiritual apathy, moral
decadence and intellectual torpor.

However, there is another side to the picture, since there were
elements within the Church which were wide-awake, zealous
and reforming despite some lapses from grace. There were
enlightened Bishops like Lewis Bayly, author of *The Practice of
Piety*, [2] and in their ranks also were more Welsh speakers. Among

[1] This edition sold for five shillings and 1500 copies were printed. It was
known as the *Beibl Coron* or the *Beibl Bach*.

[2] This extremely popular book of devotion was translated into Welsh by
Rowland Vaughan of Caergai in 1630 under the title, *Yr Ymarfer o Dduwioldeb*.
Lewis Bayly was born in Carmarthen, and it was in 1616 that he was appointed
Bishop of Bangor. His conduct as Bishop did not always accord with the high
ideals of his book since he held several livings *in commendam* and was also guilty
of nepotism.

the clergy on the lower rungs were to be found progressive ministers like Vicar Rhys Prichard who, to instruct his illiterate
flock, composed *Canwyll y Cymry*.[3] The lay adherents of the
Church contained persons of considerable worth like William
Salusbury of Bachymbyd, Sir Lewis Mansel of Margam, and
Judge David Jenkins of Hensol in Glamorgan who was prepared
to walk to the scaffold with the Bible under one arm and Magna
Carta under the other, though in time of peace he 'lived like a
heathen, and swore like a devil'. Attempts were also made under
the early Stuarts to improve the condition of the Church. The
practice of pluralism came under attack, there were serious
endeavours to improve stipends and Charles and Laud tried to
recover for the Crown the patronage of livings which had fallen
into other hands. Bishops were to be resident at one or another of
their episcopal palaces and leasing of Church property was not to
be permitted.[4]

Yet despite the existence of these abuses within the Established
Church, which were anathema to the Puritans, there were other
factors which militated against the dissemination of the faith. In
a country where the vast majority of the people were Welsh in
speech, it was hardly to be expected that a gospel presented in an
alien tongue—for the language of Puritanism was English—
would win much acceptance. In 1646 Parliament was to refer to
'the scarcity of preaching ministers in the Welsh tongue', and in
July of the same year Walter Cradock, in a sermon preached
before the House of Commons, declared that there were not in
the 'thirteene counties thirteene conscientious ministers who
preached profitably in the Welsh Language twice every Lord's
Day'. Furthermore, Puritanism was adopted most readily by an
urban middle class of merchants, traders, shopkeepers and
craftsmen because the Puritan ethos could be adapted to meet the
needs of a capitalistic society. However, representatives of the
commercial and business worlds were thin on the ground in

[3] 'The Welshmen's Candle'. Rhys Prichard was born in Llandovery in 1579
and educated probably at Carmarthen grammar school and then at Jesus
College, Oxford. In 1602 he returned home since he was appointed vicar of his
native parish. In 1613 he became rector of Llanedy and then chaplain to the
Earl of Essex. The following year he was appointed prebendary of Christ
College, Brecon. He became Chancellor of the diocese of St. David's in 1626
and vicar of Llawhaden.

[4] Supra, p. 14.

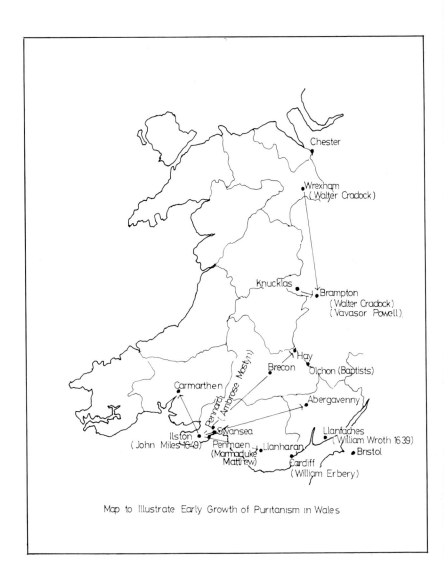

Map to Illustrate Early Growth of Puritanism in Wales

Wales. But it is still very significant that Puritanism took root in Wales in those very areas where they did exist, in places like South Pembroke, port towns in South Wales like Swansea and Cardiff, and border towns like Wrexham, areas which had also been most receptive of Protestantism earlier in the sixteenth century.

Though John Penry (1563-93) is generally regarded as the first of the Welsh Puritans, his influence was felt far more in England than in his native country. In Wales he was an isolated figure. The early leaders of Puritanism in the border counties of Wales were William Wroth, William Erbery, Walter Cradock and Vavasor Powell. William Wroth, a native of Abergavenny, became vicar of Llanfaches in Monmouthshire in 1617. He was extremely devout and had established close contacts with the Puritans in the city of Bristol. Under his influence came Walter Cradock, son of a neighbouring farmer of Trefela, near Usk, who was educated at Oxford and became curate of St Mary's Church at Cardiff. Here the vicar was William Erbery, the son of a merchant of Roath. When Laud became Archbishop of Canterbury he re-issued the Book of Sports (1633) and commanded it to be read in the Churches. This the three men refused to do. In 1635, therefore, the Bishop of Llandaff admonished Erbery and suspended Cradock, 'a bold ignorant young fellow'. In 1638 Erbery resigned and Wroth submitted. After his ejection from Cardiff, Cradock had become curate to Robert Lloyd at Wrexham, and attracted great crowds by his preaching, even at six o'clock in the morning, but he so infuriated the maltsters of the town that he was forced to leave within a year. Already, however, he had converted Morgan Llwyd, a native of Cynfal in Ardudwy, who was then a schoolboy in the town. Cradock now sought refuge at Brampton Bryan in Herefordshire, the seat of Sir Robert Harley, a Puritan landowner.[5] Here he converted Vavasor Powell, a youth who had been born a few miles away at Knucklas in Radnorshire. In 1639 Wroth, 'the apostle of Wales', without leaving the Church of England, organised his

[5] Thomas Froysell, the vicar of Clun, Shropshire, in his funeral sermon for Harley, described him in these words: 'He was the First that brought the Gospell into these Parts. This Country lay under a Vaile of darkness till he began to shine . . . His Planting of godly ministers, and then backing them with his Authority, made Religion famous in this little corner of the world'.

followers into a 'gathered' church at Llanfaches on the pattern of
the Puritan conventicles in New England. This meeting at Llanfaches in November 1639 marks the real beginning of Nonconformity in Wales.

In 1633 a group of separatists made its appearance in the
Olchon valley in the Welsh-speaking areas of West Herefordshire. Its members belonged to the Baptist denomination which a
short time previously had come into existence in England
whither it had been introduced from Holland. The origin of the
Olchon Baptists is still very obscure, but their security they owed
undoubtedly to the isolation of this remote valley among the
Black Mountains in the borderland between the Severn and the
Usk.

Puritanism, in the early decades of the seventeenth century,
was also emerging in South Wales at Swansea, and in the
neighbourhood of the town, and this development is evidenced
by three factors. In 1592/3 the parishioners presented articles
against the vicar, John After, in the Consistory Court of the
Archdeacon at Carmarthen, for not celebrating divine service in
Welsh. Payments were also made by the Corporation, usually in
the sum of 6s.8d, to itinerant ministers for sermons, and finally
many of the parishioners were giving biblical names to their

Independent Chapel, Llanfaches

children and it is a well-established fact that those who sympathised with Puritan teaching tended to adopt this practice. In the Swansea parish registers a number of such names begin to appear in the 1630s. Typical of these are names such as Ruth, Rebecca, Sara, Matthew, Moses, Debora, Joseph, Samuel and Emanuel.

The emergence of Puritanism in the neighbourhood of the town is indicated in the activities of such young Puritan ministers as Marmaduke Matthews at Penmaen and Ambrose Mostyn at Pennard. The son of Matthew ap John of Nydfwch, Llangyfelach, Marmaduke Matthews was an M.A. of All Souls College, Oxford. In 1636 he was vicar of Penmaen, near Swansea, where he preached 'against the keeping of all holy days'. Following episcopal censure of his behaviour, he fled to New England where he became pastor of Yarmouth, Massachusetts, from 1639-43.

Ambrose Mostyn was the son of Dr Henry Mostyn of Calcott, Flintshire. Born in 1610 he had matriculated at Brasenose College, Oxford, in 1629. In 1642 the parishioners of Pennard 'having never had more than four sermons a year in their parish church, and those by a man of a very scandalous life', prayed for the nomination of Ambrose Mostyn, 'a lecturer, a man of goodly sort, and one who can preach in the Welsh and English tongues'. This petition received the favourable attention of the House of Commons and on 30 April it was ordered 'That Ambrose Mostyn, a godly and faithful preacher, be at the Desires of divers of the Parishioners of Pennard . . . recommended to the said Parish to be their Lecturer at their own proper costs and charges, to preach every Lord's day in the forenoon and afternoon'.

With the outbreak of the Civil War, the Puritan ministers had fled to safer quarters in Bristol and London, though some went into hiding, and others were imprisoned, which led Morgan Llwyd to speak of the 'desolation of the Welsh Saincts'. Because the goods of Puritans had been seized by the Royalists,[6] Parliament established a Committee of Plundered Ministers, sitting in London, to look after their welfare. By the time the King was defeated, this Committee had become all-powerful in Wales and

[6] William Erbery claimed the honour of being the 'first plundered minister in Wales'.

it used for its own purposes the wealth of the Church which had been placed at its disposal. The uncompromising royalism of the vast majority of the Welsh clergy was a matter of serious concern for Parliament. Some clergy were expelled because of their delinquency and declarations against Parliament; others for holding a plurality of livings or for scandalous behaviour. But the Committee approved others and, in fact, the majority of the clergy retained their livings.[7] In the counties of Pembroke, Carmarthen and Cardigan two clergy only appear to have been ejected before 1650. Since there were few Puritan divines in Wales to take the place of the clergy who had been expelled, Parliament, immediately after Naseby, despatched Walter Cradock, Henry Walter and Richard Symonds as itinerant preachers to South Wales, although they did not commence their duties there until the Autumn of 1646. Each was allowed £100 per annum out of the sequestered revenues of the Church. In 1648 the Committee sent Morgan Llwyd, Vavasor Powell and Ambrose Mostyn on a similar mission to North Wales, Llwyd receiving £120, and Powell and Mostyn £100 each.

These Puritans were Independents since their churches were autonomous bodies with little association between them. There is no evidence of any Presbyterian movement in Wales at this time. However, in 1649, John Miles, having been baptised at a Baptist Church which met at the Glass House in Broad Street, London, returned to Wales to establish a similar church at Ilston in Gower. Soon, there were other churches at Llanharan, Hay, Carmarthen, and Abergavenny and these churches were to be effectively supervised by Miles, and this organisation constituted the nearest approach to a Presbyterian system in Wales.

This spate of Puritan activity achieved much. The Church had been completely disestablished and partially disendowed; a preaching ministry had been established with augmented salaries; itinerants had been profitably employed and the importance of Welsh as the language of the pulpit had been recognised. Nevertheless, despite these successes in Wales and the border counties, and in South Wales Puritan beliefs had been leavened further by the operations of a handful of returning

---

[7] The Committee approved or appointed over 130 ministers for evangelical work in Wales.

exiles from America, the faith continued to make only slow progress. Not unimportant among the factors accounting for this situation were the spiritual inertia of the countryside, the 'seduced' ignorance of the people and their subservience to the gentry, and finally the growing confidence of the unejected episcopal clergy.

The need, therefore, to shed light in the dark places of Wales, re-inforced by such considerations as the weight of petitions from both North and South Wales, the expert advice of Vavasor Powell and the impressions of Major-General Thomas Harrison, one of Cromwell's best cavalry officers who had been appointed to the South Wales command, led to the introduction on 29 January 1650, and to its final adoption on 22 February, of the *Act for the Better Propagation and Preaching of the Gospel in Wales*. But the way for the introduction of the Act had undoubtedly been prepared by the activities of the itinerants, both English and Welsh, in Wales before 1650 and in one sense, consequently, the Act simply represented an attempt to systematise and give direction to their activities. Wales, however, was not the only area of special concern for the supreme powers in England, for similar measures were passed for the northern counties of England, for Ireland and also for New England.

The Act, which was to be in force for three years, delegated authority in Wales to a body of seventy-one commissioners, twenty-eight representing the shires of North Wales and forty-three those in the south. Foremost among the commissioners was to be Thomas Harrison, and the Act is very significant from the administrative point of view in that it represents the only attempt made since the Union legislation of the sixteenth century to grant Wales a measure of self-government. Naturally, the commissioners were all active parliamentarians, some were uncompromisingly Puritan in their attitudes, and the vast majority had experience in administrative or military posts. Very few of the commissioners were from the Welsh-speaking areas, and neither were many recruited from among the older gentry families; though Sir Erasmus Philipps of Picton Castle and Samuel Lort of Stackpole Court were among them. About a quarter of the commissioners were Englishmen and most of these came from the border counties. The majority were gentry, or prosperous yeomen and lawyers drawn from the more anglicised areas of the country. But, significantly, among the commissioners from Wales were a number of 'new men' who had taken advantage of the turmoil of the times to enrich themselves. Among these were Colonel Philip Jones and the regicide, Colonel John Jones. The commission, however, was not the sole concern of these men. They were busily involved in other directions as well. Some sat on the Council of State or were Members of Parliament; others were active in local administration as Sheriffs or members of the various County Committees; and many, as army officers, had important military duties to perform. For all practical purposes the Act was operated by two small bodies, each consisting of fifteen commissioners. In North Wales matters were controlled very much by experienced soldiers like John Carter, George Twistleton and Thomas Madryn, while in the south the reins were held by Colonel Philip Jones, Bussy Mansel, Rowland Dawkin and John Price.

Any five of the commissioners, acting together, could examine ministers and, if they thought fit, eject them from their livings. Within three years they had ejected in all 278 persons of whom 82 were from North Wales, 151 from South Wales and 45 from Monmouthshire. Many of the clergy were ejected for pluralism, malignancy and using the Prayer Book; others for ignorance, fornication, and an inability to preach in Welsh; and some for scandalous behaviour such as drunkenness and the keeping of ale-houses. However, the authorities were not entirely insensitive to the needs and hardships of wives and children of ministers who had been evicted, and consequently the commissioners were empowered to make financial provision for them. Not all received these allowances, and even in cases where they had been granted, they were not always regularly paid.

The condition of the ejected minsiters, generally speaking, was undoubtedly hard, and they responded in a variety of ways to their fate. Those among them who had independent means attempted to provide for themselves, though often very inadequately. Others kept body and soul together by running private schools, by putting pen to paper or, swallowing their pride, accepting the charity of relatives. However, the lot of some, at least, of these ministers, was not one of utter despair because a few, even though officially ejected, continued still in their livings, while others, after appeal, were fortunate enough to have their livings restored to them. Some became schoolmasters under the terms of the Act, while others continued to hold their sequestered properties as tenants. But there were ejected ministers, also, who refused to accept their fate. They continued to hold services according to the Anglican rite in the privacy of their parishioners' houses, and even to agitate and preach openly in their former parishes to 'please their old parishioners, some of which would hear none else'. This situation was made possible by the under-current of sympathy for them among the people, the unpopularity of those who replaced them, and the inability of the authorities to supervise adquately the remoter areas.

Since it was now necessary to find others to take the place of the ejected clergy, a body of twenty-five 'Approvers' was established by the Act to select 'godly and painful men, of approved conversation . . . to preach the gospel in Welsh'. Among the Approvers were men such as Walter Cradock, Morgan Llwyd, Vavasor Powell and John Miles. Any five of these could 'approve' preachers, who would receive a stipend of £100 a year, and the funds for this purpose were to be drawn from the sequestered revenues of the Church.

But the commissioners under the Propagation Act soon discovered that it was much easier to destroy an old edifice than to erect a new one. There was a great dearth of suitable ministers and the commissioners' remedy for this 'famine of the word', of necessity, lay mainly in the continued use of itinerant ministers, some of whom were included in the body of Approvers, and many of whom had already been active as envangelists in Wales before 1650. A few appointments were made to livings and a search was made at London and the Universities for suitable candidates. Many of these, however, had already departed for the north of England, others were ignorant of the Welsh tongue and some were simply not interested and 'waived the Employment'. Of the old school of itinerants Walter Cradock betook himself to mid-Wales; John Miles was organising a string of Baptist churches from the borders of Hereford to Carmarthen; Ambrose Mostyn adopted Wrexham as his base and his activities embraced Welshpool and Oswestry; Morgan Llwyd appears in Llŷn where, apparently, he 'lost his voice', and Vavasor Powell, the 'metropolitan of the itinerants', ranged over Brecon, Radnor and Montgomery. It is rather surprising that Vavasor kept his voice since he preached in two or three places daily and, reminiscent of the great Methodist preachers of the eighteenth century, rode about a hundred miles a week and took advantage of every opportunity to preach the gospel and especially at fairs and markets.

Sixty-three new itinerants were now appointed to Wales and the vast majority of these (42) worked in South Wales and Monmouth. It is quite possible that the labours of the earlier itinerants were now beginning to bear fruit in the south and that for the harvest to be abundant it was desirable to place more itinerants there. Again, this marked concentration in the south may well indicate that itinerants found the northern shires, because of their remoteness, rather uninviting and uncongenial and the Welsh there more conservative in their views.

These itinerants had to undergo a period of probation, according to Erbery 'sometime a yeer or two', though the leading lights among them, people of the calibre of the brilliant Oxford scholar, Charles Edwards, author of *Hanes y Ffydd*,[8] were doubtless exempt. Unlike Charles Edwards, however, the majority of these itinerants were not distinguished by their learning. In their ranks were included old soldiers, substantial farmers, weavers, shoemakers, cap-makers and thatchers. Their ignorance, combined with their unconventional methods of preaching and strange doctrine, made them objects of attacks by Cavaliers. They were abused verbally as 'runners' or 'hackney preachers' and occasionally they went in fear of their lives. At Dolgellau a 'gifted brother' was dragged violently from the pulpit and had his blood 'drawne'. Anglican apologists did not spare them either. They were accused of not being able to read or understand English and Rowland Vaughan called them false prophets and doctrine-mongers. Even the older, more conservative, Puritan leaders were barbed in their criticism. Richard Baxter was so unimpressed by a Welsh itinerant whom he met in 1663 that 'it greiv'd him to talk'.

But even with this infusion of new blood, it was as well that some ministers survived the ejections. In April 1652, 127 of the 'old ministers' were still in possession of their livings in South Wales. The position in North Wales was that twelve remained in Montgomeryshire, thirteen in Caernarvonshire, seven in

---

[8] 'History of the Faith'.

Anglesey, a large number in Flintshire and a very small proportion in Denbighshire. The quality of the preachers apart, the itinerant system had severe deficiencies. A pluralism of livings had been replaced by a pluralism of counties, and the itinerant preacher was described as being 'supplied with fresh horses at every stage'. Among them also was a confusion of tongues, and there were too few of them, even though their efforts were being supplemented by teachers, and by those in settled ministries. In Breconshire, Llansanffraed had not seen a single 'Itenerent Minister' and at Michelston-super-Ely, 'now and then' only. This failure to provide an adequate preaching ministry resulted in irregular church services or even in church services not being conducted at all. According to the testimony of Alexander Griffith, an Anglican pamphleteer and consequently not the most impartial of witnesses,[9] there were '700 parishes unsupplied with any recognised minister, and that one could ride ten or twelve miles on the Lord's day where there is twenty churches and not one door opened'. The comparative failure of the system instituted under the Propagation Act, allied with uncertainty about the future, once the Act had expired, resulted in a few of the Approvers and itinerants settling down in particular districts. Walter Cradock's sphere of influence became Usk, Ambrose Mostyn's Holt, John Miles's, Llanelly, and Charles Edwards's, Llanrhaeadr-ym-Mochnant. In 1654, under the Triers, the itinerant system was to come virtually to an end.

In addition to the appointment of ministers the commissioners under the Propagation Act established schools in Wales. The object of these schools was almost exclusively a religious one and there seems to have been little or no intention that they should be directed to cultural or materialistic ends, except incidentally. The 'Approvers' were to select suitable men to act as schoolmasters at a salary not to exceed £40 a year and to be drawn, as in

[9] Alexander Griffith, having been ejected from the living of Llanwnog in the diocese of Bangor, and from the vicarage at Glasbury, under the terms of the Propagation Act, fulminated against Puritan divines like Vavasor Powell with a pen dipped in vitriol. However, despite his staunch Anglicanism, he managed to worm his way into the favour of the Triers and from 1658 he was employed as a schoolmaster at Hay. In 1660 he was restored to the vicarage at Glasbury.

COMMONWEALTH SCHOOLS.

the case of the ministers, from the sequestered revenues of the Church.

There was a strong tradition, stretching back at least as far as the sixteenth century, of religious reformers, both Catholic and Protestant, being pioneers of educational advance. In England it was John Colet, the Oxford reformer, who established St. Paul's school with Lily as its first headmaster, and this school became the prototype of the endowed grammar schools established during the course of the century. Furthermore, it was Hugh Latimer, the popular preacher, who denounced the failure of Henry VIII's government to direct monastic wealth into educational channels. 'Schools', declared Latimer, 'are not maintained, scholars have no exhibition, the preaching office decayeth'. In Germany Melanchthon and Luther organised the Gymnasia, while at Geneva the University and schools of Calvin became renowned, and were described by a Catholic contemporary as 'the mines whence cometh the ores of heresy'. The Jesuits were also in the forefront of educational reform and their schools and seminaries sprang up all over Europe. But while the Jesuits established their schools to inculcate their ideas into the minds of the young, the Protestants regarded education as the handmaiden of religion, an aid to godliness, in the sense that it was a means of opening doors to revealed truth as contained in the scriptures. After all, the essence of Protestantism lay in the right of the individual to read the scriptures for himself and to draw his own conclusions.

With this background it was not unexpected, therefore, that the Puritan authorities during the Commonwealth period should have placed a similar emphasis on education as an essential feature of their programme to puritanise Wales. The endowed grammar schools of the sixteenth and early seventeenth centuries established at such places as Christ College, Brecon (1541), Bangor (1557), Presteigne (1565), Beaumaris (1609) and Bottwnog (1616) were not interfered with in any way. Neither were the free schools, such as the one established at Llandovery by Vicar Prichard, discontinued, and side by side with these schools were the private schools and those schools run secretly by some of the ejected clergy.

The reason given for the establishment of these Commonwealth schools was to remove 'ignorance and prophaneness' and some sixty were established in the chief market towns. As between North and South Wales there was a fairly even distribution of schools, twenty-six in North Wales as opposed to twenty-eight in South Wales. [10] But within these broad areas there was a very marked concentration of schools. Thus in North Wales nineteen out of the twenty-six schools were to be found in Denbighshire (11) and Montgomeryshire (8). The other four shires had only seven between them, Anglesey, Caernarvonshire and Flintshire each with one only and Merionethshire with four. In South Wales Breconshire (9), Glamorgan (8) and Radnorshire (7) accounted for twenty-four of the twenty-eight set up. Carmarthenshire did not boast a single school. It is possibly significant that of these five shires with a greater density of schools, four were border shires, and thus subject to strong Puritan influences from east of the Dyke, while Glamorgan, with its seaboard and thriving ports like Swansea and Cardiff in close commercial contacts with Puritan strongholds like Bristol and London, contained within its boundaries the conditions conducive to the reception of Puritan doctrine. Many areas were unsupplied with schools, though the existence in some of endowed grammar schools might well account for the omission, and the situation of a few of the schools that were established was rather surprising at times. In Breconshire while a tiny, remote village like Llangorse was provided with a school, market towns like Hay and Crickhowell were not. Situations like these might well have arisen because of the influence which powerful local supporters of Parliament could exercise in high places.

The paucity of evidence is such that infuriatingly little is known about these schools. However, it has been established that they were schools free to all classes, that they were co-educational since girls as well as boys were admitted, and that they were more akin to grammar schools than primary schools is indicated by the subjects to be included in the curriculum, the employment within them of Masters and Ushers, and the phraseology of the Act itself. The school at Wrexham where Ambrose Lewis was Master and Andrew Maddock, Usher, was to 'educate Schollers in the Greek and Latin tongues', while the one at Lampeter was to lay emphasis on teaching the rudiments of Latin and English.

[10] There were five schools established in Monmouthshire.

However, the school at Carew had to be content with simply preparing its pupils 'for greater schools'. Apart from the classics, much emphasis doubtless would have been placed on the study of the Bible and books of devotion. Unfortunately, it has not been possible to establish what methods of instruction were adopted, or whether any use was made of the vernacular.

Schoolmasters were to be persons of 'approved piety', and it is not surprising, therefore, that many were drawn from the ranks of those ministers who had assisted with the propagation of the gospel. A few were ejected clergymen who, 'from mere pity', were employed in this capacity. But there were others, 'having no competent learning for a schoolmaster', who were unworthy of the occupation. Proposals were now made for the establishing of a College, supported by the state, where young men could be trained for the ministry. Unfortunately, the Restoration in 1660 was effectively to lay this idea to rest.

The Propagation Act lapsed in March 1653 and the place of the commissioners was taken in 1654 by a body known as the Triers, composed of nine laymen and twenty-nine ministers operating from London. Only two Welshmen, Walter Cradock and George Griffiths, were included. The Triers were godly, moderate men with high standards. The system of itinerant preachers was now abandoned and ministers in future were to be licensed only if they had been provided with a testimonial signed by at least three responsible persons including a settled minister. Four Receivers were appointed for Wales to collect rents and profits, and to receive also the revenues of sequestered properties which had been let, so that the new ministers would be attractively remunerated for their work. The aim was to provide the ministers with a salary of £100 a year, though this was a goal that was rarely achieved since most were paid considerably less than this. It was also proposed to re-organise the parishes by joining together the smaller ones and splitting up the larger ones. Not much progress was to be made in this direction.

Most of the old appointments to livings were confirmed and new ones were made in an attempt to plug the gaps since the Triers inherited a legacy where the country was rapidly plunging into a state of religious chaos, with churches being closed and falling into ruin, and in others, services being conducted only intermittently. The passing of the first generation of itinerants did not help, though the Triers were to find among the younger generation men of outstanding ability, such as Stephen Hughes, who was appointed in 1654 to the living of Meidrim, and Samuel Jones, who obtained that of Llangynwyd in 1657. But the shortage of suitable ministers was to prove an insuperable hurdle and led inevitably to ministers being allowed to hold more than one living, a situation which resulted in non-residence. The difficulties with recruitment also saw the itinerant system being reintroduced on a limited scale and standards of acceptance into the ministry being lowered to the point where young, inexperienced persons, with no command of Welsh, were securing appointments. It is hardly surprising, therefore, that the Triers achieved little success in Wales.

However, in addition to these official attempts to promote puritanism, there were also the activities of the Presbyterians, the Fifth Monarchy Men and the Quakers. The overthrow of episcopal authority, the disappearance of church courts, the abolition of censorship, the slackening of social conventions and the increased emphasis on the right of the individual to read the gospels for himself and to draw his own conclusions, meant that the sects were provided with an unprecedented opportunity to flourish. They were as one in maintaining that they alone had a monopoly of divine truth and that God's meaning had been made known to them by the operation of the eternal spirit within. Under these conditions, conservatives of all hues feared that the sects would spread 'like locusts from Egypt over the surface of the earth', and their fears were not unfounded, because spread they did.

Attention has already been drawn to the establishment by John Miles at Ilston in Gower in 1649 of a Baptist Church which became the spiritual mother of a string of Baptist churches in South Wales.[11] But while the Baptists were planting roots in South Wales, the Presbyterians were doing likewise in Flintshire in North Wales under the leadership of Philip Henry, though their influence was far more localised. His co-operation with the Independents in north-east Wales had the effect of giving to Presbyterianism in the area a far more liberal outlook.

But there were other sects that held and propagated views that

[11] Supra, p. 64.

were far more radical and revolutionary than those held by either the Baptists or the Presbyterians. Among these were the Fifth Monarchy Men, who believed that the second coming of Christ was imminent, and that he would rule in peace for a thousand years. In this conviction they were sustained by the interpretation which they placed upon the Book of Daniel and the Book of Revelations and, according to their calculations, the millenium would start sometime between 1650 and 1666. Consequently, any impediments to the coming of 'Y Brenin Iesu',[12] had to be swept aside. One such obstacle had been removed in 1649 with the execution of Charles I, but the Fifth Monarchists soon concluded that the Rump was quite as imperfect an instrument of government as the old monarchy had been. When in April 1653 Cromwell expelled the Rump, the Fifth Monarchists really felt that their hour had come, and they succeeded in persuading Cromwell to establish the Parliament of the Saints known as 'Barebones Parliament' after Praise-God Barbon, who was a leather merchant. The new assembly was to consist of 140 members selected by the army leaders from lists of nominees submitted by the Independent churches, and Wales was to be represented by six members, three from the north and three from the south. Their main task was the reformation of society as an essential prelude to the coming of the new heavenly King and the establishment of an earthly Utopia, and foremost among the sowers of seed in Wales were Morgan Llwyd and Vavasor Powell.

The Saints, however, were not destined to rule for long. The radicalism of the assembly disturbed Cromwell and after only five weeks its rule came to an abrupt end on 12 December 1653. Within four days, Oliver had himself proclaimed Lord Protector with his authority solidly based on military might. The Fifth Monarchists were enraged by this act and they fulminated furiously against the 'traitor', Cromwell. Vavasor Powell, having angrily denounced Cromwell at Blackfriars in London for usurping the place of Jesus Christ, returned home to continue with his agitation there, and the authorities had to keep a close watch on him, particularly after his boast in 1655 that 20,000 of the Saints were ready to rally to his support. Nevertheless,

[12] 'King Jesus'.

despite his defiance, he was quick enough to rally to Cromwell's support when the royalists in Wiltshire rose in rebellion under Penruddock. In December 1655 Powell published a petition signed by 322 people, most of whom were freeholders and tradesmen in the Welsh marches, which was bitterly critical of the Protectorate. Morgan Llwyd's name was included on the list but without his knowledge. Though Llwyd shared Powell's dismay at the dissolution of the Parliament of Saints, he was not prepared to break with Cromwell and the new regime. Furthermore, by this time, he was abandoning his belief in Millenarianism, and was coming under the influence of Jacob Boehme and the Quakers. Llwyd's misgivings at the hostile attitude of Vavasor Powell were shared by the vast majority of the Puritans in Wales. Their steadfastness was demonstrated in the petition, organised by Walter Cradock, and signed by 762 people in South Wales, in which they pledged their loyalty to Cromwell. By 1657 Powell himself had come to the conclusion that it was useless to expect the Welsh to take up arms against the Lord Protector.

But Morgan Llwyd was not alone in his belief in the inner light, for Quaker missionaries were soon active throughout Wales. In July 1653 Llwyd despatched two of his Wrexham congregation to Swaithmore in Yorkshire, which George Fox had made the centre of his missionary activities. The purpose of the visit was to inquire further into the nature of Quakerism. One of the messengers, John ap John, a yeoman of Ruabon, became convinced of the truth and importance of Fox's teaching to the extent that he became the chief apostle of the creed in Wales. Contact with the English Quakers having been established, there arrived in October at Wrexham, 'the most populous town in all Wales', two of Fox's disciples, Richard Hubberthorne and John Lawson, both of Lancashire, and the task of propagating the gospel in Wales began in earnest. In South Wales, in 1654-5, Thomas Holme launched a great missionary campaign to win converts, and this was followed in 1656 by John ap John's efforts among the Baptists of Radnorshire. Fox himself, in 1657, accompanied by John ap John, went on a crusading mission throughout Wales, a mission which started in Bristol and ended in Chester, and the counter-attack on the Quakers, launched by the Baptists in Brecon in the summer of

1656, may well have influenced his decision to do so. [13] The two leaders were accorded a mixed reception in the towns which they visited, since at times they were greeted with enthusiasm, and at other times with coldness and even hostility. Obviously encouraged by the success of this mission, John ap John, in 1658, embarked on a great preaching campaign in South Wales, though during the course of it he was to suffer considerable hardship. The Quakers had acquired an unenviable reputation as militants and their programme of radical reform, coupled with their unconventional behaviour, undoubtedly contributed to this belief. To them the sacraments were of no importance, the payment of tithes was unjustified, wives could preach, oaths were not to be taken, church services could be interrupted and, even in church, hats were to be worn. At Swansea John ap John, because of his public opposition to one of the ministers, was brought before the magistrate's court, where he was struck, and even had his nose pulled, by one Morris Bidwell without the latter incurring any reproof. He was also detained in prison for twenty weeks and at the end of that period released without trial.

Despite this persecution the Quakers made many converts in Wales, and their meeting houses were particularly numerous in the three shires of Merioneth, Radnor and Montgomery. In Glamorgan, also, their aggressive propaganda was effective, particularly when directed against the Baptists of the county and at both Swansea and Cardiff the Society of Friends made many conversions.

Both the Puritans and the faithful of the Anglican communion were equally opposed to the Quakers, the *Crynwyr*. The Friends, as the Devil's disciples, constituted a threat in their eyes to the established order in both the religious and political fields. To John Miles they were the 'plague of the times'. This, together with their strange behaviour, accounts for the persecution and suffering which, unlike the other sects, they had to endure and which was to continue unabated even after the Restoration of 1660.

Despite its limitations the Puritan Revolution had re-awakened the spiritual life of Wales. The piety displayed by so many of

[13] The broadside against the Quakers was delivered by John Miles who was instructed at Brecon to write a pamphlet as 'An antidote against the infection of the times'.

the itinerants, despite occasional lapses, certainly had its impact upon everyday behaviour. There was a marked decline, according to Henry Nicholls, in the incidence of drunkenness in Glamorgan; while in Powys, according to the testimony of Vavasor Powell, there was no working, playing or travelling on Sundays. Cradock describes the gospel 'as running over the mountains between Brecknock and Monmouth like fire in the thatch', and Cromwell himself was of the opinion that God 'had kindled a seed there'. It was this seed that was to help prepare the way for the harvest reaped so abundantly by the Methodists in the eighteenth and nineteenth centuries.

GOVERNMENT

'Rhag nerth y committee hefyd
Libera nos domine'.[14]

The County Committee made its first appearance during the period of the Civil Wars and was the brain child of the Puritan regime. It was the counterpart of the royalist Commission of Array since its function was to organise the defence of every county under parliamentary control and to use the resources of these counties to promote the general war effort. The defeat of the royalists meant that the victorious Parliament was now confronted with the task of governing the country. It was perfectly natural, therefore, that Parliament should have decided to use a device in time of peace which had proved so successful in time of war, but in the process to broaden its base and extend its functions. This involved including on the committees representatives of those older county families who were prepared to cooperate with the revolutionary authorities. The committees were designed to be essential linchpins between central and local government.

One difficulty in introducing into Wales the committee system was that only the Welsh counties of the South contained a sufficient number of gentry of standing and wealth, irrespective of whether they were Cavalier or Roundhead. Another problem was the fact that, with the exception of South Pembroke, the majority of the older gentry families were royalist in sympathy, leav-

---

[14] 'From the strength of the Committee also, Lord save us'.

ing only a hard core of parliamentary supporters among the smaller gentry, yeomen and tradesmen.

Two types of County Committees were to evolve: the Standing Committee and the Committee of Accounts. The former mobilised resources and enforced obedience to parliamentary orders while the latter, through its Treasurer, controlled finance. This system was open to abuse and, furthermore, provided opportunities for the promotion of old family feuds. Thus in Brecknock and Carmarthen, the two County Treasurers, Thomas Games and John Lewis respectively, were accused of defrauding their counties to the tune of more than £1000 between them. However, these charges must be related to a background of family antagonisms, exacerbated still further by the religious and political differences which had led originally to the Civil War.

A most important duty that fell to the lot of the County Committees, because the Roundheads, like the royalists, were determined to make the enemy pay for the war, was the sequestration of the estates of delinquents. For this purpose, *ad hoc* sequestration committees were established and it would appear that the salaried officials of these committees were drawn invariably from the limited circle of parliamentary supporters. Occasionally, erstwhile royalists intruded themselves for the express purpose of protecting their own interests and property.

In 1649 these *ad hoc* committees were replaced by two statutory Sequestration Committees, one for South Wales and another for North Wales. These two committees were empowered to levy the collective fines incurred by the two areas because of their delinquency in the second Civil War.[15] However, in 1650, there was a change of tactic since all existing sequestration committees were now abolished and their powers transferred to a Central Committee sitting at Goldsmith's Hall, London. This Central Committee then nominated three subordinate committees for Wales, one in the north, one in the south and one for Monmouthshire, and their members were to act as commissioners in their own counties. The reason for this change was the desirability of nullifying the local pull of powerful delinquents by a change in personnel, and to increase central control. These seq-

[15] Supra, p. 51.

estrators became the targets of powerful attacks in that they were men of little social standing and were dishonest, greedy and corrupt in their dealings. Of the six Breconshire sequestrators accused in 1650 of misappropriating £5000 worth of delinquent estates, for example, only one could be styled 'esquire'. They also entered into profitable deals with their victims, and even made favourable leases of the property of delinquents to relatives and friends. Perhaps the most notorious of these traffickers in sequestered estates was Colonel Philip Jones of Llangyfelach, near Swansea, who founded a new county family, with its seat at Fonmon, on the profits which he made by very dubious means during the Commonwealth period. It was said that he had increased his estate to some £4000 or even £7000 a year. Others were Edward Vaughan of Llwydiarth, Montgomeryshire, and Henry Williams of Caebalfa in Radnorshire. The sequestrators were undoubtedly the most hated men in Wales at this time, and the Breconshire solicitor for sequestration had even become the object of an armed attack in 1649.

But though the corruption associated with members of the sequestration committees, and the opportunities which they were provided with to 'hucster the common-wealth', have contributed to focusing undue attention, perhaps, on their activities, the more routine work of government was performed by the County Committees, and membership of these committees was not restricted to such a narrow circle. Professor Dodd's scholarly, probing and perceptive analysis of the composition of the early county committees has revealed six overlapping elements in their composition, though the mix naturally varied from county to county, and it also responded to the ever-changing political climate. The hard core of all these committees, naturally enough, consisted of parliamentary supporters, the new men, drawn usually from the ranks of the smaller gentry, the more prosperous yeomen or even tradesmen. Also present were representatives of the old, well-established gentry families, from whose ranks Sheriffs and Members of Parliament were drawn, and the majority of whom had either actively supported the King, or had been in sympathy with his cause during the wars. Other members were professional soldiers of proven ability and experience and, to stiffen the committees, Englishmen from the border counties were introduced who had some kind of local connection. Inevitably included were Puritan extremists, preferably such as had demonstrated their zeal on the battlefield, though the adherence of some of these was of such recent origin as to give birth to the damaging taunt concerning Sampson Lort that 'he can pray as long as there is profitt, no penny, no *pater noster*'. Finally, there were the 'neuters' and trimmers. The neutrals, during the war, had remained on the sidelines, determined to protect their own interests. On the other hand the trimmers, the 'ambodextrous', like weather cocks, changed direction with the prevailing winds. They were cynically determined to be on the winning side and their attitude is admirably summarised by Howell Gwynne, when he declared 'Heigh god, heigh devil I will be for the strongest side'. The composition of these committees indicates quite clearly that the immediate effect of the Civil War was not to change dramatically the focal point of political power, but rather to broaden its social base.

The year 1648 bore witness to a change in the composition of the committees. The flames of the second Civil War having been successfully extinguished in both North and South Wales, the military element on the committees was increased and the old county families, suspected of royalist sympathies, were removed. The net result of these purges was that the execution of Charles I in 1649 led to fewer changes on the committees than might otherwise have been expected, though more parliamentarians were now included, and, significantly, toward the end of 1649, Major-General Thomas Harrison was included on each County Committee and acted as a great unifying force. This development, together with his Presidency of the Propagation Commission, meant that he was for the next three years virtually dictator of Wales. In addition, the device of using good parliamentarians, particularly soldiers, of one county to shore up the parliamentary cause in other counties, was resorted to increasingly. The County Committees were becoming less representative of county society than of the Saints, and particularly of the Saints in arms; control was passing into the hands of a much smaller body of partisans.

The Rump of the Long Parliament, expelled by Cromwell in April 1653, was followed by Barbone's Parliament or the Nominated Parliament (July-December, 1653), and the 140

Oliver Cromwell (1599-1658)
Lord Protector (1653-1658)

representatives present, selected by the Army leaders from nominees of the Independent congregations, soon turned their attention to reform. To administer their humanitarian legislation, which embraced the relief of poor prisoners, and the better custody of idiots and lunatics, the members of the Assembly appointed small local bodies, generally not more than five to each county, and these bodies were to represent the one contribution made by this Parliament toward the committee system in Wales.

When the Saints came to grief, some of the more conservative army officers drew up a new constitution, probably drafted by Major-General Lambert, known as the Instrument of Government, by which the British Isles were to form a Protectorate, with Oliver Cromwell as Lord Protector. The first Parliament under the new constitution lasted only five months since it met in September 1654 and was dissolved in January 1655. There followed in March 1655 a minor royalist uprising in Wiltshire led by Colonel John Penruddock. It was easily suppressed but Cromwell now attempted to consolidate his position by devising a new type of military organisation. England and Wales were divided into eleven districts, and an army officer with the rank of Major-General was set over each, and given wide powers. In Wales, James Berry, once a clerk in a Shropshire ironworks, was placed in command with his headquarters at Shrewsbury. This was a brief experiment in government but it lasted long enough to leave behind it in the country an abiding hatred of militarism.

The more settled form of government introduced by the Instrument of Government, and the hatred of militarism which was the legacy of the Major-Generals, were reflected in the composition of the committees of 1657. There were some very significant changes. The military were removed from the committees other than those for their own counties. There was also a general exclusion of the Saints and the gap was filled mostly from the ranks of the old governing families now tempted back into political life by the apparent stability of the Protectorate. These committees were undoubtedly the most representative that Wales had had since the end of the first Civil War.

Two years later, in 1659, the political wheel had made yet another revolution. Oliver had died on 3 September 1658, the anniversary of Dunbar and Worcester, his son Richard had retired from politics, and moderate parliamentarians and royalists were plotting for the return of Prince Charles. The faction in power consequently had no alternative but to restore to the committees the zealots, who were now only too ready to co-operate since the Protectors no longer stood in the way of the rule of the Saints, and the royalists and 'neuters' were swept away. However, only too soon, the political climate was to change yet again and there was a further turn of the wheel. General Monck was marching on London and the moderates returned to power on the committees. The change of real significance took place on the Monmouthshire committee, where most of the Roundheads were excluded together with the extreme Puritans.

Within a matter of weeks the pattern of the Monmouthshire committees was adopted in the other County Committees of Wales. The old governing families who had been out of public life during the Interregnum were back in force, together with those royalists who had supported the new regime as a patriotic duty once it had become stabilised. On the committees also were those parliamentarians who, out of self-interest and disillusionment, were prepared to see the restoration of monarchy. The scene was being set for the return of Prince Charles.

But in addition to the multiplicity of county committees established by the Puritan authorities such as finance committees, sequestration committees, assessment committees, committees to examine and eject 'scandalous' ministers and schoolmasters, and to administer relief to poor prisoners, the old traditional organs of local administration were still operative. Deputy-Lieutenants, Sheriffs, Justices of the Peace, Coroners, Constables were all still there, though it was with some difficulty that the new untried revolutionary authorities found suitable men to occupy these positions since there was a marked reluctance among the older county families, mostly royalist in sympathy, to co-operate actively with the new regime. This situation led inevitably to the appointment as local officers of men who had hitherto remained outside the ruling clique of families and there was a marked influx, also, of Puritan magistrates. The difficulty was compounded by the fact that during the Commonwealth period not only were the responsibilities of these local officials greatly increased by central government, but they had to sit on the various county committees as well. Thus they were made responsible for implementing legislation establishing civil marriages, and the registration of births, marriages and deaths. Ordinances aimed at the reformation of manners had also to be enforced by them. These entailed the forbidding of such practices as duelling, swearing, cock-fighting, bear-baiting and horse-racing. Plays and interludes were also prohibited, gambling dens and brothels closed, and an attempt was made to reduce vagrancy, and to diminish the excessive number of ale-houses.[16] Strict

[16] In December 1655 Major-General James Berry wrote to the Justices of Caernarvon to complain that the moral condition of the county was disturbing. He asked that they should perform their duties 'like men that will be found

regulations were also issued concerning Sundays: no shops or inns were to be opened and no games to be played. How effectively they operated is open to conjecture. They probably did as well as they could and, possibly, considering the revolutionary nature of the times, the degree of success which accompanied their efforts may even have been remarkable. However, it is as well to remember that important agents of central government such as the Justices of the Peace had to rely heavily on subordinate officials like the High and Petty Constables, and these were notoriously inert and inefficient, and frequently subject to abuse. There was even among them a marked reluctance to hold these offices at all.

It was not only in the counties that changes in local administration during the Commonwealth period applied. They were also introduced into the boroughs, and it might be instructive, as a pointer to what was happening generally in the towns of Wales, to examine the changes that were effected in the administration of Swansea.

As a natural and logical policy for the victorious party to pursue, at Swansea, royalists were purged from positions of authority within the town and replaced by supporters of Parliament. The new men among the parliamentarians, who had come to the top as a result of the upheavals of the times, now took their places on the aldermanic council. In 1650 the aldermanic body had comprised seven members who had belonged to the older governing town families, and five new men, risen to prominence as a result of the fortunes of war, among whom was Colonel Philip Jones of Llangyfelach. By 1655, on the other hand, the members of the old guard numbered only five, while the new men accounted for seven. By 1657 the preponderance of the new men had become even greater, for in this year while the old guard numbered only three, the number of new men had risen to eight. The balance of power and leadership had swung

faythfull to yor trust, usefull to yor generation . . . Towns full of alehouses and the countryside rife with beggers is the reproach of our nation, and indeed Alehouses are become the pest of this Commonwealth . . . and the contagion thereof spreads exceedingly; one Alehouse makes many poor . . . and to what this mischeife will grow (yf not spedily p^{re}vented) the Lord Knows'. He begged the magistrates to exercise their authority to destroy 'this spreading Gangreene'.

from the old families to the new. A scrutiny of those burgesses who were Common Attorneys between 1646-59 only serves to corroborate the conclusions drawn above. Thus, of the nineteen burgesses who, at various times during these thirteen years, appear on the list of Common Attorneys, eleven were new men. These changes suggest that in a town like Swansea, where Puritan and parliamentary influences were strong, changes in personnel were much more marked than in the counties. However, this situation may also be explained by the fact that in the towns the ruling bodies were more compact and concentrated than in the counties, and, consequently, more easily manipulated by new forces. That similar changes in the centre of gravity of political power took place within the other towns of Wales can possibly be inferred from the readiness with which towns, generally, during the period of the Civil Wars, threw open their gates at the approach of the enemy. They invariably displayed a greater willingness to compromise with the Puritan authorities than the older gentry families in the counties.

During the period of direct rule through Major-Generals, the government radically 're-modelled' the boroughs and converted them into safe supporters. In general, the new charters granted to the towns tended to deprive the burgesses of their political power, and to vest it in smaller and more manageable bodies. In this way it was hoped to secure the return to Parliament of members who would not be troublesome to the government. In 1659, at Swansea, as a prelude to the restoration of monarchy, the Corporation simply set aside the charter and reverted to the old order of things.

The Attitude of the Welsh

It was with horror that the Welsh heard of the execution of Charles in 1649. When the axe had fallen, and the executioner's assistant held up the severed, bleeding head for all to see, a groan broke forth from the throats of the thousands of people thronging around the scaffold. Philip Henry, who witnessed the scene, commented: 'such a groan as I never heard before, and desire I may never hear again'. In Wales the King's fiercest supporters were never reconciled to the deed and withdrew from public life during the Interregnum. Other royalists, when a certain degree of stability had been established under Oliver, were lured back since they now felt that it was a patriotic duty to co-operate and government had to go on. However, to the true Cavalier, Charles was a martyr, and this conception of the King was fostered by the publication of the *Eikon Basilike* (Royal Image). This book purported to be the King's last thoughts in his cell before he was led out to be executed. Within a year of his death, it had been translated into Welsh by Rowland Vaughan of Caer-gai, who had fought for Charles at Naseby. The bards, also, were harsh and uncompromising in their condemnation of what had transpired outside the Banqueting Hall on that bitterly cold day in January, 1649. Their revulsion is reflected in these four lines of verse:

> 'Rhag addysgu lladd brenhinoedd
> Rhag hyfforddi'r peth ar gyhoedd
> Rhag trais milwyr a'u byddinoedd
> *Libera nos Domine*' [17]

The gap left by the withdrawal of most of the older county families was filled by men of lower social status who, until now, had not been included in that close circle of governing families. This happened in both county and borough and it was a development which naturally evoked deep resentment. When the stonemason became a military commander it appeared as if the old social order had been entirely overthrown, and the 'scum of the world' (*scum y byd*), low born and uneducated, had taken over. It is not to be wondered at that people despaired of events.

But the fires of resentment were fuelled further by the activities of the sequestrators, out very often simply to feather their own nests. Many royalists suffered the confiscation of their estates, while others had to pay heavy fines to compound for their delinquency. This led to a change in the pattern of landownership in Wales. New gentry families appeared within the counties, and some of these became families of the first importance, a position which many were to retain even after the Restoration of 1660. Among them were Englishmen who had entered Wales with the victorious parliamentary armies and who acquired lands there either by marrying Welsh heiresses, or by

[7] 'Spare us, O Lord, from teaching others how to kill Kings, from spreading abroad that which has been done, and from the oppression of the military and their armies, Spare us, O Lord'.

securing on favourable terms the estates of delinquents. Thus
Colonel John Carter from Buckinghamshire, a linen draper,
married Elizabeth Holland, heiress of Kinmel in Denbighshire,
while Colonel George Twistleton from Yorkshire, during his
governorship of Denbigh, obtained extensive estates in that
county and in neighbouring Flintshire. The Civil Wars and a
military regime also meant continuous high taxation and heavy
fines. Men under arms on land, and sailors before the mast at
sea, had to be paid, and the maimed had to be provided with their
pensions. Matters were exacerbated by the fact that these
demands, very often, had to be met when times were hard owing
to the failure of harvests and the consequent non-payment of
rents.

Confiscation of the estates of delinquents, heavy fines and
high taxation were certainly not calculated to reconcile the

Frontispiece of Eikon Basilike (Royal Image)

stouter royalists to the new regime; but people were further alienated by the rule of the Major-Generals. Though the experiment was short-lived, it survived long enough to leave behind it a lasting hatred of militarism. The soldier's sword could no longer be hidden under the lawyer's wig, and it was a form of government, also, that had to be supported by the imposition of yet another tax—the decimation tax—on the properties of royalists. However, the Commonwealth authorities incurred the enmity of people in ways other than by making continuous demands on their pockets. They interfered increasingly also in the daily lives of the people and the oppressiveness of the Puritan regime, as exemplified in the prohibition of pleasurable sports and pastimes, was further brought home by the strength and effectiveness of the local County Committees. In addition, the new church order was alien to most and aroused considerable anger and lasting antagonism. Civil marriages, the appropriation of church property and revenues, the persecution of the old clergy, and the preaching of strange doctrine by illiterate craftsmen served only to alienate still further the faithful of the Anglican order. In 1659, when one of the bailiffs of Caernarvon was hurled forcibly to the ground, his assailants were heard to declare: 'nid oes dym cyfraith yr rowan iw gael'.[18] This was their commentary on the hated Commonwealth regime and it possibly reflected the views of most.

Still, despite the antagonism aroused generally by what was regarded as an illegal, oppressive government controlled by strangers (*estroniaid*), the Commonwealth did have its friends, supporters and sympathisers in Wales. These were to be found mainly among the ranks of the Puritans, and the smaller gentry, yeomen and craftsmen. There were also the trimmers and timeservers, and those royalists who, for one reason or another, were prepared to compromise and co-operate. But the general attitude of the Welsh was one of hostility, and just as the vaticinatory bards of the fifteenth century had predicted with confidence the coming of a saviour King, who would overthrow a usurper, so did an equally confident royalist poet from Merionethshire, William Phylip, after the execution of Charles, foretell the coming of another—'fe ddaw brenin eto'.[19]

[18] 'There is no justice to be had now'.
[19] 'A King will come again'.

The restoration of the monarchy was greeted all over Wales, in borough and county, with the tolling of bells, the lighting of bonfires and the consuming of vast quantities of wine and ale, and the rejoicing was sincere. People had had enough of the Puritans with their narrow moral code; they were equally disenchanted with soldiers and military rule. To them the 'Merry Monarch' appeared infinitely preferable to the Saints and the Major-Generals. Consequently, it is not to be wondered at that the fires should burn long and brightly, and that the wine and ale should flow abundantly and freely, when Charles returned from exile to his native land on 25 May 1660.

Chapter 5

THE POLITICAL SCENE, 1660-1714

'Brenin a Ddaw eto'. So ran the bardic prophecy throughout the Commonwealth period and it was a prediction that was fulfilled with the Restoration of 1660. But the Crown that was restored in 1660 was not the Elizabethan Crown, since Kingship now had been shorn of some, at least, of its powers. The lustre was somewhat diminished. This was inevitable, since the events leading up to the outbreak of the Civil Wars and the execution of Charles I had left their imprint. But the revolutionary nature of the times which preceded 1660 cast a long shadow over Restoration politics, with the result that political life after 1660 came to be dominated by two overriding considerations. One was the ever-present dread of the recurrence of civil strife and the other was the deep, abiding fear, and even hatred, of popery.

In 1660 the people, and celebrated bards like Huw Morris of Pontymeibion, joyously welcomed the return of Charles II because to them he stood for the restoration of the old order in church and state. The Rule of the Saints and of an oppressive military regime were behind them. The King epitomised in his person the blessings of unity and peace, and from pulpit and printing-press the message was driven home inexorably. The scars of war had to be healed, and people who had been on opposite sides of the great divide, reconciled. Consequently, the divine right of Kings, and the need for passive obedience to the will of both King and magistrate, were doctrines that were now preached openly and in the new climate of moderation 'enthusiasm', in whatever form, was something to be abjured. But the fear that the fabric of society might yet again be rent, that the spectre of civil war might become a reality, was heightened by such events as the Venner and Monmouth rebellions in 1661 and 1685 respectively, and the Derwentdale and Rye House Plots, the former in 1663 and the latter in 1683. These machinations and insurrections created an atmosphere of unrest, even panic, and the suspicions regarding Charles II's religious policy, particularly his toleration of Catholics, and a growing conviction

Stuart Wales

The Government of Charles II. Engraved frontispiece to *England's Glory*, 1660 (1661)

concerning James II's intentions with regard to his co-religionists, served to heighten passions still further until, in 1688, yet another King 'went on his travels'.

Yet despite the unease that pervaded society concerning the recurrence of civil strife and the fear and alarm generated by the religious policies of both Charles II and his brother James, the keynote of Welsh political life after 1660 was undoubtedly stability; a stability which stemmed from the domination of the great landed families, the nature of the electoral system and the fact that the actions and attitudes of Welsh Members of Parliament were not governed by adherence to any fixed set of political principles. For them, the appellations 'Whig' and 'Tory' were labels stuck on empty bottles, though in some of the elections that were contested, the first faint echoes of division along party lines begin to be heard.

Following the defeat of Charles I in the Civil Wars many of the older families paid a heavy price for their loyalty to their sovereign. Many suffered sequestration of their estates, while others had to compound for their delinquency by paying fines. On the other hand, support for the winning side led to families that had hitherto been obscure, and had lain outside the narrow governing circle, coming to the top, and many were to remain there even after the Restoration. There was also an infusion of new blood from outside, since successful parliamentary officers acquired large estates in Wales, either by marrying heiresses, or by taking advantage of their official positions. [1] Consequently, a change in the pattern of landownership can be discerned.

From 1660 onwards the wealthier landowners in Wales were enabled to extend their patrimonies quite considerably. Many of the Cromwellian families, from their ill-gotten gains, had become families of the first importance during the period of the Interregnum, and they retained their status after 1660. But the Restoration also meant the re-emergence of those older Tudor families who had refused, on the whole, to co-operate with the revolutionary governments and had remained consequently in cold storage. Many of these families came back crippled financially by confiscations, fines and mortgages, and after 1660 they were burdened with further exactions. The more substantial and

[1] Supra, pp. 87-88.

fortunate among them, through investment in the funds, by
effectively exploiting the mineral resources of their estates, by
negotiating advantageous marriages, or securing positions at
Court, were able to improve their condition. But there was both
rise and fall, and while the star of the great landowner was in the
ascendant, the lot of the smaller squires, dependent on rents and
the sale of farm produce, deteriorated. The latter courted disaster by trying to emulate their social superiors. However, the
ever-increasing costs of elections, the burden of hospitality, and
rash enterprises, saw many of them sink lower in the social scale.
They became prey to moneylenders, and some were compelled
to sell out and become tenant farmers, while others deserted the
land to try to retrieve their fortunes in the professions, and more
especially at the Bar. Though in the second half of the seventeenth century there was little change in the total number of
families from which Wales drew her Members of Parliament—
they remained around a hundred—parliamentary elections,
both borough and county, came to be dominated by a small
number of great houses which only allowed an outsider in when
an heir was not of age. This was in stark contrast to the days when
the smaller squires would arrange among themselves the dis-
position of the county and borough seats, and thus obviate the
danger of any one family achieving a monopoly position. Thus,
Montgomeryshire came to be dominated by the Vaughans of
Llwydiarth, Denbighshire by the Myddeltons of Chirk, Anglesey by the Bulkeleys, Radnorshire by the Harleys, Glamorgan
by the Mansels of Margam or Briton Ferry, Pembrokeshire by
the Owens of Orielton and Cardiganshire by the Vaughans of
Trawscoed; and this electoral dictatorship applied to the
boroughs as well. Not one of these great families had suffered
unduly during the 'distempered and bedlam times' represented
by the Civil Wars and their aftermath because their purses were
large enough to accommodate the fees of the finest lawyers in
defence of their interests. However, it is worthy of note, that
these were not the families which gave Wales her standing in
British politics between Restoration and Revolution. That
honour belongs to the representatives of the depressed class of
small squires who attempted to repair in the law courts their sink-
ing fortunes at home, and who provided England during this
period with a Lord Chancellor, two Secretaries of State, two

Speakers of the House of Commons, a Chief Justice and most of James II's law officers. [2] But these were 'political adventurers' and they did not represent the interests and values of any community in Wales.

Just as these opportunists had turned their backs on Wales, so were the great landlords likewise to forget their roots. It did not take them long to establish that they had more in common with their English counterparts across the border than with their social inferiors at home. From these they were becoming increasingly divorced by cultural, as well as economic and political, interests, since they soon forgot the language and ceased to interest themselves in its literature. By the end of the century the process of anglicisation was complete. The Court gentry had become servile English lackeys.

Though increasingly estranged from native society, these great families still appreciated the importance of a seat in the House of Commons, since it conferred on them the mantle of superiority within their own shires, and they were able not only to enjoy the delights of the London social scene, but were also presented with the opportunities to promote family interests there as well. Furthermore, as Members of Parliament, they occupied the most prestigious offices at county level, such as that of *Custos Rotulorum*, or Deputy-Lieutenant, and the Justices were chosen by them from the ranks of the smaller squires that moved within their orbit. To these was delegated very largely the task of conducting the routine business of county administration. The supremacy of this small, exclusive group of great families was strengthened still further in 1710 by an Act of Parliament which decreed that only the gentry possessed of landed property to the annual value of £600 could represent the counties, while the borough members had to own land to the value of £300 *per annum*. This legislation was to remain on the Statute Book until 1858.

But the stabilising political influence of this small clique of dominant families was confirmed still further by the nature of the electoral system and the growing indifference of the small squires toward politics. Parliamentary representation of a permanent

[2] These were Judge George Jeffreys, Lord Chancellor; Sir John Trevor of Trevalun and Sir Leoline Jenkins, Secretaries of State; Sir William Williams and Sir John Trevor of Brynkynallt, Speakers of the House of Commons; and Sir John Vaughan of Trawscoed, Chief Justice.

nature had been conferred on Wales by the Act of Union, 1536/43, when twenty-seven members were to be returned to Westminster, fourteen representing the counties and thirteen the boroughs, and Professor Dodd has drawn our attention to the development of a 'Welsh Interest' in Parliament, a Welsh Interest which failed to survive the upheavals of the Civil War period and the Interregnum. The county member was returned by the forty shilling freeholders and the size of the electorate varied considerably as between counties. At one extreme was Caernarvonshire, with five hundred voters, and at the other, Pembrokeshire and Denbighshire, with two thousand each. In between there were six shires with between one thousand and one thousand five hundred voters, and four with less than one thousand. It would appear, therefore, that in the counties the ratio of voters to total population varied between 1.8% and 4%. The situation in the boroughs was not so straightforward since there was no uniform franchise, and matters were complicated further by a system of out-boroughs or contributory boroughs. These had evolved in the sixteenth century as a result of the provision in the Act of Union that Welsh Members of Parliament were to be paid and, in the case of the towns, the wages of the borough member were to be levied not only on the shire town, but also on 'all other ancient boroughs' within the county, though these, by the terms of the Act of 1536, were not allowed a voice in the election. This obvious injustice was remedied in the supplementary measure of 1543. Willingness to contribute toward the member's wages, therefore, no doubt determined what persons were entitled to vote, and which boroughs were to participate in the elections. However, there were two boroughs that, from the very start, constituted single borough constituencies: Haverfordwest and Brecon. The right to vote, in the majority of boroughs, was vested in the freemen, and admission to the ranks of the burgesses could be achieved by one of four avenues: birth, marriage, apprenticeship, and gift. In other boroughs the right to participate in elections was vested not in the general burgess body, but in a small oligarchy of ruling families. But whichever situation applied, during the second half of the century the boroughs came increasingly under the domination of the great landed families and, as mere appendages to county seats, became subject to the same electoral pacts between families, with the end result that few seats were contested. When there was conflict, this stemmed more from family feuds involving precedence and prestige than overtly political issues. Though the percentage of voters to population in the boroughs was appreciably higher than in the counties, the position overall was that in a country with a population that could hardly have exceeded 400,000, only some 4% had the right to vote. The great landowner was safely enthroned, and there did not exist in Wales at this time a powerful middle class to dispute this supremacy. Moreover, it was not until the days of Morgan John Rhys and Jac Glan-y-gors in the eighteenth century, that the *werin*, the people, were taught that they also were endowed with certain inalienable rights.

The growing indifference of the smaller squires towards politics also helped to consolidate the authority of the great landowners. The lack of interest on the part of the former may well be related to the fact that they could no longer afford to proceed to the Universities, or the Inns of Court, and this was to lead to an ever-widening gulf between Westminster and the Welsh countryside. When the Duke of Beaufort, as President of the Council of Wales, summoned the Welsh magistrates to Ludlow to ascertain their feelings concerning James II's proposed Declaration of Indulgence, more than half of the three hundred and twenty that were expected to be present stayed away on one pretext or another, while those who did attend were not prepared to commit themselves. It was quite apparent that they no longer had the desire to get involved in politics.

However, the path to Ludlow was no longer a well-trodden one. Neither was it paved with gold. For twenty years no court had sat there, and consequently the Welsh gentry had grown unaccustomed to attendance at the Welsh 'Capital'. The Council had been restored, along with Monarchy, in 1660, and like the Monarchy it had been deprived of some of its powers. This applied to its criminal jurisdiction, and to its authority over the four English border shires which, ironically, despite their earlier opposition, supported by petition the revival of the Court. The Council now existed purely as a court for civil actions, the councillors all being lawyers, and its administrative functions were limited to the President's role as Lord Lieutenant of all the Welsh counties. At the time of its re-establishment, the Council was

Ludlow Castle: the 'capital' of Wales in the sixteenth and seventeenth centuries

provided with two successive Welsh Presidents. One was the
Earl of Carbery, the luke-warm royalist commander in West
Wales during the Civil War, and the other was the Marquis of
Worcester, later Duke of Beaufort, the Protestant heir to
Raglan. Carbery, who was greedy, oppressive, and a nepotist,
not unexpectedly, considering his track record, failed to restore
the prestige of the Court. Beaufort, according to Dryden,[3] a fair-
minded man, attempted to accomplish this by means of a quasi-
royal tour of his domains in 1684 and this 'progress' through
Wales was to prove a great personal triumph, since it was widely
and enthusiastically acclaimed. But neither President resided at
the castle at Ludlow, each preferring to conduct his correspond-
ence from his own home. When the Council finally disappeared
in 1689, and for half a century events had been moving inexorably in that direction, there were few in Wales to champion its
cause, for Ludlow had ceased to epitomise, in any sense, the
ambitions and aspirations of the Welsh gentry.[4]

Finally, the stability of the period may be explained by the
absence, very largely, of political labels except for electoral purposes. The conduct at Westminster of the majority of the Welsh
members was not in the nature of a response to adherence to any
set of political principles, whether Whig or Tory. Before 1642
there were matters which they held in common since they regarded themselves as the custodians of Welsh interests, and to some
extent they reflected opinion within their areas as they 'com-
municated to the House such business as they brought from their
countries'. However, by 1660, most of the burning issues which
had concentrated their attention before the outbreak of hostilities, and which had contributed to making British politics so real
and vital to them, had been resolved. Neither the Tudor land
settlement, nor considerations of coastal defence against the
Spaniards, nor the menace of Ireland, pre-occupied them any
longer. Consequently, their interests switched to England, and
to London particularly, since Ludlow as a political, social and

[3] John Dryden, 'Absalom and Achitophel', pt. 2, l. 941.
[4] The unpopular member for Beaumaris, Sir William Williams, an eminent
lawyer, is the only known Welsh champion of the Council and he was in no
sense representative of the Welsh gentry. It is most probable that he opposed
abolition on patriotic grounds rather than as an upholder of the royal prerogative.

cultural centre had ceased to exercise any attraction for them. The sole occasion when they spoke with one voice occurred in 1696 and related to the lordships of Denbigh, and Bromfield and Yale, in north-east Wales. William III had proposed granting these to one of his Dutch favourites; but the opposition that Robert Price of Giler, descended from a line of small Denbighshire squires, but who had himself taken silk, was able to arouse in the House of Commons compelled William, very sensibly, to drop the scheme. The main preoccupation of most was the furtherance of their own selfish interests and, in this respect, they shared with their English counterparts, with whom they had such affinity, in the general corruption of the times and the low standard of public and private morality. The Restoration Court set no example of moral probity, since its standards were notoriously lax, and the 'Merry Monarch' himself shared his bed with a succession of mistresses, a situation which was not lost upon Dryden:

> 'Then Israel's monarch after Heaven's own heart
> His vigorous warmth did variously impart
> To wives and slaves, and, wide as his command,
> Scattered his Maker's image through the land'.

The tone of the Court was reflected in society, at all levels, and this degeneracy undoubtedly represented a reaction against the strict Puritan code of the Commonwealth.

The stability of post-Restoration politics, reinforced as it was by an undercurrent of fear of renewed strife and dread of popery, meant that in Wales loyalty to Crown and Church was a cornerstone of people's beliefs. Even before the restoration of monarchy in 1660 the old governing families, who had withdrawn from public life during the Commonwealth, were back in force on the County Committees, and the scene was being set for the return of Charles II. Some loyalists had endeavoured to hasten the restoration by taking up arms on behalf of their sovereign across the water, and in North Wales many of the squires had been involved in the Booth rebellion of 1658.

In Wales, elections to the Convention Parliament, which was instrumental in restoring the Stuarts, resulted in the return of a majority of members who were moderate Roundheads, prepared to come to some arrangement over the restoration of monarchy. A substantial number were Cavaliers who, from a sense of patriotic duty, had decided to co-operate with the Commonwealth authorities. There were few unyielding royalists on the benches—possibly only four. Contested elections were minimal and about half the members possessed previous parliamentary experience. But the royalist tide was gaining in force, and the changing political atmosphere was reflected in the composition of the Cavalier Parliament, which assembled in 1661 and was not dissolved until 1678. The old pre-war parliamentary families came swarming back in force, and at least six uncompromising loyalists were elected. Of the members of the Convention, only four were returned to this Parliament. About half a dozen seats were contested in the boroughs. Breckockshire was the only contested county seat and there, after three successive polls, Edward Progers of Gwernvale, a Catholic, and a favourite of Charles II, was finally returned. By 1678, loyalists constituted about two-thirds of the membership, since during the life of this Parliament there were twenty-four by-elections. The royalist tide continued to run strongly until 1667, to the fall of Clarendon, who was made a scapegoat for the disasters of the Dutch War 1665-67. Among those prominent in encompassing his downfall were some Welsh members, particularly Sir John Vaughan of Trawscoed. Before being 'dropped', Clarendon had alienated many members by attempting to dominate Parliament in the interests of the Crown by building up a 'Court' party in the Commons, to which many of the Welsh representatives were attracted. However, those members suspicious of Clarendon's designs now formed an opposition 'Country' party. Clarendon's policy of building up a body of support for the Crown in Parliament was continued by Danby, an intolerant Anglican, and from 1673 onwards some twenty-two of the Welsh members, county as well as borough, were pensioners of the Crown. Reaction to this policy was swift; and anger at these attempts to manipulate the Commons, allied with a growing disenchantment with the King's foreign and religious policies, led, during the last years of this Parliament, to the return of members who were sons of old parliamentarians. In 1677 Sir Richard Lloyd, an eminent judge and member for Radnorshire, was succeeded in the county seat by Richard Williams of Caebalfa, whose father had represented the county in Cromwell's parliaments; and in 1678, at Brecon, after the decease of the ardent royalist, Sir Herbert Price, the seat was occupied by a son of Bussy Mansel, who had been a leading parliamentary supporter in Glamorgan.[5]

The principal means employed in building up the Court or Tory party was financial and lay in the power of the purse. Pensions and offices were in the King's gift and the readiness with which Welsh squires, particularly those from North Wales, were prepared to accept these is possibly a sad reflection on their standards of public morality. However, their venality can be very largely explained on the ground that many had suffered grievous losses owing to their attachment to the royal cause during the Civil Wars and to these the grant of a pension, or an office, was in the nature of compensation for their losses, rather than a lure to corrupt them. Thus John Robinson, the member for Beaumaris, whose support for the King in Cheshire and Anglesey had led to the confiscation of his estates, was in receipt of a secret service pension of £400 *per annum*, while John Wynne of Melai, whose father had given his life for the King, received not only a pension of £400 a year, but also the office of Steward of Denbigh. But there were other offices and perquisites at the King's disposal, and many a needy Welsh squire was only too ready to accept the loaves and fishes from the royal hand.

These developments meant that, with the weakening of the traditional bonds linking Welsh members, they were now to find a new one, since the majority became involved in the pursuit of common political aims embracing loyalty to Crown and Church. This re-orientation saw them being merged with English party groups, since only in this way could they be effective, and it also resulted in a wedge being driven between them and their compatriots in the Commons, and between them and their constituents at home.

The elections for the new Parliament in 1679 were held against a background of panic caused by the Popish plot. In 1678 a scoundrel, Titus Oates, declared the existence of a plot to murder Charles and place on the throne his brother, James, with the aid of the French army, and for the restoring of Roman Catholicism in England. Two incidents occurred which served to give

[5] Supra, p. 45.

some degree of credibility to Oates's story. Firstly, highly incriminating papers were discovered in the room of Coleman, the Jesuit secretary of the Duchess of York, whom Oates had cited as being implicated in the plot; secondly Godfrey, a highly respected London magistrate before whom Oates had laid a sworn deposition, was found murdered in a ditch outside London. The Earl of Shaftesbury and the opposition seized upon the supposed plot as the very opportunity they had sought to discredit the Roman Catholicism of the Court, and to break up Charles's connection with France. Parliament, without one dissentient vote, declared a 'damnable and hellish plot' to be in existence, and Catholics were now tried and executed on the flimsiest evidence. In Monmouthshire, the spiritual home of Welsh papists and recusants,[6] there was considerable disaffection already, since Catholic Justices of the Peace, basking in the favour and protection of the Worcesters at Raglan and the Morgans of Llantarnam, were alleged to be discriminating in favour of their co-religionists. Interwoven with all this was an element of family rivalry, since Sir Trevor Williams, the county member, and John Arnold of Llanthony, in their opposition to the Marquis of Worcester, were inspired as much by personal animus arising from Worcester's arrogance and his policy of family aggrandisement, as by concern for the Protestant faith. Worcester had also made enemies by using his position as President of the Council to influence elections in order to secure the return of candidates favourable to the Crown. In Wales the whole sordid story was given a more sinister twist when one of Oates's accomplices, William Bedloe, declared the existence of another plot, whereby Lord Powis was to seize Chepstow castle and then unite with prominent Catholics to restore popery. The agitation inevitably caused by these revelations led to an intensive persecution of the Catholics and a number of Catholic priests became martyrs for their faith. The Jesuit, David Lewis, a native of Abergavenny, 'tad y tlodion',[7] was hanged at Usk in

[6] Of the thousand Roman Catholics returned in the census of 1676 one-half lived in Monmouthshire, while the remainder were about equally divided between Breconshire and Flintshire.
[7] 'Father of the poor'. He was 'unkenneled' by a Monmouth Justice of the Peace since he was found 'under ground under a Clay Floor cunningly contriv'd in a poor despicable cottage' at Llantarnam.

1679, and in the same year another Jesuit, Philip Evans, and a secular priest, John Lloyd, perished at Cardiff. Others were to die in gaol. Over the border at Cwm, on land belonging to the Earl of Worcester, in the parish of Llanrothal in Herefordshire, the Catholic seminary was ransacked and the Jesuit priests imprisoned.

The Popish plot, and the revelation that Danby had asked for subsidies from France to enable Charles to dispense with Parliament, both events shamelessly exploited by Shaftesbury, meant that in the Parliament which assembled in March 1679, the first of the three Exclusion Parliaments which met between 1679-1681, the Country Party had a tremendous majority. Even in Wales the Court suffered a series of set-backs, since many of the 'pensioners' lost their seats, and members critical of the administration were returned, including old parliamentarians of pre-Restoration days like Bussy Mansel, who represented Glamorgan. Even a great territorial magnate like the Earl of Worcester received severe rebuffs in the counties of Brecon and Monmouth, since in Brecknockshire Edward Progers, high in the favour of Charles II, was replaced by Sir Richard Williams of Caebalfa, while in Monmouthshire, his chief enemy, Sir Trevor Williams, secured a borough seat. And the heightened interest in politics was reflected in the greatly increased number of contested seats.

This Parliament, which sat from March to July 1679, immediately became involved in the Exclusion Controversy, a move to prevent the openly Catholic James, Duke of York, from succeeding his brother, Charles, as King. The Country Party, the Whigs as they were now coming to be called, introduced an Exclusion Bill, by which the succession would fall to Charles's illegitimate son, the Duke of Monmouth—an unfortunate choice—rather than to James, and two Welsh lawyers, Edward Vaughan and William Williams of Llanforda were included in the ranks of those who drew up the Bill. Charles, who had also benefited from the excesses of the Whigs themselves, gained a tactical victory by adopting Halifax's proposal of a scheme of 'Limitations' to safeguard the Protestant religion.

Shortage of money soon compelled Charles to summon another Parliament, which met in October 1679, but apart from minor redistribution as between borough and county seats, there was little change in the Welsh membership. This Parliament was so strongly opposed to the Court that on the day it should have met, 7 October, 1679, it was prorogued. When, after a recess of a year, Parliament finally assembled, with William Williams as Speaker, Shaftesbury introduced another Exclusion Bill, which was more extreme than the first. The Bill passed the Commons but was rejected by the House of Lords, largely owing to the eloquence of the Marquis of Halifax. In January 1681 the Commons resolved that no further supply should be granted until the Exclusion Bill was passed. Charles now dissolved Parliament, but not before it had voted for the imprisonment of five Catholic peers, including Lord Powis, in the Tower. It was during the recess of this Parliament that new party labels were introduced. Opponents of the Court had petitioned against prorogation or dissolution, while their opponents had expressed abhorrence of their actions. The Petitioners and Abhorrers later came to be known as Whig and Tory.

In the interval before the assembling of a new Parliament, attempts were made throughout the Principality to ensure the return of members more supportive of the Crown. Worcester described his own county of Monmouth as being 'as ill-affected as any in England', and within the area of his jurisdiction he instituted a purge of magistrates, which resulted in twenty-seven Justices of the Peace, mostly in the south-east and Montgomeryshire, losing their Commissions. A change of Sheriffs, a crucial office at election time, followed, and the charters of the borough corporations of Brecon, Carmarthen and Cardiff were remodelled to permit a greater degree of royal control.

On 21 March 1681 writs were issued for a third Parliament, to meet at Oxford, where it would be out of reach of the London mob. Whether it was because of the precautions taken to ensure the return of better-affected members, or whether it stemmed from a growing fear of the renewal of civil strife, the elections resulted in some resounding successes for the Court. The Denbighshire seat, contested by Sir John Trevor of Brynkynallt, a court barrister, and Sir Thomas Myddelton of Chirk, ended in riotous scenes at Wrexham. Supporters of Myddelton had their windows broken, their candidate's town house was attacked, and those who had 'got a lap of good ale . . . were disposed to fight it out'. Although Tory gains were not sweeping, they managed

to retrieve some lost ground. Sir John Hanmer recovered
Flintshire, while in neighbouring Merionethshire the seat went
to Sir Robert Owen, the grandson of Sir John Owen, the royalist
Colonel. In South Wales the Court achieved fewer successes.
John Arnold, in defiance of Worcester, again won Monmouth,
while Sir Edward Mansel, no friend of Worcester, recovered the
county seat in Glamorgan with the result that his kinsman, Bussy
Mansel, had to sit for Cardiff. Sir William Wogan, a future
judge and a spokesman for the opposition, though losing Haverfordwest, was 'kicked upstairs', since he won Pembrokeshire. In
Radnor borough Sir John Morgan of Kynnersley, descended
from good Roundhead stock, won the day.

The Whigs came to the Oxford Parliament armed, hoping in
this way to compel acceptance by the King of their Exclusion
plan. This was a fatal miscalculation because the nation, now
recovering from the fear of the Popish plot, was possessed by a
dread of civil war. Charles, with his finger on its pulse, sensed
this and dissolved Parliament after it had been in session for only
a week.

But faction still lurked under the surface and in Monmouthshire there were 'unlawful parliamentary stirs' over 'barrels of
ale' being organised by Sir Trevor Williams and his henchman,
John Arnold, who had 'most of the youth of the country at his
command'. Numerous sectaries also showed their hand and
together they clamoured for the release of their hero, Shaftesbury, who had been imprisoned in the Tower. However, neme-
sis was at hand, and after the discrediting of the Whigs by
Shaftesbury's flight abroad to Holland, and the Rye House plot
(April, 1683), hatched at the Green Ribbon Club when Whig
conspirators planned to assassinate the royal brothers on their
way back from the Newmarket races, the government turned on
its enemies. In Wales, Worcester instructed the Deputy Lieutenants in all the shires to disarm 'dangerous' persons, and Sir
Trevor Williams and John Arnold were proceeded against in
King's Bench and both received crippling fines.

Charles's successful *coup* was followed by a perceptible cooling
of political passion, and the succession of James II was effected
peacefully. There were no upheavals of any description in
Wales, and neither did Welshmen join in the Duke of Monmouth's rebellion following his landing at Lyme Regis in June

1685. Beaufort had been commissioned to raise a regiment of ten companies for the defence of Bristol and the south-west against the rebels. That Welsh soldiers fought at Bristol, and probably at Sedgemoor, is indicated by the fact that in April 1686, at Brecon, the Justices ordered that the maimed soldiers of the county should appear at the next Sessions and hand in their certificates to enable them to receive their pensions. It was also laid down that no person should be added to the list of the maimed until his certificate had been examined.[8] However, it was in an altogether calmer atmosphere that the elections to James II's only Parliament were held in the spring of 1685 and, almost everywhere in Wales, Court influences prevailed. Even South Wales, following the example of North Wales in the previous election, toed the line.

THE GLORIOUS REVOLUTION

Not a dog barked at James's succession. The Welsh gentry, apart from a few personal enemies of Worcester, who had orchestrated some opposition in Monmouthshire, had refused to have anything to do with the fanaticism which had characterised the conduct of the Whigs in the Exclusion crisis and their fear of extremes in politics only served to strengthen their attachment to Crown and Church. Welsh lawyers—and Wales and the border counties were to provide seven of the King's principal legal advisers—were equally desirous to serve the new sovereign, and the zeal of one of them, Judge Jeffreys, was demonstrated in his Bloody Assizes held in the West, when ferocious penalties were imposed on the unfortunate rebels. This firmness, even cruelty, must have impressed James because shortly afterwards Jeffreys was elevated to the office of Lord Chancellor. Meanwhile, a cousin of his, Sir John Trevor of Brynkynallt, had become Speaker of James's only Parliament, and his occupancy of this exalted office was such that he was rewarded by being made Master of the Rolls and later a Privy Councillor. It is quite apparent that at this stage Welsh lawyers and Members of Parliament sniffed no danger in the King's designs. These were only to become apparent to them a few years later.

[8] Professor Dodd had maintained that lack of time would have prevented these troops from being used against Monmouth.

The Parliament over which Sir John Trevor presided as Speaker assembled in May 1685. It was undoubtedly more favourable to the Court, owing to the remodelling of the borough charters which had taken place under Charles II, than any that had sat since 1661. However, the Crown did not take long to dissipate the goodwill of this very amenable assembly, and the slide to disaster began when, despite the Test Act 1673, James started to appoint Catholics as officers in the army, the son of the Catholic Earl of Powis being given a commission in the Duke of York's regiment. Control of the army was an essential preliminary, as far as James was concerned, toward the realisation of his twin aims of restoring Catholicism and the establishment of his own personal despotism. The significance of the use of the King's dispensing power was effectively hammered home when a camp of 13,000 men was established at Hounslow Heath for the express purpose of overawing the City of London. These measures, however, aroused opposition in the House of Commons and James promptly prorogued Parliament. It was not to meet again during the reign. The King now proceeded to fill offices of state, as well as military and naval offices, with his co-religionists. He also attempted to secure the support of the nonconformists by granting a general toleration. In April 1687, exercising his Suspending power, he issued a Declaration of Indulgence. If James expected a favourable reaction in Wales to this he was to be disappointed, since only three addresses of thanks were received from the Principality, and it is doubtful whether these reflected the feelings of the mass of nonconformists. This rebuff led to Circuit judges being instructed to cajole Grand Juries in the counties to express their appreciation, but only the Grand Jury of Merioneth obliged.

In July James dissolved Parliament and he followed this up by taking systematic steps to ensure the return of a Parliament of the complexion he wanted. To test the temperature of the water, he instructed Beaufort to summon the magistrates and Deputy Lieutenants to Ludlow and ascertain their views regarding the abolition of religious tests. The response was far from satisfactory since more than half stayed away, and those present were non-committal.[9]

[9] Supra, p. 97.

Nevertheless, James pressed forward with his schemes for remodelling the corporations, and he also attempted to remould the representation of the counties. Nominations of dissenters suitable for commissions of the peace were now sought, and Beaufort submitted a list of ten names, five each for North and South Wales. The remodelling of the corporations proved equally difficult, though a beginning was made in Montgomery, Conway and some of the Glamorgan boroughs. At Swansea the charter was changed to enable the Crown to remove officials by Order in Council.

In 1688 James issued his Second Declaration of Indulgence. It was followed a week later by an Order in Council by which Bishops were to distribute the Declaration throughout their dioceses, and have it read in every church on two successive Sundays. Sancroft, the Archbishop of Canterbury, and six other bishops, [10] petitioned the King to be relieved of this duty. When the petition was found circulating in print, they were tried for seditious libel. Despite the efforts of the prosecuting counsel, Sir William Williams, who was Solicitor General, the Crown failed to secure a judgement against the seven bishops for their 'false, malicious and seditious petition', and another Welshman, Sir John Powell, who hailed from Carmarthenshire, was on the Bench of Judges that acquitted them. [11] Among the bishops freed was William Lloyd of St. Asaph, 'one of the most learned, laborious and successful bishops that ever occupied the see', and the rejoicing with which the verdict was received in London must have had some echoes in Wales.

The crisis in James's affairs was heightened by the birth to James and Mary of Modena, only two days after the committal of the seven bishops to the Tower, of a son. The opposition, which had been prepared to wait patiently for the death of James, and the accession of his son-in-law, the Protestant William of Orange, was now forced to act. The new Prince of Wales would undoubtedly be brought up in his father's faith particularly as Lady Powis, a confirmed Catholic, was appointed his governess. It is hardly surprising, therefore, that though the birth might

[10] The others were the bishops of Bath and Wells, Bristol, Chichester, Ely, Peterborough and St. Asaph.

[11] He subsequently became Recorder of Brecon and a Judge of Great Sessions.

have been received with rapturous delight by Welshmen occupying official positions at Court, the reaction in Wales was far more restrained and at Oxford, whose liberties the King had so grossly infringed since, with Cambridge, it was the fountain from which came the stream of Anglican bishops and clergy, the news was received in sullen silence.

James, determined to make a personal appeal to his people, now embarked upon a royal progress of the border counties. His tour took him to Badminton, Gloucester, Worcester, Ludlow, Shrewsbury, Whitchurch and Chester. Wherever he went he was greeted with demonstrations of loyalty and he even received a letter of thanks from a group of Monmouthshire dissenters. Though he did not actually cross the border into Wales, he did endeavour to repair some of the damage inflicted by his policies through acts of conciliation. Dispossessed magistrates such as Robert Davies of Gwysanney, Flintshire, and John Griffiths of Carreglwyd, Anglesey, were restored to the commissions of the peace and all municipal charters granted since 1679 were annulled. But matters were rapidly coming to a head and, just as Charles I had turned to Wales as a recruiting ground for infantry troops in time of need, so did James II now grant a commission to Beaufort to recruit an army of 10,000 men there, including a

The Seven Bishops returning from the tower (1688)

special regiment to be known as the Prince of Wales's Regiment, to be raised in South Wales by Colonel Thomas Carne of Ewenni. In Glamorgan the county militia was placed in a state of readiness to resist the impending invasion from Holland. Though James had not drawn up any plans for North Wales, since it was not in the direct line of attack, local squires like Sir Robert Owens, Thomas Mostyn and Robert Pugh of Penrhyn Creuddyn offered to raise, on their own initiative, local forces, an offer which was surprisingly rejected by James.

Meanwhile, William had landed at Torbay and the gentry of the west flocked to his standard. When, finally, the King joined his army in November, the moment for decisive action was gone. Bristol was soon lost and so also was Ludlow. Many of James's officers deserted him, even Beaufort's own son, the Marquis of Worcester, joining William near Oxford. James, in desperation, now issued the writs for a free Parliament, but events took an entirely different turn when the King decided not to await the outcome of the elections, but to flee abroad instead. Loyalist hopes in Wales were dashed by this act. The spectre of an Irish Catholic army, coming to the rescue of the King as in the days of Charles I, once again haunted people, and the few Irish soldiers that did arrive in London created considerable alarm, which soon spread to Wales. At Dolgellau a mob, fearing that an Irish army was on the way, forced open the gaol and freed the prisoners, the gaoler, David Owen, being assaulted in the process with clubs and swords. Such was the panic that, on the following day, when strangers were seen descending the mountain toward the town, they were mistaken for Irish and fired on. One of the unoffending party was killed before it was realised that they were Excise Officers pursuing their lawful duties. At Welshpool there were clashes in the streets between Protestants and Papists sparked off by a duel between the borough member, Charles Herbert, and Owen Vaughan. Powis castle was attacked, its parks and ponds destroyed, and the house itself 'reduc'd to such a Condition as some of ye Lewd Houses at London'. After a search of the house of the Pughs at Penrhyn had proved fruitless, the frustrated Constable and his assistants maliciously defaced the private chapel which the family had only recently repaired for private worship. In Anglesey, there were affrays at Holyhead when news was received that James had landed in Ireland.

James II receives news of the landing of William of Orange (1688)
From the painting by Edward Matthew Ward, R.A.

However, the Convention Parliament had now met and, despite James's attempts to leave the country in a state of complete anarchy by destroying the writs for the new Parliament and throwing the Great Seal into the Thames, his schemes were to be frustrated, and William and Mary were proclaimed joint sovereigns. Elections to the Convention Parliament had been conducted quite smoothly in Wales with most returns unopposed. There were families in Wales, both Protestant and Catholic, like the Barlows of Slebech and the Carnes of Ewenni in the South, and the Earl of Powis and the Pughs of Penrhyn in the North, who never wavered in their loyalty. But the vast majority of the Welsh gentry either accepted, or even welcomed, the turn events had taken, even Beaufort being reconciled to the new Court. Apart from some well established gentry families, opposition in Wales was largely confined to a handful of clerical non-jurors, and town corporations like that at Abergavenny, which was deprived of its charter because its burgesses refused to take the Oath of allegiance. The Welsh squires, though they displayed little enthusiasm for the principles of 1688, accepted the Revolution because it ensured stability. It was 'Glorious' because the land was spared the horrors of internecine strife and the prospect of bloodstained fields of battle. But the relationship between the Crown and Wales could never be the same again. The magic was gone. The Crown, and the Council at Ludlow, as well as being focal points of unity, had enshrined the hopes and aspirations of the political nation. After 1689 the Council was no more, and the Kingship had been shorn of much of its glamour, prestige and authority. Parliament did not provide an adequate substitute since there was no such special relationship, and Welsh members were increasingly drawn into the vortex of English politics to the neglect of issues which were of special relevance to Wales. It was only the occasional pebble that caused ripples on the surface as far as specifically Welsh matters were concerned. There was objection to the importation of cattle from Ireland, and considerable concern expressed over the need to promote the cloth trade even to the extent of compelling people to be buried in woollen cloth.[12] A vigorous campaign was conducted to abolish the Council in Wales, and an equally vigorous defence of the Court of Great Sessions,[13] was skilfully conducted by Sir John Vaughan of Trawsgoed. Within the Commons, also, there was a well orchestrated furore over the grant of the lordships of Denbigh, and Bromfield and Yale, to a Dutch favourite, Bentinck, who had been created Duke of Portland.

Despite the stability which the new sovereigns helped to guarantee, Welsh loyalty to them at the outset was lukewarm, and William's attempt to provide lands in north-east Wales for one of his favourites was as ill-advised as it was unpopular. However, news of the attempted assassination of the King served to conjure up once again the Popish bogy and when, in 1696, the National Association for his protection was established, this body was received with considerable enthusiasm in Wales. The Glamorganshire roll alone contained 760 signatures, though it is

---

[12] Act for Burying in Woollen only, 1667. Clergy officiating at funerals had to make a declaration that '. . . of the Parish of . . . Taketh oath the deceased was not put in, wound up or wrapt up or Buried in any shirt, Shift, Sheet or Shroud or in anything whatever made or mingled with Flax, Hemp, Silk, Hair, gold or silver or other than what is made of Sheep's wool only. Nor is a coffin lined, or faced with any cloth, stuff or other thing whatsoever made or mingled with any other material but sheep's wool only'.

[13] Great Sessions was finally abolished in 1830.

significant that nine Members of Parliament did not sign, possibly an indication of Jacobite sympathies. William's stock in Wales was further improved by his assumption of the role of Protestant champion against Catholicism and the ruthless ambitions of Louis XIV of France, and by his conquest of Ireland, which was described by Robert Harley, who represented the Radnor boroughs, 'as a very great mercy'. The Welsh openly rejoiced in his triumph over the Irish in the battle of the River Boyne in 1690, and even greater glory came his way after the defeat of the French fleet at La Hogue in 1692.

The reign of Anne witnessed a further improvement in the Court position in Wales. The High Church Party, favoured by the Queen, renewed its attack on toleration and particularly the practice increasingly adopted by dissenters of conforming occasionally to enable them to hold office. Matters were highlighted when Sir Humphrey Edwin, a rich wool-merchant with extensive estates in the Vale of Glamorgan, became Lord Mayor of London in 1697. After taking the sacrament on the day of his election according to the rites of the Church of England, he shortly afterwards proceeded in full regalia to a Presbyterian Meeting House. Angry Tories reacted, however, in a very ham-fisted manner, since they now attempted to bring in a bill against Occasional Conformity by tacking it on to a money bill, hoping in this manner to push it through unnoticed.

Tory anger was further inflamed when the Whig government in 1710 sought to impeach Dr Henry Sacheverell, a High Churchman, for preaching a sermon before the Lord Mayor and Aldermen of London in which he denied that 1688 had been a revolution, and accused the Whig ministry of being hostile to the Church. Sacheverell was convicted by the House of Lords, but on a very marrow margin, by sixty-nine votes to fifty-two. He was forbidden to preach for three years, and his sermon was ordered to be burnt. This mild sentence was interpreted as a moral victory for the Tories, and, as far as the Welsh members were concerned, there were 17 Tory votes in favour of the Doctor and 7 Whig votes against. The living of Selattyn in the diocese of St. Asaph was now conferred upon him, and the journey to his new living was greeted by great throngs of people en route. Fifty thousand awaited him at Shrewsbury, and the local gentry were lavish with their entertainment as well. These demonstrations on the part of the Welsh gentry and people were clearly indicative of the Tory complexion of the country, and this situation was further reflected in the composition of the last Parliament of Anne's reign, when about three-quarters of the Welsh members were Tories.

It was not unexpected, therefore, that there should have been considerable sympathy for the exiled Court at St. Germain and at clandestine meetings, from especially designed cups, Welsh squires drank to the health of the King across the water. Among them were gentry of no mean rank, such as Lewis Pryse of Gogerddan, Sir Charles Kemeys of Cefnmabli, and Sir John Philipps of Picton Castle in Pembrokeshire. But though the Marquis of Powis was prepared to follow his King into exile, few others were prepared to make similar sacrifices. Most Jacobites in Wales, mindful of their own interests, and doubtless remembering also the unavailing and ruinous sacrifices of so many families in the cause of monarchy earlier in the century, preferred to remain at home, and to confine their declarations of loyalty to heady mutterings in their cups and attendance at secret society meetings. In 1709/10 Jacobites assembled at Aberystwyth in the town house of the Pryses of Gogerddan to toast their absent King, and in 1710 the best known of the Jacobite societies, the Cycle of the White Rose, was established with its headquarters at Wynnstay, near Ruabon, the home of Sir Watkin Williams Wynn, the greatest landowner in the area. It was now strongly rumoured abroad that the Pretender was preparing to return to seize the throne, and at Wrexham, on 10 June, Jacobites openly celebrated his birthday. But the succession of the Hanoverian George I was accepted peacefully enough in Wales and when English Jacobites, in the '15 rebellion, attempted to dethrone him, the attempt evoked hardly any response from the Welsh.

Chapter 6

THE CHURCH AND DISSENT

The Curch

1660 witnessed the return, not of the Fifth Monarch, Jesus, as Morgan Llwyd and the dreamers of the Puritan Revolution had prophesied, but rather the restoration of the 'Merry Monarch', Charles II. This event was the work of the Presbyterians who had remained hostile to Cromwell and military rule. In Wales, apart from those Puritans who felt that they had in some way incurred the displeasure of the Almighty,[1] the return of Monarchy was welcomed with acclamation and genuine rejoicing. Even prominent parliamentary officers, and lukewarm Puritan ministers, displayed considerable gymnastic suppleness when addressing themselves to the new situation, and it was a course of action that could pay handsome dividends.

Together with the restoration of the Monarchy, 1660 also witnessed the re-establishment of an intolerant, persecuting Anglican Church. Cromwell's policy of toleration had enabled the sects to proliferate, and despite the promise of liberty to tender consciences contained in the Declaration of Breda, there had been no settlement of the religious problem when the Convention Parliament was dissolved on 9 December. Hopes of reaching an acceptable settlement floundered with the diminishing influence of the Presbyterians in the Cavalier Parliament, and the failure of Anglicans and Presbyterians to reach agreement at the Savoy Conference 1661. Bishops, despite their ignoble role during the Interregnum, came back and recovered both their lands and their seats in the House of Lords. Restored also was the Prayer Book. But the Church did not completely recover its old position. As with Monarchy, the hands of the clock could not be turned back to 1649, though Charles II was officially to date his reign from the 30 January in that year in the fond hope that the eleven intervening years simply constituted an unimportant interlude. The supremacy of Parliament over

---

[1] One compared the Restoration to a dog devouring its own vomit.

the Church was now an undeniable fact, and bishops were never to recover the position which they had once held in political life. The boundaries of the four Welsh bishoprics remained unchanged, which meant that St. David's extended from its headland in Pembrokeshire to the boundaries of Herefordshire. But if bishoprics were overlarge, so also were parishes with their churches, in many cases, badly sited. Restoration bishops, possibly, were not of the calibre of those appointed to the Elizabethan Church. On the other hand, they were superior to those who succeeded them during Hanoverian times. The religious life of Wales undoubtedly suffered from the fact that Charles II, naturally enough, granted high office in the Church to those who had demonstrated their loyalty to the Crown. There was nothing unusual in political appointments of this nature, for they had been common enough ever since the Middle Ages. The danger lay in the continuation of the practice from age to age. Nevertheless, it was pillow talk, rather than politics, that obtained for Henry Glemham the bishopric of St. Asaph, since his niece happened to be Lady Castlemaine, who was one of the King's many mistresses. According to Pepys, no Puritan himself, Glemham was a 'drunken, swearing rascal and a scandal to the Church', and as an old royalist soldier he was more accustomed to camp life than to the cloisters. The impact which the Welsh Bench made was also diminished by the practice of bishops, because of the poverty and remoteness of their sees,[2] of regarding them simply as stepping stones to preferment to richer dioceses elsewhere. They were birds on the wing and the brevity of their stay in Wales precluded any possibility of their being reformers or innovators. Many of the bishops were also non-resident, since, in addition to their bishoprics, they held other benefices particularly deaneries, in England. Thus, Bishop Tyler of Llandaff was dean of Hereford and persons seeking ordination at his hands had to travel to Hereford. William Lucy, bishop of St. David's, though resident in his diocese, still conferred benefices on non-residents, and in this context he was to report to Archbishop Sheldon: 'The R^t Reverend Father in God William [Nisholson] Ld Bpp of Gloucester holds in

---

[2] The poorest, by far, was Llandaff at £500. St. David's, the largest, was worth £900. On the other hand, Bangor and St. Asaph were each worth £1400.

Comendam wth his Bppricke the archdeaconry of Brecon, a canonry in the Cathedral Church of St. David's with the vicarage of Llandilo-Vaure in the County of Carmarthen, hee maintaines noe licensed curates nor provides licensed preachers'. Lucy was, furthermore, a flagrant nepotist to boot, since his four sons were unashamedly appointed to various preferments within his diocese. It would appear that age was no impediment to the holding of a bishopric, since William Beaw, who had fought with distinction on foreign fields, was offered a 'little bishoprick', Llandaff, in 1679 and was still there when he died in 1706 at the great age of ninety-seven. However, on the credit side, it must be stated that, certainly down to the 1690s, most of the bishops, and this had applied to the Elizabethan bishops as well, were Welshspeaking. Among them, also, were scholars of distinction. Humphrey Humphreys, who was elevated to Bangor in June 1689, was one of the most eminent antiquaries in Wales. Certainly, in Edward Lhuyd's view, he was 'incomparably the best Skill'd in our Antiquities of any person in Wales'. His desire to promote the use of the Welsh tongue led him, in 1690, to issue visitation queries in Welsh to ascertain the state of his diocese. William Lloyd, bishop of St. Asaph, was a ready controversialist and, among other achievements, wrote a series of substantial pamphlets against Popery; George Bull, who was appointed bishop of St. David's in 1705 by Queen Anne, when he was seventy years old, because of his knowledge of the early fathers, was described as 'one of the glories of anglican scholarship'.

The restored Church was to be bedevilled by the weaknesses which had reduced its effectiveness in the past, and foremost among these was its poverty. It was estimated in 1708 that half the livings of St. David's were worth less than £30 a year, and a quarter worth less than £10 a year. In the North Wales dioceses the situation was considerably better, since in St. Asaph only four livings were worth less than £30, and as many as seventy were worth between £50 and £100 a year. In Bangor, also, ten livings only were worth less than £30, while there were forty valued between £50 and £100. These revenues had been largely impropriated by laymen, who also held the patronage of livings, and this was particularly true of the south. This situation inevitably led to unworthy sycophants, and persons not distinguished by their scholarship, being appointed to benefices, and to miserably low stipends being paid to curates. Though it has been correctly attested that many of the ministers ejected between 1660-2 were replaced by graduates, more places were filled by non-graduates, and in the diocese of St. David's, of the clergy admitted to holy orders, less than a quarter had associations with Oxford or Cambridge. Bishop William Lloyd of St. Asaph stated that it was not practicable to fill every living with a degreed person. What was more important, among a monoglot population, was to appoint clergy with a command of Welsh. He further declared that, in his experience, 'of those I have ordein'd the graduates have not been allwaies the best scholars, being often shamefully outdone by men that never saw the University'. Stipends were abysmally low, and curates could be paid as little as £10 a year, though the tithe might be worth as much as £100.[3] Charles II, in 1660, had directed that the stipends paid to vicars and curates should be augmented out of the revenues 'appropriated' to the higher clergy of cathedrals but, apart from Llandaff, the response to this missive would appear to have been disappointing. It is not to be wondered at, therefore, that there should have been considerable pluralism, with its attendant evil of absenteeism, among clergy 'pinched with poverty', and plurality returns indicate that there were twenty-eight pluralists in St. Asaph and fifty-one in St. David's. In these circumstances, it is understandable that many a demoralised curate turned to drink for some measure of consolation.

Still, among the clergy, there were those who were only too aware of the shortcomings of their fellows and of the Church in general. These were conscientious in the performance of their duties and authors of good works. John Jones, dean of Bangor (1689-1727), founded and endowed at least nine Charity Schools. Furthermore, he distributed Welsh literature among his parishioners and assisted in the establishment of parochial and diocesan libraries. In his will he left generous bequests for the religious education of poor children. Again, according to the testimony of Sir John Philipps, as early as 1701, the work of establishing Charity Schools had been undertaken by a group of thirty-one clergymen, who had sought the sponsorship of the

---

[3] It would appear that the Duke of Somerset drew £900 a year from parishes in Carmarthenshire but disbursed only £70 in stipends to six curates.

Archbishop of Canterbury. In their ranks, also, were writers of repute, and of the 140 active Welsh authors between 1660-1730, no fewer than forty were drawn from the ranks of the clergy. Moreover, they displayed their zeal in the pulpit, and by the early decades of the eighteenth century, in the majority of churches, if sermons were not heard every week, they were most certainly heard on alternate Sundays.

In the reign of Anne, who had endeared herself to Anglicans by her generosity—Queen Anne's Bounty—there were unmistakable signs of regeneration in Church life.[4] At St. David's, under the influence of the saintly George Bull, there even appears to have been an evangelical revival. That the people of Wales were capable of great devotion is indicated in the warm tribute paid to them by Erasmus Saunders in his *A view of the state of Religion in the Diocese of St. David's* published in 1721. 'There is', he says, 'I believe, no part of the nation more inclined to be religious, and to be delighted with it, than the poor inhabitants of these mountains. They don't think it too much, when neither ways nor weather are inviting, over cold and bleak hills to travel three or four miles, or more, on foot, to attend the public prayers, and some times as many more to hear a sermon, and they seldom grudge many times for several hours to gather in their damp and cold churches to wait the coming of their minister, who, by occasional duties in his other curacies, or by other accidents, may be obliged to disappoint them or to be often variable in his hours of prayer'. Sometime in the 1710s, thirty-one of the inhabitants of Llandysul drew up a petition deploring the fact that their late minister had neglected his duties, and begging for the appointment of a good minister who would satisfy their spiritual needs. There had been faint stirrings in the bosom of the Church at a much earlier date. In 1683, at Minera, the parishioners established a fund to pay the salary of an 'honest and Godly minister', while the freeholders of Maenordeifi, in 1688, had expressed disquietude at the absence of their rector, David Phillipps, and the unsatisfactory moral character of the curate he had left in charge. Church services were now improved, sermons delivered more frequently, communion

[4] Moneys originally paid to the Pope, but appropriated by the Crown at the Reformation, were by this Bounty transferred to the Church for the purpose of increasing stipends in the poorer parishes.

celebrated more regularly, and serious efforts were made to restore public catechising. Furthermore, the overseas mission was not neglected, since the S.P.G. (Society for the Propagating of the Gospel) was conspicuously active in the American colonies. In Pennsylvania, resident missionaries were maintained—one of the earliest being a Cowbridge man, Henry Nichols—and Welsh ministers and schoolmasters were sent out and they were to achieve impressive successes in winning converts, even among the Quakers.

However, missionary enterprise was not confined to Pennsylvania. Welsh missionaries were soon to be found in most of the colonies established along the Atlantic seaboard of America, in Newfoundland, and in the West Indies. Of the 700 missionaries, clergymen and schoolmasters who went out to the plantations between 1695 and 1740 no fewer than 80 were Welsh. They provided not only for the spiritual needs of the colonists, but also introduced Christianity to the Indians and the negroes. Churches, schools and colleges were established, and Bibles, Books of Common Prayer and other devotional literature and tracts distributed. It was in 1702 that Dr Humphrey Humphreys, at that time bishop of Hereford, proposed 'the sending of a great Welch Bible and Common Prayer Book to the Welsh Congregation in Pennsylvania', and these were the first books to be sent out by the S.P.G. They were probably received by Evan Evans,[5] Rector of Christchurch, Philadelphia, for the use of St. David's Welsh Church, Radnor. Welsh Bibles were in great demand since it has been estimated that between 1650 and 1700 about 12,000 Welshmen emigrated to North America, mainly to Pennsylvania and Virginia, and a large proportion of these were monoglot Welsh.

But laymen as well as clergy contributed to this missionary effort in North America. In 1674, Edward Morgan gave 60 acres of pasture-land toward the maintenance of the minister of St. Catherine's Church in Jamaica, West Indies, while in South Carolina, sometime before 1696, a certain Richard Morgan left

---

[5] He had been a curate at Wrexham before setting out for Pennsylvania. His bilingual preaching, and that of his temporary assistant, John Thomas, met with considerable success especially among monoglot Welsh families with an Anglican background which had turned Quaker for lack of Anglican ministrations in their mother tongue.

a large sum of money for the founding of a free school, probably the first in the colony.

The S.P.C.K. (Society for the Promotion of Christian Knowledge) also supported the efforts of the Danish East India Mission, the first Protestant society to send workers to India. One of the chief Welsh supporters of the Mission was George Lewis of Fort St. George, Madras, chaplain of the East India Company, but another who interested himself in the work of the mission in India was Sir John Philipps. In 1712 he conceived the idea of sending a printer and printing press to India, and that he succeeded in realising his aim is shown in a letter which he wrote in 1713 to his wife who was in Bath at the time, doubtless taking the waters: 'there is a Catechism in ye Portuguese language just come from Tranquebar in ye East Indies, being printed there from the press we sent over which has filled us with surprise and holy joy'.

Despite its imperfections, and they were many, the Church was held in real affection by the mass of the people, possibly more so in the conservative north than in the south. Bard and ballad-monger testified to the popularity of the Church, and it is extremely significant that the early Methodist leaders were never to leave its fold, and later ones to depart from it only with the greatest reluctance.

DISSENT

But the tang of bitterness was in the air and despite the early attempts to arrive at some compromise, the nonconformists were only too soon to experience the full fury of the Anglican backlash exercised through a formidable array of disciplinary agencies such as royal proclamations, parliamentary acts, the courts and episcopal visitations. Vavasor Powell, the Fifth Monarchy man, who had been such a thorn in Cromwell's side, was quickly arrested and, until his death after a painful illness in October 1670, spent most of his time in prison. It was during his incarceration that he wrote an account of Puritan suffering entitled, *The Bird in the Cage, Chirping*. While Powell was languishing in prison, John Miles who, in 1649, had established a Baptist Church at Ilston in Gower, and organised a string of subsidiary churches in South Wales, was evicted and, in 1663, fled to America, taking his flock with him, and established the town of Swanzey,

Massachusetts. Other Puritan clergymen not confirmed in their livings by the Act of Indemnity and Oblivion, and who did not find a short route to a dark and musty cell, were, like Miles, ejected so that former incumbents could be restored to their livings, and to enable lay patrons to exercise their right of advowson. Before the passing of the Act of Uniformity 95 Puritan ministers in Wales were to suffer this fate.

In 1661 all attempts at comprehension of Presbyterians and the sectaries within the Church, which was the aim of moderate men on both sides, were abandoned, since the government associated nonconformity with treason. Church and state now embarked upon a draconian persecution of the dissenters, which caused considerable emotional havoc. Henry Maurice, in his diary, recorded that in Llŷn he 'found the christians thereabouts very fearful so that they came together very late in the night'. Between 1661-65 the Cavalier Parliament, all of whose Welsh members were Anglicans, passed four penal acts, known collectively as the Clarendon Code. These laws, however, were not the work of Clarendon, still less of Charles. They stemmed from the Cavaliers' desire for revenge for their long years of suffering and for the restoration of their lost acres. Despite their severity, these laws were to prove the salvation of Puritanism. In the white hot heat of persecution, the dross fell away, since Puritans now parted company with opportunists and self-seekers, and they rid themselves also of the taint of materialism which they had acquired during their years of liberty.

By the Corporation Act, 1661, membership of municipal bodies was confined to those who received communion according to the rites of the Church of England. This was followed in 1662 by the Act of Uniformity, a legislative measure with which Archbishop Laud would fully have concurred, and which had been anticipated since 1660 by the evictions of Puritan divines which had taken place. Ministers and teachers were to assert their 'unfeigned consent and assent' to everything contained in the Prayer Book and to take an oath of non-resistance. In England, the operation of this Act was to have a very considerable impact, since about 2000 clergymen were expelled from their livings. In Wales, on the other hand, the effects of this measure were far more limited, since some thirty-one ministers only were ejected, though it must be borne in mind that ninety-five had already been removed during the previous two years and others had anticipated the Act and fled. The Act, however, created a great divide in Welsh religious and social life because, in the eyes of all uncompromising Anglicans, nonconformists were heretics, and the bitterness at the rupturing of Church unity was to endure long. Ellis Wynne gave expression to his feelings in 1703 when he lashed out at nonconformists for leaving the Church without rhyme or reason, and until his dying day in 1767 Theophilus Evans was not to miss a single opportunity of denouncing those guilty of 'schism'

The Conventicle Act 1664 made attendance at meetings for religious worship, other than those held in accordance with the rites of the Established Church, where five persons outside the family were present, punishable by imprisonment for the first and second offence, and transportation for seven years for the third. When Archbishop Sheldon inquired about the effectiveness of this Act, the Welsh bishops proved quite secretive. The bishop of Bangor even denied the existence of any conventicles within his diocese, although it was generally known that dissenters were meeting there. In 1670 the Act was renewed with even stiffer penalties being imposed. Elizabeth I had declared that she had no desire to open windows into men's consiences. Sir John Vaughan of Trawscoed now struck a similar note, when he observed that 'as long as persons conform outwardly to the law, we have no inquisition into opinion'.

In 1665 the Five Mile Act laid down that no clergyman or schoolmaster was to come within five miles of a city or corporate town unless he declared that he would not 'at any time endeavour to any alteration of government either in Church or State'. Since Puritan congregations were to be found mainly in the towns the aim of the Act was the suppression of dissenting schools. Acts, however, do not always achieve what they are meant to bring about, and in 1672, according to the testimony of Bishop Lucy, there were dissenting schools in Brecon, Carmarthen, Cardigan, Haverfordwest, Swansea and 'severall other places'.

The code of persecuting laws was completed in 1673 with the passing of the Test Act. This laid down that the holders of any civil or military office should take the sacrament according to the rites of the Church of England, take the oaths of Supremacy and

Allegiance, and make a declaration against the Catholic doctrine of the Mass. It was as a consequence of this Act that the Duke of York resigned as Lord High Admiral, and Clifford relinquished his office of Lord Treasurer.

As a result of this code of laws, for a whole generation, down to the passing of the Toleration Act in 1689, the nonconformists were to endure the most barbaric treatment and the tender plant of dissent wilted under the storm. But it survived, growing in the process ever stronger and deeper roots, until in the eighteenth and nineteenth centuries the flower of nonconformity was to blossom in all its glorious radiance. The sheer ferocity of the treatment meted out to the nonconformists is exemplified by the fact that Vavasor Powell was not alone in having to languish in prison. Other dissenters had to endure similar privations. The Baptist, Henry Williams of Ysgafell, in Montgomeryshire, spent nine years in gaol and was deprived of most of his earthly possessions. However, his tribulations did not end there, since his delicate wife was roughly handled, and his father killed, by brutal soldiers. And the persecution was not confined to the living. It extended to the dead as well, since Anglican ministers are known to have refused to bury them in consecrated ground. In Breconshire, in the parish of Llanfihangel Brynpabuan, the minister had the body of a young Baptist woman exhumed and buried at the crossroads, a place usually reserved for suicides, while at Llangollen the corpse of a friend of Vavasor Powell was allowed to remain unburied in the churchyard for ten days.

The most vigorous persecution was undoubtedly reserved for the Catholics. Though their numbers were small—according to the religious census of 1676 there were only 1085 of them altogether, concentrated in the three shires of Monmouth, Brecon and Flint—they still constituted a threat in the eyes of the Protestants, and this situation was exacerbated by the favour shown towards them by both Charles II and his brother James. Suspicions as to Charles's intentions were aroused by the secret Treaty of Dover 1670, but the floodgates were really opened by the Popish Plot 1678, and the cry of 'no popery' once again reverberated throughout the land. In the case of papists, the penal laws were consistently applied, and the Jesuit College at Cwm was destroyed by Herbert Croft, bishop of Hereford. Catholic and Jesuit priests were hunted down mercilessly, and in

1679 four of them were put to death. The papists never recovered from this persecution, and despite James's efforts on their behalf, their numbers continued to diminish.

Severely repressive, also, was the persecution of the Quakers; and the ill-treatment which they had endured, even during the Interregnum, was to continue after the Restoration. Theirs was a very aggressive creed. Not for them the comparative safety of a distant farmhouse. They had to shout their message from the rooftops, and they incurred the antagonism not only of the Anglican authorities, but of the other sects as well. As early as 1662 an Act was passed which forbade five or more Quakers from assembling together outside their own homes, and by imprisonment—between 1660-89 five of them were to die in gaol —fines, confiscation of their goods, and the destruction of their meeting houses, every effort was made to silence them. The fury of this persecution in the end weakened the resolve of the stoutest

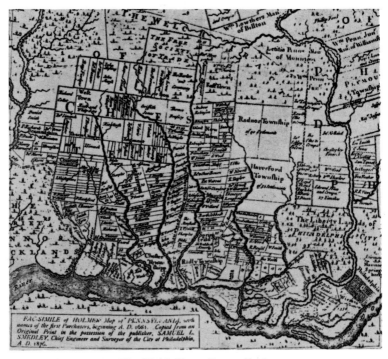

The Welsh Tract, Pennsylfania

hearts, and when they heard that William Penn, as a 'Holy Experiment', was to found a colony in America based on religious toleration, many decided to join him. In 1681 twelve Quakers from North Wales visited Penn in London and purchased from him 30,000 acres of land in Pennsylvania for £600, the capital being raised through the establishment of seven companies. The first batch of Quakers left in 1682, landing at Philadelphia, and most of those that followed came from Merionethshire and Montgomeryshire. The 'Merion' tract was founded, and then the 'Radnor' and 'Haverford' settlements, the whole movement being completed by communities established at 'Montgomery' and 'Gwynedd'. This development represented the first substantial migration of Welshmen to the New World. But the compulsion to emigrate was not caused by persecution alone. Many were captivated by the Utopian conceptions of Penn; others by tales of a land flowing with milk and honey; while many a small squire, who was losing out to the great Leviathans in his native county, hoped to recover both riches and status on the other side of the Atlantic. In 1683 Thomas Lloyd, the brother of Charles Lloyd of Dolobran, left for Pennsylvania and he was soon to act as Deputy-Governor for Penn during the latter's absences in England. In the early days of the settlement, the Welsh Quakers were to play an important part in its affairs, and in 1700 Rowland Ellis of Dolgellau, who had emigrated in 1686, was elected to the state assembly. But while the Quaker church in Pennsylvania flourished, in Wales Quakerism decayed, and the loss through emigration of so many of its more enterprising members must have been a not unimportant factor in accounting for its decline.

The hand of persecution fell heavily on the Independents also, but they survived. Imprisonment failed to silence Vavasor Powell, who was like a bird in a cage, and after his decease in 1670, his mantle fell on the shoulders of worthy and talented leaders such as Henry Maurice and Stephen Hughes. An invitation to Maurice to become pastor of the 'gathered' church of the Independents of Brecknock, with its centre probably at Llanigon, led to ten years' missionary work in the county. His crusading zeal was such that Bishop Lucy credited him with bringing the Puritan invasion up to the gates of Brecon. Another of the great apostles of nonconformity was Stephen Hughes, the son of a Carmarthen mercer. In 1654 he had been given the living of Meidrim. The Restoration, however, saw him ejected from this living, and during the period of persecution he appears to have been extremely active as a preacher in Carmarthenshire. 'A plain, methodical, affectionate preacher who insisted much upon the substantial things of religion', he was sufficiently moderate to be permitted to preach in parish chuches, since he was acceptable to some of the Anglican clergy and gentry. But though a powerful and effective preacher, he is possibly best remembered for his services to education, and as a publisher of Welsh devotional books.

For the Baptists, also, it was not all unrelieved gloom; there was a silver lining. Though John Miles had fled to America in 1663 taking his congregation with him, in 1667, owing to the endeavours of William Jones, Cilymaenllwyd, a new church was established at Rhydwilym on the borders of Pembrokeshire and Carmarthenshire. Despite the persecution, this church was to flourish, and by 1689 there were 113 members drawn from nearly twenty adjacent parishes. Nevertheless, in 1683, following what was by now a well-charted route, the Arminian Baptists from Radnor emigrated to Pennsylvania and settled at Pennepek on the outskirts of Philadelphia. In 1701 they were joined by sixteen Baptists from Rhydwilym, but the two bodies failed to agree,[6] and so the Rhydwilym Baptists moved on and bought 30,000 acres of land in Delaware, on what came to be known as *The* Welsh Tract. Here, Welsh was the order of the day, since church records were kept in that language and ministers officiated in it.

That nonconformity survived at all was due not only to the courage and fortitude displayed by the faithful, but also to the fact that the harshness of the persecution was not continuous, and dissenters experienced periods of relative calm, when flagging spirits could be revived and broken bodies mended. These respites from persecution may well have stemmed from the authorities' fear of a Puritan backlash in the form of armed insurrection if matters were pushed too far. The intensity of the persecution varied from place to place and from time to time, but

[6] The new arrivals were stricter in their religious practices, and more wedded to the mother tongue, than the Pennepek congregation in which the Welsh element had been in a minority from the first.

it was at its fiercest at times of increased national tension. Thus the years 1660-62, 1664-67, 1670-72, 1678-79 and 1681-84 represent peak periods in the persecution and they all relate to developments at the centre such as the Restoration, the Treaty of Dover and the Popish Plot, which generated deep passion or alarm. Though there were bishops like William Lucy of St. David's and Humphrey Lloyd of Bangor who were uncompromising in their attitude towards dissent, and Lucy had described the nonconformists as 'dangerous to the King and Kingdom and an affront to the established religion', there were others who were far more conciliatory, and more than prepared to enter into a dialogue with them in an effort to persuade them to return to the bosom of the Church. While Bishop Lucy was very critical of the Brecon magistrates for not silencing an unlicensed preacher, Henry Maurice, who had come near the town, [7] William Lloyd, bishop of St. Asaph (1680-92) held conferences, mainly at Wrexham and Oswestry, with the leading dissenters of his diocese, with John Evans the Independent, the Quakers Charles and Thomas Lloyd of Dolobran, and Philip Henry and James Owen, the Presbyterians. All these public disputations were to prove abortive. But the Brecon magistrates were not the only ones without eyes to see, or ears to hear. Throughout Wales, though the majority could not be described as culpably negligent, there were Justices and Constables who 'openly declined all engagements in these persecutions', who 'winked at Conventicles', and some even left the bench rather than become instruments of persecution, and it is doubtful whether nonconformity could possibly have survived if the law had been diligently applied. But there was a limit to what could be achieved through raw courage, blind magistrates and, presumably, faith in the Almighty. To survive, self-help was required and the fact that nonconformists met in widely-scattered farmhouses, in caves, woods, and other out-of-the-way places, and displayed considerable skill in discovering loopholes in the law, made detection and prosecution more difficult. It is in these meetings

[7] Lucy writing to the Archbishop of Canterbury, early in 1673, said: 'there is also one Morrice who (as I can learne) has noe licence, a teacher errant, who Leades a body of 200 or 300 after him in the face of this Country, having the last weeke preached heire neere this town [Brecon], not at all checked or disturbed by the Justices of the Peace'.

at secret places that the foundations were laid for many of the Baptist and Independent churches of today. There were times, also, when nonconformists were afforded the opportunity of getting a second wind. Such an occasion was March, 1672, when Charles II issued his Declaration of Indulgence suspending the penal laws and allowing them freedom of public worship, 'which meetings shall be open and free to all persons'. Licences were to be issued to enable nonconformists to hold their meetings, and the first licence in respect of Wales was for Marmaduke Matthews at his own home in Swansea. Charles, by thus exercising his Suspending powers, placed the dissenters in a very difficult situation since though they wanted toleration, they had no desire to achieve this by unconstitutional means. Throughout Wales, 185 licences were taken out, invariably by agents; 136 in South Wales, and forty-nine in the north, and of this total no fewer than 126 were taken out by Independents. These were stronger in Wales than in any other part of the British Isles.[8] The marked concentration of dissenting congregations in South Wales, particularly in Brecon, Glamorgan and Monmouth, can be accounted for by the fact that this area had always been more open to English Puritan influences than the more conservative north. The number of licences taken out was not a true reflection of the strength of dissent in Wales. Many nonconformists were suspicious of the King's motives, since he had acted not so much to help them, but rather to aid his co-religionists, the Catholics, and nonconformist ministers are known to have preached without being in possession of a licence. Furthermore, to apply for a licence could be interpreted as an acknowledgement of the King's supremacy in religious matters. The toleration was short-lived, since the Indulgence was cancelled in March. 1673.

Further Declarations of Indulgence were issued by James II in 1687 and 1688, but the King's action was regarded with suspicion and misgiving, because the Revocation of the Edict of Nantes in 1685 by his cousin, Louis XIV of France, had heightened fear of Popery. In addition, James's pilgrimage to St. Winifred's Well, Holywell, in 1686, had left people in no doubt as to their sovereign's religious sympathies. By this time, however,

[8]According to the census of 1676 there would appear to have been 4,221 sectaries in Wales, 2398 in the diocese of St. David's, 905 in Llandaff, 643 in St. Asaph, 247 in Bangor, and 28 in outlying parishes of the diocese of Hereford.

there was a growing awareness that Anglicans and nonconformists would have to learn to put aside their differences and live together in some sort of amity. Archbishop Sancroft, following his acquittal together with six other bishops, issued Articles to his clergy in which he enjoined them 'to have a very tender regard to our brethren, the protestant dissenters', and 'on occasion to visit them at their houses, and receive them kindly at their own'. When William landed at Torbay in November 1688, the climate of opinion was such that it was not only possible, but even inevitable, that the Toleration Act should be passed in 1689. Though many of the disabilities on dissenters continued—the Test and Corporation Acts remained on the Statute Book[9]—they were now provided with the opportunity of erecting their chapels and ordaining their ministers. Furthermore, in 1691, as a response to the Act, the Independents and Presbyterians established a Common Fund in London to support their churches, and to make provision for the education of ministers, though this development led to some resentment against 'gwŷr y Fund' (Fund people) as some churches were not prepared to sacrifice their independence in return for fund support. The plant of nonconformity had weathered the storm. Now was the time for real growth.

NATURE OF DISSENT

There was nothing exclusive about the dissenters. They included in their ranks a fair cross-section of the population. Nevertheless, socially, the majority were drawn from the ranks of the middle section of society. These included minor gentry, substantial yeomen and farmers, merchants and artisans. In a congregation at Denbigh in 1715 it would appear that one member was worth £4,000 to £5,000 a year, and three worth £500 each. Humble labourers also figured prominently, and possibly constituted the largest single social stratum. An analysis of the ten dissenting congregations in Monmouthshire, with a total membership of 1,300, has shown that there was one squire, 37 gentlemen, 115 yeomen, 85 farmers, 137 merchants and 167 labourers. The presence of persons of wealth and standing

---

[9] These were only repealed in 1828 though annual Indemnity Acts passed since 1727 had made it possible for them to hold office.

undoubtedly represented an element of strength and encouragement since they were in a position to extend their patronage and protection to the humbler members of the flock.

Together with their naked courage, though there were some timorous ones in their midst, the dissenters were characterised by their zeal, their readiness in debate, their knowledge of Biblical texts, their addiction to family devotions, and the emphasis which they placed on the importance of education and literacy. Their preachers, trained and educated at nonconformist academies like Llwynllwyd in Breconshire, appreciated to the full the value of the sermon from the pulpit. In an age in which the majority were still illiterate, and which did not boast—or have cause to regret—either radio or television, this was by far the most effective means of disseminating their views. Although the Methodists claimed that their sermons were arid, dissenting ministers preached with considerable evangelical fervour, and the play which they made with people's emotions often culminated in whole congregations being reduced to tears. And church membership was taken seriously. Conduct unbecoming a Christian, or non-observance of the Sabbath, could lead to members being expelled. After 1660 their churches tended to be organised on a county basis. Though there might be just the one county church, it would have several branches, and the minister, travelling from church to church on horseback, was hard pressed at times to provide services for all the scattered congregations, however small the membership. In Cardiganshire, the church at Cilgwyn had congregations in at least eight different places, though they constituted the one church. The itinerant minister was certainly a unifying factor. But the various congregations would combine on occasion for communion, and they were also subject to a common code of discipline. While in the early years of nonconformity Presbyterians, Baptists and Independents were found together in the 'gathered' church, by the end of the century there was a growing tendency for churches to separate according to doctrinal belief, and the days of the gathered churches were over.

It was very largely owing to the unselfish dedication of these ministers that nonconformity was enabled not only to survive the years of persecution, but also to display symptoms of growth. John Evans, the Presbyterian minister and theologian, collected

Sir John Philipps   Howell Harris

statistics of nonconformity between 1715-1718, and, allowing for his natural inclination to exaggerate the strength of protestant dissent, it would appear that at the death of Anne there were about 89 nonconformist congregations in Wales, with a total membership of some 17,700. They thus constituted about 5% of the total population. Their main strength was in the south, in the shires of Pembroke, Carmarthen, Cardigan, Glamorgan and Monmouth. Building on such sound foundations, it is hardly surprising that Methodism in the eighteenth century should have achieved such resounding success. [10]

[10] Howell Harris, in his diary, paid tribute to the efforts, and the abiding influence, of a Puritan giant like Vavasor Powell whose memory he still found green in his native Radnorshire, and observed how the path of the Methodist movement had been made easier since the new revival was able to link itself, over the years of persecution, with the old.

Chapter 7

FROM DARKNESS INTO LIGHT

BACKGROUND

The Protestants had always placed considerable emphasis on the value of education since they wanted to create as literate a ministry and laity as possible. The right of the individual to study the Scriptures for himself, and to draw his own conclusions, was of the very essence of Protestantism, and the ability to read was the key which would unlock the door to revealed truth as contained in the written Word. During the Interregnum, as part of the effort to Puritanise Wales, the revolutionary authorities, under the terms of the *Act for the Better Propagation and Preaching of the Gospel in Wales* (1650), had established about sixty schools in the chief market towns, and even Owain Glyndŵr's dream of a University in Wales was revived. The University never materialised, and the Commonwealth Schools, more like grammar than primary schools judging by their curricula, created *de novo* and *ad hoc*, and with no corporate traditions to sustain them, disappeared in 1660 with the Puritan authorities that had created and maintained them. Glamorgan, in 1662, according to Bishop Lloyd of Llandaff, 'was utterly destitute of schools'. Despite the uncharitable attitude of Anglican clergymen and Tory squires towards dissenters, as exemplified in the Clarendon Code, one of the characteristic features of the age ushered in by the 'Merry Monarch', was a concern for piety and good works. Solicitude for the physical and spiritual welfare of one's fellows came to be regarded as a kind of open sesame to eternal salvation. The Vicar Prichard had given expression to this view, [1] and it was a note that recurred time and again in Restoration literature. Religious reformers believed fervently that good deeds redounded to the greater glory of God, and men of means were exhorted to assume responsibility for the welfare of the underdog, the old, the infirm and the poor. This belief in the efficacy of good works was

[1] The couplet reads as follows:
  'Y maint a roech i'r tlawd a'r truan
  Storio'r wyt i ti dy hunan'.
['That which you give to the poor and the wretched, you are storing up for yourself'.]

134

soundly based on the Biblical commendation, contained in the Sermon on the Mount,[2] that the merciful would be blessed, and the need to lay up treasures in heaven by charitable deeds here on earth towards one's fellow man, was a message that was given considerable prominence.

This emphasis on piety and good works represented a reaction against the low standards of private and public morality, themselves an indirect by-product of the strict Puritan regime. There were those who were appalled by the vice, profanity, gambling and drunkenness so prevalent in society, and they were determined on a 'Reformation of Manners'. Societies were formed for this purpose,[3] the first being established in London, and, by prosecutions in the law courts—made possible by an impressive apparatus of funds, lawyers, informers and witnesses—it was hoped to mend men's ways. These societies soon spread out from London; and in Wales, through the influence of Sir John Philipps of Picton Castle, they were very active in Carmarthenshire and Pembrokeshire.

However, this movement was not exclusive to England. Similar developments were taking place in Germany under the guidance of Philipp Jacob Spener, a Frankfort pastor who had been profoundly influenced by Lewis Bayly's *Practice of Piety*. The Pietist movement, as it was known, had as its core, personal redemption, piety and good works, and in this respect represented a reaction against Luther's central doctrine of Justification by Faith Alone. Spener's most famous disciple was Hermann Francke, who became a Professor at the new University of Halle. Francke's theology, like Spener's, was eminently practical, since he also emphasised the need for the care of the poor, and the provision of schools, colleges and orphanages. It was as a result of the influence of these Pietists, and especially of Francke's *Pietas Hallensis*,[4] that the London reformers came to the conclusion that penal action alone was insufficient. What was also required to achieve higher moral standards was to diminish

---

[2] Matthew V, 7.

[3] Dr Josiah Woodward published a history of these societies in 1697 in a booklet entitled: *An Account of the Religious Societies in the City of London, and of their Endeavours for the Reformation of Manners*.

[4] This was an account of 'the Orphan House and other Charitable Institutions at Glauche, near Halle'.

the ignorance of the masses through a system of religious education.

The Church in the Post-Restoration period, where education was concerned, was rather supine since it embarked on no new initiatives. Most existing Anglican schools were old foundations, endowed before the outbreak of hostilities in 1642. In 1665, though information is, unfortunately, not available for Bangor and Llandaff, it would appear that in the diocese of St. Asaph there were only five schools, and in that of St. David's, the largest diocese in Wales, embracing more than half the territory of the Principality, only fourteen. In a great number of cases, possibly most, these schools were conducted, not by schoolmasters appointed for that particular purpose, but by local clergymen. Thus, of the fourteen schools recorded in the diocese of St. David's, eight were administered by clergymen, leaving only six to be run by persons who were schoolmasters and nothing else; and three, possibly four, of these were soon attracted to the ranks of the clergy by fatter salaries. In 1665, at Christ College, Brecon, the Master was the thirty-three-year-old Meredith Penry who, since 30 November, 1661, had been rector of Llan-

Christ College, Brecon

hamlach, and since 9 February 1662/3, vicar of St. John the Evangelist with the very important 'chapel' of St. Mary's. To enable him to perform his duties as schoolmaster, Penry kept a curate at Llanhamlach, and another, Hugh Jones, at Brecon, who also acted as Usher to the school. The salaries paid to the Anglican schoolmasters do not appear to have compared favourably with those paid by the Puritan authorities during the Commonwealth since, at Brecon, while the Puritan Master and Usher had received £40 between them, Meredith Penry got only £13.13*s*.4*d*. and Hugh Jones only £6.6*s*.8*d*., both sums together amounting incidentally to the original endowment of £20 per annum. The paucity of evidence is such as to make judgements concerning the curricula of these schools rather tentative. Doubtless, the endowed schools corresponded very closely to those of English grammar schools, with the emphasis very much on the teaching of Latin and Greek grammar—and among the teachers in St. David's and St. Asaph there were six M.A.'s, three B.A.'s and an Oxford undergraduate—with some provision for religious education. They provided a free education for a specified number of poor scholars, and were conducted in English. In other schools, run by a licensed master, children might be taught simply 'to reade and write', and at Boughrood, Rice Powell is described as keeping school in his own home 'and boardes many schollars'.

The Puritans were certainly not as moribund. Though the Commonwealth schools vanished from the educational scene in 1660, the Act of Uniformity 1662, by which dissenting teachers were banished from their classrooms, as well as dissenting ministers from their pulpits, resulted in many of the ejected clergy, though unlicensed, turning to keeping schools as a means of making a living. So successful were they that the Cavalier Parliament felt constrained, in 1665, to introduce the Five Mile Act, by which Puritan ministers were forbidden to teach in any public or private school, or to take 'any boarders or Tablers that are taught or instructed by them', on payment of a penalty of £40 for each offence. It is understandable, perhaps, considering the nature of the times, that the Anglican authorities should be determined to shield the young from what they regarded as the fanatical and corrupting influence of nonconformity, but at the same time the persecution is indicative of a certain bankruptcy of ideas on the part of the Church, since a policy of negative repression could never be an adequate substitute for one of positive action as exemplified in the establishment of new schools. Furthermore, it was a policy that was bound to fail, since it only succeeded in arousing sympathy for the oppressed, particularly in that great Puritan stronghold, London.

However, despite the Five Mile Act, many nonconformists continued to keep school, and one such minister was Samuel Jones, who had been ejected from the living of Llangynwyd in Glamorgan. He was a fellow of Jesus College, Oxford, and a scholar of considerable repute. He opened his school in his own home at Brynllywarch, near Bridgend, either in 1662 or 1672, and it was possibly after 1688 that he began to accept students of mature age who wished to be trained for the dissenting ministry. It was in this manner that the school became a dissenting academy, though it was not connected with any particular denomination since ministers of several religious sects were educated there. Such was the reputation of the academy established at Brynllywarch that even young men not intended for the ministry came there to be educated, and particularly did this apply to the sons of the local gentry.

The Act of Indulgence 1672, suspending the penal laws and ushering in a degree of greater tolerance, might well have tempted some nonconformists, particularly those who had been schoolmasters during the Puritan regime, to open schools. Certainly, Bishop Lucy of St. David's refers to unlicensed schools having been established at Brecon, Carmarthen, Haverfordwest, Swansea, Cardigan, and various other places. Stipends of £6 and £8 per annum were paid to the teachers, and it is quite evident that some of these were women.

THE WELSH TRUST

During the Restoration period Anglicanism absorbed much of the Puritan ethos and this was reflected in the new spirit of tolerance and co-operation that became very evident during this era. Men of liberal views in both the Anglican and dissenting camps decided to get together to improve spiritual and moral standards and to effect this through education. It was this desire to improve 'manners' (conduct) through education that led to the establishment in 1674 of the Welsh Trust, which represented the first attempt by a voluntary agency to establish schools in Wales. People of very differing religious hues became patrons. On the Anglican side were the future bishops, Tillotson and Stillingfleet, while the nonconformists were represented by zealous Puritans like Richard Baxter, William Bates and Thomas Firmin, London's leading philanthropist. All were moderate men who prided themselves on their 'latitude'. Furthermore, they were bent on demonstrating that philanthropic endeavour was infinitely preferable to the promotion of religious divisions. The lion, indeed, was to lie down with the lamb.

The principal architect of the Welsh Trust was Thomas Gouge, a Puritan divine who had been ejected from the living of St. Sepulchre, in Southwark, London, in 1662. His attention had first been drawn to the low moral state of Wales by reading the *Life* of Joseph Alleine, the nonconformist minister of Taunton, published in 1671. Gouge was 'set all on fire', and, as an ejected minister he had the time and, despite his considerable losses in the Fire of London, 1666, he also possessed the means, to embark on the evangelisation of Wales. His first flirtation with Wales occurred in 1671-2, when he undertook some itinerant preaching on the 'skirts of Wales'. It was this experience that convinced him of the need to establish schools and to provide devotional literature in Welsh. The realisation of these twin aims necessitated the raising of funds, and, on his return to the Capital, he established the Trust. The movement, therefore, from its very inception, was London-based. To Charles Edwards, author of *Hanes y Ffydd Ddi-ffuant*,[5] the Trust was further evidence of the benefits that continued to accrue to Wales from the union of the two countries. The patronage of the Lord Mayor and Council of Aldermen of the City of London conferred on it an immediate respectability, and 'Broad Church' bishops and clergy responded readily to his appeal for support. Nor did the clarion call go unheeded among the Welsh gentry, since some of the leading families like the Mansels, the Mostyns, the Awbreys and the Phillippses of Picton, lent their patronage.

Within these Charity schools established for the education of poor Welsh children, the emphasis was on the teaching of reading, writing and arithmetic, a severely practical curriculum.

[5] 'History of the Unfeigned Faith'.

The medium of instruction was English, since it was held, and especially by the Puritans, that because English was the key which unlocked so many doors, the interests of the children would best be served by their acquiring a mastery of that language whereby they would be 'more serviceable to their country and live more comfortably in the world'. Furthermore, the London patrons of the movement did not regard Welsh as a fitting vehicle for the communication of eternal truths. Stephen Hughes of Meidrim, who was closely associated with Gouge in this work, disliked this emphasis on English from the very start, and he expressed his misgivings about Gouge's plans to instruct Welsh children in the English tongue as early as 1672. He was adamant in his belief that only by giving instruction in the language of the hearth could children be taught effectively. The books mainly employed in the instruction of the pupils were the Bible, the Church Catechism, the Apostles' Creed, *The Practice of Piety* and the *Whole Duty of Man*. The schools, therefore, aimed not only at producing pupils who would be good in this world and happy in the next, but also to mould children who would be useful citizens, since they would have been taught obedience to the powers that be, irrespective of whether that authority was wielded by magistrate or minister. The leaders of society were still suffering from the hangover left by the Civil Wars. A further legacy from the period was that, while the high peaks of the Protestant faith figured prominently in the instruction provided, at the same time there was inculcated into the minds of the young a hatred of Popery, because they were taught that the Church of Rome was the mother of ignorance and superstition and her ways were those of the Devil.

By 1675, 2,185 children were receiving a free education in eighty-seven schools situated in the chief towns of Wales, and the number of pupils in each varied between ten and sixty. With the exception of Merioneth and Montgomery, there were Charity schools to be found in every shire in Wales, with a particularly marked concentration in the shires of South Wales. Three hundred and fifty-two children were being taught in twelve schools in Monmouthshire; 341 in sixteen schools in Glamorgan; 346 in sixteen schools in Pembrokeshire and 266 in eleven schools in Carmarthenshire.[6] After 1675 a very marked decline

[6] The statistics for the other counties are as follows: Brecknockshire 20 +

set in and, by 1678, only thirty-three schools were still in existence. The number of children taught had been reduced significantly: in Monmouthshire to 235; in Glamorgan to 330; in Pembrokeshire to 219 and in Carmarthenshire to 154. The tree in blossom had been well and truly shaken, and the decline is attributable in the main to the opposition of the Welsh bishops. The shadow cast by the Civil Wars meant that charitable endeavour was regarded with suspicion; and the persecution of Anglican clergy, and the proscription of the Litany, were too recent to be forgotten. The hostility of the bishops, particularly of Humphrey Lloyd of Bangor and William Lucy of St. David's, was most destructive. Lloyd, having described Gouge as an 'itinerant emissarie of the leading sectaries', then proceeded to accuse him of 'drawing the credulous common people into a disaffection to the government and Liturgy of the Church', with 'insincerite, not to say false dealing'. The bishops were further alienated by the decision in Bate's case of 1670, which allowed patrons to appoint masters to schools which they had founded, since this verdict effectively undermined their control over appointments. They also found intolerable the publication by the Trust in 1678 of a new edition of the Welsh Bible, since this was an area which the bishops had always regarded as exclusively their own. In 1681 political events at the centre served to exacerbate an already volatile situation. The Rye-House plot, [7] hatched by some of the more desperate spirits, presented the government with the opportunity of executing the chief aristocratic Whig leaders, notably Russell and Sidney. A vigorous persecution of the dissenters, Shaftesbury's great allies, was now begun through a ruthless enforcement of the Clarendon Code. The dissenters had been thrown to the wolves, and the Anglican clergy turned 'the force of their zeal almost wholly' against them. Finally, it is undeniable that the Trust schools failed because the language of instruction for children, who were predominantly monoglot Welsh, was English, and Stephen Hughes had early sounded the alarm bells.

pupils in two schools; Cardiganshire 193 pupils in seven schools; Radnorshire, 100 pupils in three schools; Caernarvonshire, 80 pupils in four schools; Denbighshire, 230 pupils in eight schools; Flintshire, 209 pupils in seven schools and Anglesey, 48 pupils in one school.

[7] Supra, p. 106.

In 1681 the Trust came officially to an end but some of the schools established by it survived, and it is most significant that the S.P.C.K. was later to report the existence of schools at thirty centres where Charity schools had been established. Representing a continuation of the work of the Trust, the S.P.C.K. also undoubtedly owed a great deal to the Trust's spade work as a voluntary agency providing a form of elementary education. The Trust constituted an essential link between the state-inspired educational provision of the 1650s, and the voluntary efforts of the eighteenth century. This continuity of educational and religious experience related not only to ideas, but also, to a quite remarkable degree, to personalities as well. In this sense, the Charity schools of the eighteenth century can be regarded as the Trust's educational offspring.

Though the establishment of schools undoubtedly represented the most important aspect of the work of the Trust, the provision of religious literature in Welsh did not lag far behind in importance. In this work, Gouge received considerable support from Stephen Hughes, the son of a Carmarthen mercer. In 1654 he had been appointed to the living of Meidrim, which he held until his ejection at the Restoration. Despite the penal code he continued to preach in Carmarthenshire and to keep school there. Such was his industry that throughout Wales he was referred to as the Apostle of that shire. After his marriage to a Swansea lady, he took up residence in the town. Like John Penry and Morgan Llwyd before him he wanted to assuage the spiritual thirst of thousands of souls.[8] He endeavoured to meet this demand through his activities as an itinerant preacher, and also by publishing devotional books in Welsh. As early as 1672 he was unhappy with Gouge's plan to teach Welsh children in a foreign tongue, English. He appreciated clearly that to preach and teach successfully in Wales, the vernacular had to be employed. Little is known about him between 1660 and 1670, but from the latter year onwards he embarked vigorously on his life's work of publishing Welsh books, a task in which he received active support from both Anglicans and nonconformists. In 1672 he published four parts of the work of the Vicar Rhys Prichard, together with

[8] 'Torri syched ysbrydol miloedd o eneidiau'.

the Book of Psalms, the New Testament and the Catechism.[9] It was during his stay in London at this time that he met Thomas Gouge and Charles Edwards. Charles Edwards was yet another ejected minister, and it was in this manner that there began a fruitful association between the three men that was to last over ten years. Other publications followed, but it was in 1678 that he made a reality of one of his dreams. In 1672 he had been unable to lay his hands on more than fifty Bibles, but in 1678, in co-operation with Gouge and the Trust, he published a cheap edition of the Welsh Bible. Eight thousand copies were produced, and 1,000 copies were given free to the poor, and other copies were placed in the Charity schools for the benefit of the pupils. In 1681 he published another edition of the work of the Vicar Prichard, and gave it the title by which it has been known ever since, *Canwyll y Cymry.*[10] After Gouge's death he continued to publish Welsh books at his own expense, and his efforts made a great contribution to the preservation of the Welsh language among the Welsh people.

THE S.P.C.K.

Though the Welsh Trust came officially to an end with the death of Thomas Gouge in 1681, its work was continued by another philanthropic organisation, the S.P.C.K. The S.P.C.K. undoubtedly benefited inestimably from the activities of Gouge and his associates, since it was able to breathe new life into dying embers. On the other hand, the Society differed markedly from the Trust in one very important respect. While the Trust had been non-denominational, and had included eminent Anglicans as well as nonconformists, the S.P.C.K. was composed solely of members of the Church of England. The S.P.C.K. was founded in London in March 1699 by five philanthropists, and the influence of the Pietist movement in Germany, associated mainly with Spener and Francke, hung heavily over the movement. Of the founder members, four were laymen and one a cleric. The laymen were Lord Guildford, Chief Justice Hooke,[11] Colonel Colchester and Sir Humphrey

[9] '*Llyfr y Psalmau, ynghyd â Thestament Newydd ein Harglwydd* and *Catechism Mr Perkins.*
[10] 'The Welshmen's Candle'.
[11] The first meeting was held in Hooke's London house.

Interior of a Coffee-House

Mackworth. The one cleric was Dr Thomas Bray, who was of
Welsh descent, and had received his early education at the
grammar school in Oswestry, a town situated just over the
border from Welshpool. Though Mackworth was the only
Welshman in their midst, the others, with the exception of
Guildford, all had Welsh associations, and when Sir John Philipps of Picton Castle joined the Society in April, the native Welsh
element was significantly strengthened. The aim of the Society at
home was to attempt to combat the vice and profanity so prevalent in society, through the establishment of schools and the distribution of religious literature. But the need to save souls
applied also to the the colonies, and in North America there was a
great missionary effort to carry the light of the Gospel into dark
places. Indeed, at the commencement, Dr Bray had placed more
emphasis on the needs of the 'Plantations abroad' than on the
work of the Society on the home front, and for two years the work
of training missionaries, dispatching them abroad, providing for
their dependants and sending out books was carried on by the
S.P.C.K, It was only in 1701 that the Society for the Propagating
of the Gospel was established as a quite separate entity.

The Society operated through a system of residing and corresponding members. The former lived in or around London, and

included bishops and influential laymen. The corresponding members, on the other hand, lived in the localities, and were to be found, for the most part, in the chief market towns. They kept the Society's central committee, which usually met at one of London's most popular coffee houses,[12] informed of religious and educational conditions in their own areas, distributed publications and remitted contributions to the Society's headquarters at London. These members had to be of good moral character and, particularly important, of unimpeachable loyalty to the Crown and Church.

SCHOOLS

Between 1699 and 1740, the S.P.C.K. successfully established 96 schools in Wales, though Flintshire had none. The first schools were founded by Dr John Jones, dean of Bangor, who in 1699, informed the secretary 'that he has set up schools for the poorer sort at his own charge'. As with the Welsh Trust, most of these schools were to be found in the counties of South Wales— and more especially south-west Wales—since 74 of them were located in the six shires of Cardigan (2), Carmarthen (14), Pembroke (31), Glamorgan (12), Brecknock (8) and Monmouth (7).[13] Another characteristic which these schools shared with the Trust schools was that the curriculum was virtually the same. The three 'r's' were taught, and the main text-books used were the Bible, the Church Catechism, the Prayer Book and some books of devotion. The main emphasis was placed on teaching the children to read the Bible, and on Catechising them, so that they would reject the dogmas of both nonconformity and the Church of Rome. However, pupils did receive instruction in some useful trades, though this aspect of their education was not given the prominence that it was given in the English schools. Thus, the boys were taught a craft, while the girls were given instruction in sewing, spinning and knitting. Furthermore,

[12] In the reign of Queen Anne, the London coffee-house had reached the height of its popularity. It was the centre of news, the haunt of the idler and of the man of fashion, the rendezvous for appointments and the mart for business men. Such meetings as those of the S.P.C.K. would have been held in private rooms.

[13] In the other shires of Wales the numbers were as follows: Anglesey (3), Caernarvon (3), Merioneth (2), Denbigh (6), Montgomery (6) and Radnor (2).

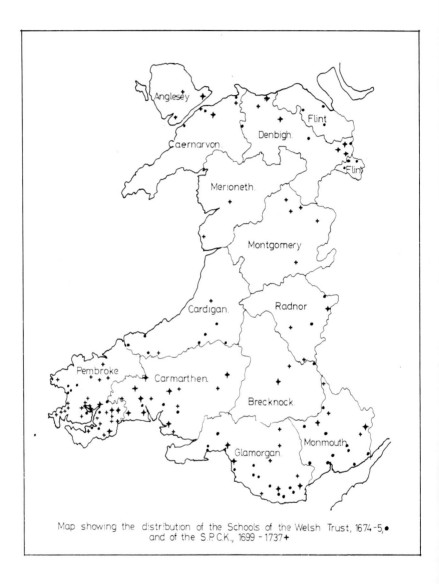

Map showing the distribution of the Schools of the Welsh Trust, 1674-5, ●
and of the S.P.C.K., 1699 - 1737 +

unlike the Charity schools in England, music was introduced into a few, at least, of the Welsh schools. The medium of instruction in most of them, as with those of the Trust, was English and this factor considerably reduced their effectiveness. The policy was possibly appropriate in schools situated in the market towns of the marches, and in the anglicised areas of South Wales, but in the Welsh heartland, and in North Wales, it had little relevance, since the children were monoglot Welsh. John Morgan, the vicar of Matchin, in Essex, in a letter to his friend, Moses Williams, a great Welsh scholar and a tireless worker for the Society, declared that to teach Welsh children through the medium of English was as laughable and unreasonable as teaching English children through the medium of Latin and Greek, and it is most significant that agents and teachers of the Society in Denbighshire, Flintshire and Montgomeryshire, had arrived at the same conclusion as early as 1700. In the circumstances, it was inevitable that in certain of the S.P.C.K. schools, masters, with the full approval of the founders, were providing instruction in Welsh as the only means by which any real educational progress could be effected. Broadly speaking, the situation was that in South Wales, where most of the schools were situated, the children would have been taught in English, while in the north, the medium of instruction, in most cases, was Welsh. Occasionally, objection was raised to the use of English on grounds other than educational, and, surprisingly, among those who objected was Lewis Morris, Deputy Steward of Crown Lands in Wales. His opposition was based on the fear that the teaching of English would encourage the Welsh to migrate to England, 'to the utter ruin of the place of their nativity'. From this, it appears that concern over rural depopulation and its consequences is not exclusive to sociologists and politicians in the twentieth century. Doctor John Jones, one of the most powerful patrons of the Society in North Wales, manifested his disquietude over the use of English by establishing a string of twelve Welsh schools himself, and in his will provided endowments for them on condition that 'the children were to learn Welsh perfectly'. It is undoubtedly true that it was the use of English in so many of these schools that prompted Griffith Jones of Llanddowror to establish the first specific Welsh-medium schools.

Usually the Society's schools were established in parish churches, though unoccupied houses, suitably altered, were also frequently used. According to a report from Haverfordwest, the schoolmaster there had 'a good house to live in and a large room for the school'. The course of study lasted four years, and the school day extended from 7 a.m. to 5 p.m., the morning session finishing at 11 a.m. and the afternoon session beginning at 1 p.m., although it was customary during the cold, dark, winter months to start at 8 a.m. and finish at 4 p.m. The teachers were invariably vicars or curates who had undertaken the work in order to supplement their meagre earnings.[14] As it was, the payment they received as schoolmasters was pitiful enough, since it amounted to only £4 or £5 a year. Later, their salaries were to be augmented through the admission of fee-paying pupils, though the Society had opposed this initially. The masters were expected to be not only members of the Church of England, but also 'of a sober life and conversation, not under the age of twenty-five, one that frequents the Holy Communion, hath a good government of himself and his passions, of a meek temper and humble behaviour, of a good genius for teaching, who understands well the grounds and principles of the Christian religion . . . who can write a good hand and who understands the grounds of Arithmetick'. Among them were teachers of considerable repute. Griffith Jones, who was later to establish in Wales a system of Circulating schools, taught in the school at Laugharne from 1708 onwards and, apart from being well-known for his hasty temper, established quite a reputation for himself as a pedagogue, while Lewis Evans of Carmarthen was renowned as a translator and 'excellent grammarian'.

To maintain standards, a regular system of inspection of the Society's schools was instituted, and in Wales this work was performed by the chief organisers of the movement in the counties. In Pembrokeshire, the agent entrusted with this work was John Pember; in Carmarthenshire, John Vaughan; in Glamorgan, James Harries; in Monmouthshire, Herbert Pye; in Brecknock and Radnorshire, Humphrey Jorden;[15] in Anglesey and Caernarvonshire, Dr John Jones, and in Denbighshire and Flint-

---

[14] In S.P.C.K. letters it was even said that 'many poor clergymen are not able to purchase more than bare food and raiment for their families'.

[15] A minister, he was a great benefactor of the movement, since in the

shire, John Price. Judging by their reports, the standards within the schools appear to have been most satisfactory, the main grievance being the difficulty experienced in finding a sufficient number of competent teachers. Sir Humphrey Mackworth appears to have been most difficult to please, since he rejected for his works' schools two Welshmen who were afterwards to become successful teachers in England.

The role of the patron was central to the success of the Society in establishing schools, for although the S.P.C.K. sponsored their establishment, unless there was very special need, it did not actually provide them. In general, the schools were maintained by voluntary subscription, endowments and church collections, and even sacrament money was occasionally used for this purpose, a practice that was frowned upon by some, at least, of the bishops, and particularly by Adam Ottley, when he was bishop of St. David's. By the early eighteenth century there was a growing realisation that voluntary effort was not enough and that a system of state aid should be introduced, and in Wales the first correspondent to appreciate this was John Vaughan. In relation to the schools the contribution of the Society was mainly the provision of books and materials, and for this purpose the headquarters of the Society in London became a great distributing centre. However, in an effort to get children to attend, allowances were occasionally made for clothing, and even free meals were provided, as at Pembrey in Carmarthenshire and Llanfyllin in Montgomeryshire. At Llanfyllin, all the children 'were to be cloath'd' and 'a meal as their dinner is allowed to 'em that live very far from school'.

One of the greatest patrons of the Society in Wales was undoubtedly Sir John Philipps of Picton castle, Pembrokeshire. He was the son of Sir Erasmus Philipps, one of the Commissioners under the *Act for the Better Propagation and Preaching of the Gospel in Wales* and a member of the Welsh Trust. In 1679 John Philipps entered Westminster School as King's scholar, and from there he proceeded to Trinity College, Cambridge. He left Cambridge without a degree, and this failure may well be attributable to his extravagant life-style, because his father warned him against indulging in 'foolish frolics'. In 1695 he entered Parliament as

counties of Brecknock and Radnor he paid for the schooling and books, annually, of 57 children in four small schools.

member for Pembroke boroughs, and later he was to represent Haverfordwest. His reforming zeal alienated some of the hard-drinking, fox-hunting Tory squires within that august chamber, and a fellow member was provoked to invite a friend to contrive some means of ridding the House 'of this ghostly authority'. In 1697 he married Mary, the daughter and heiress of Anthony Smith, a wealthy East India merchant. From 1695 to the time of his death in 1737, he was a leading figure in the religious and philanthropic movements of the day. On more than one occasion he presided over the S.P.C.K., and was a member of the Society for the Reformation of Manners, the S.P.G., the East India Mission[16] and the Holy Club.[17] He was a great patron of the Charity schools, and was a considerable influence in the lives of young reformers like the brothers John and Charles Wesley, George Whitefield and Griffith Jones. His main sphere of influence was south-west Wales, the two shires of Pembroke and Carmarthen and, at his own expense, he founded twenty-two schools in the former shire and several in the latter.

While the influence of Sir John Philipps was paramount in Pembrokeshire, in neighbouring Carmarthenshire the unquest-ioned leader of religious and educational life was John Vaughan of Derllys, a close friend of Philipps and a relation by marriage. John Vaughan was instrumental in establishing schools and lib-raries—he was the pioneer of free libraries and children's lib-raries in the home[18]—and extremely active in the dissemination of Welsh religious literature. He was also an advocate of county grants for the education of poor children. It was as a result of the influence of these two enlightened squires that the S.P.C.K.'s greatest success was to be achieved in this part of Wales.

[16] Supra, p. 122.

[17] In 1729 a number of undergraduates and clergymen at Oxford had formed themselves into a group for the purpose of mutually studying and practising religion. They organised a routine of Bible-reading, prayer, fasting, prison visitation, and teaching slum children. This group came to be dubbed the 'Holy Club'.

[18] He proposed that 'all parents thro' the Kingdom, and especially those of estate and abilitie, be exerted to bestow on their children a small library consisting of good practical books such as the Society should name, to the value of 3, 4 or 5 pounds, to be fixed in cases with locks and keys, like those for ye Carmarthen Librarie'.

Sir Humphrey Mackworth, a leading industrialist,[19] and a founder member of the S.P.C.K., was also active. Through marriage to Mary, the daughter of Sir Herbert Evans of Gnoll, Neath, he came into possession of leases which gave him a virtual monopoly in the working of coal in the area. He also smelted copper at Neath and later, in 1698, acquired considerable interest in the Cardiganshire lead mines on the Gogerddan estates. In 1706, his Company of Mine Adventurers made provision for the payment of £30 a year 'to a minister to read prayers, preach and catechise the children' at a works' school at the Esgair Hir mine in Cardiganshire, as well as £20 a year for a Charity school at Neath 'for the children of the miners and workmen'. It was he, who, in 1719, because of the difficulty in getting a schoolmaster at Neath, advised the Society 'to send them one of the best schoolmasters in London to be used as an itinerant teacher to set up new schools and train an usher in every school to carry on the work', an idea that was to be taken up later by Griffith Jones of Llanddowror.

Female patrons were not unusual and between 1699 and 1740 over thirty women supporters were attracted to the movement. Jane Herbert, Whitefriars, Cardiff, bequeathed £500 for the endowment of a free school in the town, while at Gresford, Denbighshire, Dame Margaret Strode gave £500 for teaching and clothing three poor boys and three poor girls in the parish. There was a further stipulation that the children, when apprenticed, were to be placed only with members of the Church of England.

DEVOTIONAL LITERATURE

The other aspect of the work of the S.P.C.K. was the provision of religious literature in Welsh. With the funds at its disposal, it was able, over a considerable period of time, to finance the publication of thousands of devotional books and tracts, and to sponsor two editions of the Welsh Bible, one in 1718, of which 10,000 copies were printed and sold, and the other in 1727. The editor in both cases was Moses Williams, who had also produced in 1717 *A Catalogue of all Printed Books in Welsh*. There was no other organisation in existence at this time which could have undertaken the work, and it is more than possible that the literary

---

[19] Infra, pp. 164-5.

revival of the eighteenth century owed a great deal to the herculean publishing feats of the S.P.C.K., which undoubtedly enriched the Welsh language. In addition to the publication and distribution of Welsh books, and these books were either distributed free, or at cost price, the Society established four diocesan libraries. The first was established at Carmarthen, where Edmund Meyricke, canon and treasurer of St. David's cathedral, had made a house available for this purpose. Others quickly followed at Cowbridge, Bangor and St. Asaph, and each library was presented with books to the value of £60. Together with the four diocesan libraries, eight parochial libraries were also established. John Vaughan of Derllys had wanted these libraries to be used by all, [20] provided that assurances were given that all the books borrowed would be returned undamaged, but it was generally felt that the need of the clergy was paramount, since their poverty precluded the possibility of their being able to buy books, and it was essential that they should 'administer wholesome and sound doctrine'. Prisoners in gaols were not overlooked, and in 1711 John Vaughan had requested that the prisoners in Carmarthenshire should be provided with books. It was not long before prisoners in all the 'twelve county gaols of Wales' were similarly provided. Down to the end of the eighteenth century, and long after its schools had closed their doors, the Society continued with its publishing activities, and it is worthy of note that institutions and agencies other than those under its own patronage were to benefit from its efficiency and generosity.

It was between 1699 and 1715 that the S.P.C.K. achieved its most conspicuous success in Wales since, in this period, 68 out of the total of 96 schools were established. The heightened activity of these years is most significant, since it co-incided with that regeneration of church life, though short-lived, which was taking place during the reign of Queen Anne. However, after 1715, the leaves began to fall, the autumn had arrived only too soon, and between the death of Anne and 1727 only a further 28 schools were established and after 1727 none at all.

---

[20] In 1706 he wrote to the central committee desiring that 'the inhabitants of every parish may have the perusal of the books in the Welsh Libraries as well as the Clergy and Schoolmasters and more especially housekeepers'.

Many factors accounted for this decline; not least the Schism Act 1714,[21] passed by the High Church party, which removed from dissenters the education of their children since this was to be transferred to persons licensed by bishops of the Established Church. The Act re-opened old wounds, and led to a perceptible cooling of dissenting enthusiasm towards the movement. Inevitably, the Act led to the energies of dissenters being channelled into opening Charity schools of their own. Furthermore, gentry and clergy who entertained Jacobite sympathies, some of whom were among the strongest supporters of the S.P.C.K. in Wales, were alienated by the intense pressure exerted on schoolmasters to demonstrate openly their loyalty to the Hanoverian George I, even to the extent of offering daily prayers for him. Thomas Lewis of the Fan, Caerffili, withdrew his support for the three schools which he had established at Merthyr Tydfil after he had been fined the very considerable sum of £10,000 for his Jacobite activities. The S.P.C.K. schools were also losing ground to the privately endowed schools, 61 of which were founded between 1699 and 1740, though the majority were established after 1714, when the Society's schools were in decline. Perhaps the principal reason for the decline was the use in the majority of the schools of the English language as the vehicle of communication. Not only was the practice 'unconstructive' educationally, but it also led to the building up of strong passions beneath the surface. The generally held view that educating poor children made them unfit for labour, and the poverty of the homes from which these monoglot Welsh children came, were also factors not conducive to success, since these considerations made it very difficult to convince parents, living at subsistence level, of the value of education. Repeatedly, from Pembroke, came reports that 'The masters cannot prevail upon the parents of poor children to keep them constantly at school'. Often they did not possess the means to even clothe their children properly to enable them to attend school. Furthermore, it was often difficult to release the children from their labours on the farm, or in the workshop, since they were needed to perform relatively undemanding physical tasks like lifting stones, fetching animals, frightening birds away from growing crops, and hoeing. This was a difficulty which Griffith

---

[21] This Act, together with the Occasional Conformity Act, was repealed in 1719 though after 1714 it had been effectively nullified by a Whig government.

Jones was later to overcome by holding his Circulating Schools during the three winter months when work on the farms was at its slackest. In Arfon, according to the testimony of John Jones, the main obstacle to the success of the schools was the necessity for poor children to keep body and soul together by begging for food daily from door to door. It is hardly surprising, therefore, that but few of the poor children of Wales were enabled to attend these schools. The fortunate ones who did, tended to be the products of homes which were reasonably well provided.

It is difficult to evaluate the success of these schools in Wales. The fact that English was the medium of instruction in most would undoubtedly have been counter-productive, especially in those areas with a monoglot Welsh population. Furthermore, the inability or unwillingness of parents, because of their abject poverty, to send their children to school meant that the number of children who benefited from this form of primary education would not have represented a high proportion of the population. Again, much of the learning was sterile since children learnt by rote, and without any real comprehension or understanding. Sir John Philipps had experience of children who could repeat the Catechism, or parts of the Scriptures, perfectly, and yet did not know the meaning of words like 'resurrection' or 'grace', or the basic tenets of their faith. It is possible that Wales benefited more from the work of the S.P.C.K. in the fields of religion and literature than in education, because it is questionable whether the Society's schools left any lasting impression. On the other hand it can be asserted with confidence that the S.P.C.K. did succeed in keeping interest in education alive, stimulating both clergy and gentry into thinking seriously about the besetting ignorance of the poor, and attempting to do something constructive about it.

Chapter 8

THE INDUSTRIAL PULSE

In the seventeenth century, as in earlier ones, agriculture was still the predominant occupation. Nine out of every ten Welshmen lived and worked on the land, and the other tenth had some connection with it, however tenuous. Even town dwellers had close associations with the surrounding countryside. It was not until the revolutionary changes that took place in industry during the eighteenth century, and more particularly the nineteenth, that the urban dweller became quite distinct from the countryman, and the industrial worker easily distinguishable from the farmer or farm labourer. In the seventeenth century the lines of demarcation between town and country, between farmstead and workshop, were very blurred. The mercer or cordwainer living in a borough invariably pastured animals, or grew corn, in the meadows or arable fields outside the town walls which belonged to the general burgess body, while the miner or copper smelter very often had a strip of land adjoining his cottage on which he grazed an animal, or grew vegetables, to provide for his own table. Furthermore, to meet the needs of society at large, people skilled in various trades and crafts were required. In great demand was the blacksmith, since horses had to be shod, as indeed did cattle, before being taken along the long, difficult roads to London by the drovers, and in industry, on the land, and in the home, iron tools, implements and utensils were required; the carpenter was needed for building, and to make tools and furniture; the tanner produced from the hides of animals the leather which was then cut by the saddler, the glover and the shoemaker; road traffic made demands on the services of the wheelwright; yarn had to be spun and woven into cloth, which was then stitched by the tailor to make clothes; and dwellings required the expertise of the stonemason and the thatcher. Craftsmen such as these were to be found in every community and they were people who prided themselves on their skills.

THE AGRARIAN FRAMEWORK

Though agriculture was by far the most important occupation in Wales since it engaged the attention and energies of the vast majority of the people, no far reaching changes were introduced into its practices during this period. In Wales agriculture was backward, even primitive, and this situation was dictated by a lack of enterprising landlords, the innate conservatism of the farmers, a chronic shortage of fluid capital, the barrenness of the soil, an unfriendly climate and the topography of the country since two thirds of the land was to be found 500 feet above sea level. This geographical feature resulted in an agriculture being practised on the higher levels which differed markedly from that followed in the lowlying fertile regions. On the farms situated on high ground, animal husbandry held sway, with the emphasis on the rearing of cattle, particularly store cattle, sheep and goats. However, architectural evidence, such as the large number of barns to be found there, indicates that some corn was grown particularly as a winter feed for animals. In the more fertile lowland areas and river valleys such as the Vale of Glamorgan, Pembroke, Anglesey, Llŷn, the border lowlands of Denbighshire, the Vale of Clwyd, the Severn, Usk, and Wye Valleys, lowland Cardiganshire, and the Gower peninsula, mixed farming was pursued on an extensive scale since here were the 'pleasant meadows and . . . pastures, the plains fruitful and apt for tillage, bearing abundance of all kinds of grain'. In these areas, in addition to the breeding of cattle and sheep, cereal crops such as wheat, barley and oats were grown and agricultural by-products such as milk, butter, cheese and hides were exported to England, Ireland and France and served to supplement the meagre incomes of farmers.

A feature of this pastoral economy was the practice of transhumance, when the herds and flocks were moved in the springtime from the valleys to feed on the mountain pastures. The family, or part of it, left the winter home or *hendre* and took up temporary residence in an upland summer dwelling known as the *hafod*. This practice was, however, becoming less common in the sixteenth and seventeenth centuries as smaller farmers and younger sons turned the former *hafotai* into permanent farms.

But the backbone of the economy was cattle rearing, and the cattle, together with sheep, were sold by private transaction, particularly during the summer season, to drovers and middlemen at the numerous fairs held throughout the country. The cattle, having been shod, were then taken by the *porthmyn* overland to be sold at the great cattle fairs held at Smithfield, Barnet and elsewhere. Following sale, they were fattened on the rich pasture lands in the Home Counties before being slaughtered to feed an ever growing urban population.

The incentive to rear cattle and sheep in greater numbers, and to produce more of the by-products of agriculture, provided by the price rise, and by the growing demands of a rapidly increasing population, led to the trends towards the consolidation of farms and enclosure of common and mountain land, being accelerated in the seventeenth century. But the Welsh gentry could not be described as 'improving landlords'. Their prime concern was profit and not the introduction of improvements in agricultural techniques, and they failed signally to act as conduits for the free flow of new ideas to their tenants. There were a few improving landlords in Wales, and a veritable luminary in the reign of Elizabeth had been George Owen of Henllys. He had laboured hard to convince the farmers of his beloved Pembrokeshire of the advantages of improving the quality of the harvest through the use of marl, lime and seaweed as fertilisers, and by introducing some system of crop rotation. Towards the end of the seventeenth century Henry Rowlands, the antiquary from Plas-Gwyn, Llanedwen, and Edward Wynne of Bodewryd, Anglesey, were equally enthusiastic in their promotion of the introduction of new methods, but it must be avowed that their exhortations on the whole fell on deaf ears, and they failed to effect any significant changes in Welsh agricultural practices. Farm implements remained crude, and the wooden plough employed in Wales drawn by four oxen, though horses were gradually replacing them in the seventeenth century, remained in use in parts of the country until the 1870's. Wales had to wait a little longer before she could reap to the full the benefits of an Agrarian Revolution.

WOOLLEN CLOTH

In the later Middle Ages cloth manufacture was a widely scattered domestic industry, concentrated mainly in the South Wales counties of Pembroke, South Carmarthen, Glamorgan and Monmouth. The spinning and weaving were performed in the home by the farmer, his wife and children, and the cloth they produced was very coarse in texture, poorly made and expensive. Until almost modern times the industry was mainly a means of supplementing the income of a people mainly devoted to animal husbandry. During the early part of the sixteenth century, cloth manufacturing was still one of South Wales's leading industries[1] and in 1566-7 over 5,000 pieces of cloth were exported from Carmarthen. Gradually, the industry migrated to mid and North Wales, and towns in South Wales like Haverfordwest, Pembroke, Usk, Carmarthen and Brecon 'decayed' as a result. The extent of the decline in South Wales can be gauged from the fact that by 1586-7 the number of pieces of cloth exported from Carmarthen had fallen to 2,000, and by 1603 the export trade had virtually ceased. The reasons for this decline in cloth manufacturing in the south are to be found in the competition from the well-organised cloth industry in the West Country, the inhibiting effect of guild organisation in the towns which led to the migration of the industry to the countryside, and finally the changing nature of Welsh exports with coal replacing cloth as the main item in this trade. This development stemmed from the fact that Contiental buyers, like the Bretons, preferred coal to cloth in exchange for their salt and wine. South Wales then reverted to its medieval role of exporting raw wool coastwise to Bristol and the West Country.

In mid and North Wales cloth manufacturing was again a widely scattered domestic industry, though by Elizabeth's reign three counties, Montgomery, Merioneth and South Denbigh, had attained a position of pre-eminence. Within these three shires, on the banks of rivers and streams, dozens of fulling mills sprang up, the first being established at Garthgynvor in Merioneth about 1546, and the area was referred to as 'gwlad y pandai'.[2] While fulling mills in South Wales had been widespread since the fourteenth century, they did not become common in mid and North Wales until the latter half of the sixteenth century and the beginning of the seventeenth. The introduction of these mills effected considerable changes in the struct-

[1] It was the Flemings, established by Henry I in Pembroke, who had helped to make South Wales the centre of medieval Welsh cloth manufacture.
[2] 'Land of the fulling mills'.

ure of the industry since, while the carding, spinning and weaving continued to be performed in the cottage or farm-house, the cloth could now be taken both for dyeing and fulling to one of the many *pandai* in the area. A contemporary observer declared: 'I thincke and judge that God and Nature hathe appoynted thinhabitants of those partes to lyve by cloathing onley'. The conduct of the industry in widely scattered cottages, the lack of capital, and the need for ready cash and a quick return resulted in marketing being controlled by middlemen. These were the Shrewsbury Drapers, who by 1562 had attained a monopoly position with regard to the sale of all Welsh cloth, with Oswestry as their chief entrepôt. Indeed, by 1619, at Oswestry, these Drapers were reputed to be transacting £2,000 worth of business each week.

In 1539 Leland had noted that Oswestry 'standeth mostly by sale of cloth made in Wales', and, fifty years later, Camden found the town 'a place of good traffic for Welsh cottons, especially which are of a very thin or if you will slight texture, of which great quantities are weekly vended here'. While the cloth makers of South Wales in earlier times had disposed of their products through local fairs, or by way of one of the many seaports of the area, the manufacturers in mid Wales were not so blessed. There were few fairs, and the creeks and harbours of Cardigan Bay, apart from small boats used for off-shore herring fishing, did not possess the shipping. The cloth-makers, therefore, had to look eastwards for an outlet for their products and Oswestry proved to be most conveniently and strategically situated.

At Oswestry there was a weekly market conducted in 'certain houses anciently reserved for the market', and drapers from Shrewsbury, having attended a six o'clock service at St. Alkmund's church, would arrive to buy the cloth offered for sale. It would appear that the eighteen-mile journey from Shrewsbury to Oswestry was beset with perils, and even as late as the 1580s those drapers undertaking the journey had to take precautions against attack, since they were enjoined to 'wear their weapons all the way, and go in company—not to go over the Welsh bridge before the bell toll six'. In addition to the Monday market, there were also three big fairs, in May, August and November. But the dissatisfaction of the Shrewsbury Drapers with Oswestry as their main market grew apace, and in 1621 it was resolved that they would no longer buy Welsh cloth there. In the same year, the trade was thrown wide open by royal proclamation, and by 1633 the cloth trade in Oswestry had virtually ceased, and Shrewsbury reigned supreme as the market for Welsh flannel and cloths. Business was conducted in a spacious room on the second floor of the Market Hall, which had been erected in 1596. Trading began at mid-day, and continued until 6 p.m., and although the monopoly of the Drapers' Company was nominally terminated by an Act of 1624, in reality it was to continue for centuries after that date. The company dictated prices, and it took a lion's share of the profits as well. This stranglehold exercised by the Shrewsbury Drapers was resented by the cloth makers, who failed to see why the Company should intrude itself between them and the London merchants who disposed of the cloth. However, since the Company was responsible for finishing the cloth, employing at one stage 600 shearmen for this purpose, Welsh weavers were never in a position to trade in the open market, and this factor must have exercised an inhibiting influence on the expansion of the industry.

A factor which had undoubtedly favoured the development of the industry was the exemption enjoyed by it for so long from parliamentary legislation, owing to the coarseness of the cloth, and its production in isolated and widely scattered dwellings. But as the industry developed, and as cloth began to assume some importance as an export commodity, legislation was introduced which aimed at protecting the consumer, and ensuring that the sale of cloth did provide the Crown with a valuable source of income.

The first statute relating to Welsh cloth was passed in 1541. This Act required cloth to be folded, instead of being rolled, so that faulty workmanship would be revealed. In the following year, legislation was introduced which established specific requirements as to the length, breadth, weight and quality of Welsh friezes and cottons.

Further legislation was now passed establishing the machinery for the supervision and inspection of Welsh cloth. Despite these Acts the quality did not improve, and in 1637 a letter from the Drapers' Company of Shrewsbury, complaining of the poor quality of Welsh cloths, was referred by the Privy Council to the Lord President and the Council in Wales and the Marches. A controversial feature of Welsh cloth was its length, since unlike English cloths, which were twenty-four yards long, the pieces in Wales could be one hundred or even two hundred yards in length. Following this complaint, the length of Welsh cloths was fixed at 24 ells.[3]

Welsh cloth often contained a quantity of wools from outside Wales and in the early seventeenth century it was reported to the Privy Council that wool from Kent, Sussex, Berkshire, Worcestershire, Wiltshire and Norfolk was often sent via Oswestry— where £1,500 was paid per week for such wools—to North Wales and draped into cloth to be sold in London.

The extent of the industry can be estimated, perhaps, from Sir Julius Caesar's assessment that in the early seventeenth century, in Wales and Shropshire, 100,000 people 'do live by the making of these cottons', and in 1624 over 300,000 goads[4] of Welsh cloth were exported from London and probably another 50,000 from Bristol. From these ports, Welsh cloth was dispatched for sale in France, Guernsey, Italy, Spain, Portugal, the Netherlands, Ireland, the Canaries, Madeira, the Azores, Russia, Malaga, New England and Leghorn.

What the industry in Wales required was an infusion of capital but the gentry failed signally to appreciate the opportunities. Though, generally speaking, they had an eye to the best chance, they were not prepared, for the most part, to sink capital into a large-scale development of the industry, and a glorious opportunity went begging. Sir John Wynn of Gwydir, on the other hand, devised a scheme for developing woollen manufacture in the Vale of Llanrwst by employing 300 immigrant Irish weavers, all to be housed within a mile of Gwydir. But it was a vision that was not shared by others and it attracted little official notice. The suggestion of an unknown clergyman that the development of the cloth industry could be a means of remedying the 'petty thefts, idleness and extreme poverty' of Wales was to attract even less attention.

In the period under review, the cloth industry was an unorganised, widely scattered domestic industry without the capital to enable it to compete with cloth manufacture in such English centres as the West Country, the Cotswolds, East Anglia

[3] An ell was 45″ in length.
[4] A goad was a measure 55″ in length.

and the West Riding of Yorkshire. It complemented the earnings
from a mainly pastoral economy, but it was an activity that
brought little enough reward to those who produced the rough,
unfinished cloth in countless cottages scattered over the Welsh
countryside.

INDUSTRY

The twin axes on which Welsh economic life revolved in the
seventeenth century were still the rearing of cattle and sheep,
with cloth manufacture a close adjunct of the latter. However,
the mineral wealth of the country was being exploited not only by
native landlords eager to supplement their incomes, but also by
English entrepreneurs possessed of both the capital and the tech-
nology, and the Act of Union 1536/43 by extending the prerogative of the Crown over Mines Royal to the whole of Wales, had
given a very considerable boost to this process.

COAL

Coal mining in Wales had long antecedents, since it is possible
to trace the history of the industry back to Roman times, because
it is certain that the Romans had worked coal in the Forest of
Dean area and elsewhere. During the later Middle Ages coal was
worked on a small scale in both North and South Wales, especially at Ewloe in the Flintshire coal-field and at Kilvey, near
Swansea, in the South Wales coal-field. However, it was made
use of only in those areas which lay in close proximity to the coal-
pits. Outside these areas, the older fuels like wood, peat and turf,
held the upper hand, even at the end of the seventeenth century.
This situation can be ascribed to the prevailing prejudice against
the use of coal for domestic heating—an antipathy that certainly
lasted until James I's reign—and to the difficulties of transportation. During the Middle Ages its use was confined mainly to the
burning of lime, which was used both as a fertiliser and to make
mortar. It is quite possible that coal was used also in the smithies.

The sixteenth century, and particularly the reign of Elizabeth,
witnessed considerable development in the North Wales coal-
field in Flintshire and Denbighshire, where numerous new sink-
ings were made. But the main development took place in the
South, at Gelliwastad and Llansamlet, in the neighbourhood of
Swansea, and at Cadoxton, near Neath. While Swansea and

Neath were the main centres of coal-mining operations, there was activity also in other parts of the South Wales coal-field, which extended from Pembroke in the west to Monmouth in the east. From the point of view of the future development of coal-mining in Wales, it was this activity in the South Wales pits that was to prove of most significance.

Several factors accounted for the expansion of the industry during the sixteenth and seventeenth centuries. The proximity of the coal outcrops to the sea was certainly a very important one at work, since this simple geographical feature went a long way towards overcoming the problem of transportation of a bulky commodity like coal, which was so much easier when undertaken by water than by land. Another, undoubtedly, was the change in the ownership of mineral property following on the Reformation because, if the ecclesiastics had continued in possession of their holdings, they would, perhaps, have hindered the growth of coal-mining under Elizabeth and the Stuarts by being less able to undertake the investment of the large capital sums so necessary to promote this growth. But undoubtedly the crucial factor at work underlying the expansion of the industry was the fuel shortage. This shortage, particularly of wood, owing to its prodigal use in the smelting furnaces, was common to most parts of the island and led to an ever-increasing demand for coal as a substitute both in the home and in industry. South Pembrokeshire, with its limited supply of timber, was probably the region of Wales which first appreciated the value of coal as a domestic fuel. George Owen of Henllys, the historian of the county, declared in the early seventeenth century that there 'coal was burned in chimneys and grates of iron and, being once kindled, giveth a greater heat than light and delighteth to burn in dark places . . . The hard coal is so pure that fine cambric or lawn is usually dried by it without stain or blemish, and is a most good dryer of malt, therein passing wood, fern or straw'. In the larger houses of South Wales coal, as a result of the revolution in domestic architecture, and the increased building of dwellings in stone and brick, came into much greater use after mid-century, and deliveries of coal direct from the pit were not uncommon. In South Wales, however, it was not so much the local demand for coal that proved the great stimulus to the industry. Far more important was the need for coal in England, particularly the

West Country, and in the Channel Islands and France. In these areas, coal was used in the home, and for such industrial purposes as burning lime, brewing and distilling, and the making of salt, glass, bricks, pottery, alum, soap and paper.

The Welsh gentry were not slow to appreciate the possibilities of exploiting the coal reserves of their estates, and among these entrepreneurs were families such as the Mansels of Margam and Briton Ferry; the Herberts of Swansea, the Myddeltons of Chirk and Brymbo, the Mostyns in Flint and the Evanses of Gnoll, Neath. Gradually, however, the active participation of these landowners in coal-mining operations declined. They discovered that it was far less risky to lease their rights in return for rents and royalties.

After the Restoration, considerable expansion took place in the Welsh pits. The coal industry, as was to be expected, had suffered serious decline during the Civil Wars and Commonwealth, and the blockade of Welsh ports by the parliamentary fleet, the universal horror excited abroad by the execution of the King in 1649, the attacks of French privateers on shipping, and the wars with Holland (1652-54) and Spain (1655-58) had all contributed greatly to that contraction. But the industry recovered, and this was reflected in the high level of exports during the second half of the century.

One of the foremost developers during this period was undoubtedly Sir Humphrey Mackworth. A man of vision and a philanthropist, he was also dynamic, ruthless and ambitious. When, in 1686, he married Mary, the sole beneficiary of Sir Herbert Evans of Gnoll, Neath, he came into possession of sufficient capital to enable him to realise his fondest dreams. His wife's grandfather, David Evans, as well as his father-in-law, had obtained leases which gave them a virtual monopoly of coal-mining in the area. These were renewed for Mackworth who actively developed the mines on his wife's estates. He was an autocrat by temper—his opponents accused him of aiming at 'universal monarchy' in Glamorgan—and he further strengthened his position of dominance in the area by assuming the office of Constable of the Castle, and exercising his right of choice of portreeve of the borough from the three nominees put forward by the burgesses. Certain irregularities in the manner in which he conducted the office led to Bussy Mansel and certain of the burgesses challenging him in court. In the 1690s he re-organised the working of the town pits by introducing steam engines, improving ventilation and linking the pits to the town quay by the construction of canals and tramways. At the end of the seventeenth century he collected £1,200 in rents from his estates, and a further £700 from his coal-mines. According to one estimate he profited to the extent of £40,000 from his mines during a ten-year period. The daring adventurer and speculator was indeed reaping an abundant harvest.

Mackworth's restless energy and overweening ambition brought him into headlong conflict with neighbouring coal proprietors, notably Sir Edward Mansel of Briton Ferry, and his Company of Mines Adventurers, which had been financed by very dubious means, became bankrupt in 1709. The whole· matter was, in 1710, the subject of investigation by a select committee of the House of Commons which, in its findings, declared Mackworth 'guilty of many notorious and scandalous frauds'. He was saved from further penalties by the fall of the Whig administration in that year. Yet this same man was extremely pious and benevolent, and it is difficult to reconcile this aspect of his life, which included the writing of devotional works, and the promotion of the education of poor children, [5] with the questionable nature of some of his financial dealings. There is a strange, even inexplicable, dichotomy in his character. But however unsavoury some of his actions may have been, it is still undeniable that he bestrode his narrow world like a Colossus, and, through his undeviating pursuit of wealth and success, coal-mining in the Neath area was to be greatly expanded.

Great as was the contribution of Sir Humphrey Mackworth to the development of coal-mining in South Wales after 1660, the discovery about 1709 by Abraham Darby at Coalbrookdale that coke could be used to smelt iron ore instead of charcoal, was to exercise an even greater impact. Coal, as a result, ceased to be merely the handmaid of the metal industries. It assumed an entirely new importance, and this revolutionary discovery was to lead to an enormous expansion of coal-mining in the Taff, Cynon and west Monmouthshire valleys. In North Wales,

[5] Supra, p. 151.

metal-working at Holywell and Mold stimulated production in the Flintshire mines, and at Minera and Bersham it led to increased activity in the mines of Denbighshire.

Though, technologically, the industry had made certain limited advances in the second half of the century, coal-mining still remained a singularly unattractive occupation. Wages were low and hours of work extremely long, lasting from 6 a.m. to 6 p.m., with an hour's break for lunch. In some parts of Glamorgan, miners worked an eight-hour shift, from 3 a.m. to 11 a.m., and then supplemented their meagre earnings by labouring in the fields, or by loading ships, in the afternoon. Mining was also a hazardous occupation since coal-dust could damage lungs irreparably, and there were also the dangers of flooding, falling roofs and gas. Choke damp could cause a person to suffocate to death, while the deadly fire-damp, which became increasingly dangerous as pits during the century went deeper, could cause explosions that were horrendous in their toll of human life and disfigurement. The dangers from fire-damp or methane gas were vastly increased since miners, while picking at the coal face in a sitting position because of the low head-room, worked by the light of a naked flame. William Waller, writing about 1700, described the perils confronting the miner in the following words: 'the work is dangerous, dark and unwholesome and the miner, in fear of being crushed to death or choked with damps in poisonous air, sick at first on going into the mines, many fall from the high ladders made of raw hides, with loads on their backs and many die for want of air'. It is hardly surprising that when the week-end, or a Saint's Day, brought a welcomed respite from their labours, the miners should seek consolation in drink, or an expression for their frustrations in outbreaks of unruly behaviour.

The increased activity in the coal-mines of Wales was reflected in the expansion of the export trade, both coastwise and foreign, and by 1688 coal constituted about 90 per cent of Welsh exports. Where Swansea, Neath and Briton Ferry were concerned, coal continued to be the main item, almost the sole one even, of export in the seventeenth century. It was primarily a seasonal trade, conducted mainly between spring and autumn, and the vessels employed ranged in size between 15 and 80 tons. Since trade in commodities other than coal was slight, only occasionally were items of general cargo such as cloth, salt, wine, butter, pitch, resin and skins, included in the manifest. Though, by mid seventeenth century, coal was being conveyed up the rivers Severn and Wye to Gloucester, Worcester, Monmouth and Hereford, the main direction of the coastal trade from the South Wales ports was to the West Country. Abroad, the chief markets for coal from the Swansea and Neath areas were the Channel Islands and France. The trade with Southern Ireland was conducted mainly from the Pembrokeshire coal-field by way of Milford Haven and its creeks of Tenby and Carmarthen. Pembrokeshire culm, which was cheap, commanded a ready sale in Ireland, since it was required for brewing. During the course of the seventeenth century the sale of culm was extended to the east-coast towns of England and to the Continent, to France and, in a few instances, to Spain.

In North Wales, coal mined in Flintshire was taken to the Chester market. From Chester and its creeks, including Mostyn, much of it was taken to Dublin and Northern Ireland. In 1638-9, a total of 7,709 chaldrons of coal was shipped across the Irish Sea. After 1712, exports to Ireland showed a remarkable increase and this expansion applied not only to Flintshire, but also to the South Wales ports. So important did this traffic become that, for a while, it surpassed in importance the foreign trade.

Though the South Wales coal-field at this time had not developed into a 'Black Klondyke', the increased activity there in the sixteenth and seventeenth centuries was a clear pointer to things to come. Valleys, like the Rhondda, still retained their pristine greenness. But in the following two centuries all this was to change; the fair face of Gwalia was to be disfigured by industrial scars, and the land came to be referred to as 'gwlad y pyramidiau'.[6]

IRON

Wales, and particularly South Wales, possessed a number of advantages which favoured the development of an iron industry. There was an abundance of iron ore, plentiful supplies of timber and almost limitless amounts of water. In the Middle Ages, iron

---

[6] 'Land of the pyramids'.

had been worked at Glyntawe in Brecknock, and at places like Llandovery, Neath, Blaenavon, Ebbw Vale and Margam in South Wales, and in Flintshire in North Wales. However, the industry had been on such a small scale that it had not even sufficed to provide for domestic needs, and during the early decades of the sixteenth century occasional cargoes of iron were finding their way into West and North Wales. By the late sixteenth and early seventeenth centuries the process had been reversed, and cargoes of iron were being exported from Newport, Cardiff and Swansea to Southampton, Bristol, Minehead, Bridgwater, Fowey, Weymouth, and even France.

In Henry VIII's reign, under the stimulus of national need, a new era opened for the iron mining industry. The search for minerals was extended to Crown estates in Wales and especially to the lordship of Glamorgan, which had come into the hands of the Crown after the battle of Bosworth. In 1531 an iron mine was developed at Llantrisant, though it was on a very small scale since only three miners were employed.

It was the demand for ordnance for national defence that provided the main impetus to expansion in the iron industry in the sixteenth century, and in this respect it was the discovery of the process of casting iron guns which was to prove most revolutionary. In 1596 Edmund Mathew of Radyr was casting ordnance at his furnace at Pentyrch near Cardiff, and in 1602 he was charged with having sent ordnance overseas from Cardiff contrary to government regulations.

The iron industry in Monmouthshire was given a further fillip in Elizabeth's reign with the establishment in 1568, with monopoly rights, of the chartered company of Mineral and Battery works by William Humfrey and his German associate, Christopher Schutz. Schutz, who hailed from St. Annenberg in Saxony, was described by Humfrey as 'a jewel such as all Germany hath not the like . . . the lantern of Germany as touching mineral and metal affairs . . . cunning in all manner of melting and well known to be expert in all mineral works'. The company established a wireworks at Tintern to meet the demand for wire emanating mainly from the woollen industry. Wool had to be carded and wire was extensively utilised in the making of the cards used for the purpose. By 1603 some 600 men were employed at Tintern. The presence of the wireworks stimulated the demand

Arms of the Society of Mineral and Battery Works
As they are blazon'd

for iron and helped to provide the necessary impetus for the establishment of works at Pontypool, Monkswood, Trevethin, Pontymoel, Abercarn, Machen and Blaina. Prominent among the early iron masters associated with these works was Richard Hanbury, a London goldsmith, whose family was to play such an important role in the industrial history of Monmouthshire.

The grave crisis that confronted the industry in England in the latter half of the sixteenth century, owing to the rapid diminution of the timber supplies, led to a number of Sussex iron masters moving into Glamorgan and beginning industrial operations there. The way for this incursion had been prepared in the 1540s, when Sir William Sidney of Penshurst, in order to obtain haematite ore for his iron works at Robertsbridge, had sought supplies in Glamorgan. By mid-century a William Relfe had settled in the parish of Llanwonno and established a forge at Pontygwaith and a furnace at Duffryn, Mountain Ash, at a cost of £170. On Relfe's decease in 1582 his estates passed to another Sussex iron-master, a Thomas Morley. However, Morley was imprisoned for debt and in 1586 his interests were purchased by Thomas Mynyffee, described as of Aberdare and Radyr. By 1570 Edmund Roberts of Hawkhurst had interests in a furnace at Pentyrch-Radyr in the lower Taff valley; and by 1600, further west in Glamorgan at Coity, two other ironmasters from the Weald, John Cross and John Thornton, were in possession of ironworks.

The introduction during the course of the century of the indirect method of smelting meant that cast-iron hardware could be produced, and this led to the development of a new market. There is evidence which suggests very strongly that a furnace in Merthyr, presumably at Pontyryn, produced fire-backs as early as Edward VI's reign.

In North Wales, the most important iron-producing district was sited around Chirk. Sir Thomas Myddelton, in the years preceding the Civil Wars, had an ironworks at Pont-y-Blew on his Chirk estate, the ore being brought from Ruabon. Further west, at Nannau in Merioneth, on land belonging to Hugh Nannau and his son, attempts by English speculators to work iron failed. The property was leased in 1597 to John Smith of Newcastle-under-Lyme, who replaced the old works there by a blast furnace and forge, the capital being supplied by William Dale and William Grosvenor. The works failed to make a profit and in 1604 they were closed.

During the Civil Wars the iron industry was crippled as a result of heavy material damage, but the most serious obstacle to the expansion of the industry continued to be the shortage of timber. Until the great technological break-through effected by Abraham Darby in the early decades of the eighteenth century, charcoal remained the only really satisfactory fuel for the smelting of iron.

Nevertheless, the second half of the seventeenth century witnessed considerable advance in the industry as a result of a more scientific approach to the problem of iron manufacture. The forging of iron gradually became divorced from smelting, and this development was accentuated when coal began to be used to supplement charcoal in the forge. In consequence, the forges moved in the direction of the coal-fields, leaving the furnaces on their former sites dependent on diminishing supplies of charcoal. Gradually, the industry progressed from the stage where it consisted of isolated furnaces and forges under individual or family ownership, to the situation where it was controlled by small co-operative groups of partners. It was this re-organisation of the industry through a large capital outlay, and the amalgamation of small owners into larger groupings, with more effective and centralised management, and improved techniques, that constituted the most significant development in the industry in the century extending from 1650-1750.

This progession is exemplified by developments at Mathrafal. The Quaker, Charles Lloyd of Dolobran, had taken advantage of the opportunity provided by the sale of sequestrated lands in Montgomeryshire, to acquire in 1651 the manor of Caereinion in the lordship of Powys, together with Mathrafal. He shortly commenced iron-working operations on the estate, establishing a forge in the park at Old Mathrafal. After the Restoration, Lord Powis recovered his estates, and the Mathrafal forge passed into his possession. The forge was now leased to a group including William Wilson and his sister, Sarah Wilson, Robert Smith of Chirk, Ellis Jones of Sedgewick and, later, Robert Swift. Apart from some vicissitudes, the forge at Mathrafal appears to have remained under the control of these lessees until about 1693.

Though adventurous Welshmen were prepared to sink capital into the industry, the chief pioneers were Englishmen. Under their influence there was a mushroom growth of forges, but only a few of these entrepreneurs prospered. Success went to the skilful and the prudent. Most of those engaged, owing to lack of experience, over-confidence, high overheads and local opposition, were to taste the bitter fruit of failure.

TINPLATE

Closely associated with the iron industry was the making of tinplate. Before the late seventeenth century tinplate, which was an alternative to the more expensive brass and pewter ware, had been imported from South Germany and Bohemia, where it had been known as early as 1600. The industry was introduced into

Wales from the Forest of Dean during the Restoration period. Between 1660 and 1688 Andrew Yarranton conducted experiments in producing tinplate in the vicinity of Pontypool. However, his attempt to place the venture on a commercial footing failed, and it was not until the 1720s that John Hanbury brought the art to such a high degree of perfection that Pontypool became a pioneering centre in the production of tinplate.

The Non-ferrous Metals

LEAD

Lead, again, has a very long history in Wales, since it was mined in pre-Roman times. However, even during the period of Roman occupation, the workings were on a very small scale, the demand arising mainly from the use of lead for commemorative purposes, coffins and, more especially, water pipes.

During the Middle Ages there was increased activity in the lead mines in Wales owing to the growing demand for lead for the building of castles, churches, and the more lavish town houses, and also owing to the initiative shown by abbeys such as Margam. The later Middle Ages witnessed a decline in the industry, in which the plagues of the period played a significant part by reducing the supply of labour quite dramatically.

During the Tudor period, lead was mined in Glamorgan, Denbighshire and Flintshire, though the enterprises were all on a small scale. The first real stimulus for the industry was provided in 1568 with the establishment of the Society of Mines Royal which was given monopoly rights in all the Welsh counties except Monmouthshire. In 1583 Customer Smythe acquired a lease of the company's mines in Devon, Cornwall and Cardiganshire for a rent of £300 a year. His manager, Charles Evans, reported most unfavourably on the condition of the mine at Cwmsymlog in Cardiganshire when he took over. Evans made the existing works safe and then proceeded to extend them. Furthermore, he effected economies in the costs of smelting. At Holywell in Flintshire there was also increased activity, since a smelting mill was erected by two London merchants, though there was considerable local opposition to the operations.

The Cardiganshire lead mines really began to flourish when Hugh Myddelton, the banker and youngest son of Richard

Myddelton, and brother to Sir Thomas Myddelton of Chirk, took out a fourteen-year lease on them in 1617 at an annual rent of £400. He was a man possessed of enormous energy, and so successful was he in overcoming the technical problems linked with the mining operations, that it was estimated he made a profit of £2,000 a month from his works at Cwmsymlog. On 21 February 1625, in recognition of his New River project, designed to improve London's water supply, his lease of the Cardiganshire mines was confirmed for a further period of thirty-one years. However, his enjoyment of the lease was to last only a further six years since he died in 1631.

Myddelton's mantle descended on the shoulders of Thomas Bushell who had learnt the art of mining under the wing of Sir Francis Bacon. Sir Hugh's widow, Elizabeth, sub-let the mines to Sir Francis Godolphin, the Cornish mineowner, and Bushell as joint partners. Godolphin soon died and, after his decease, Bushell negotiated the transfer of Godolphin's share of the lease to himself. In 1637 he secured confirmation of the lease from the Privy Council. Bushell was confronted with considerable problems in the mines, since Lady Myddelton's manager and men had attempted to ruin the mines, before they were handed over, by throwing rubbish into them and destroying some of the pumps. Despite this inauspicious beginning, compounded by the opposition of local gentry like Sir Richard Pryse of Gogerddan, Bushell persevered, and his active prosecution of the work brought success, since the mines eventually yielded a return of £5,000 a year. To improve efficiency and working conditions he drove adits upwards into the mountain and this technique not only simplified drainage, but also made unnecessary the haulage of waste material upwards through the mouth of the shaft. Ventilation was improved by the use of bellows worked by two men, the air being conveyed to the workings by means of a pipe. Since the ore was rich in silver, in 1637 he was authorised to establish a mint in the royal castle at Aberystwyth for the coining of all the bullion mined in the Principality of Wales. This concession by the Crown was important, since it obviated the necessity of transporting the silver to the Royal Mint in London, a long, irksome and expensive journey.

During the Civil Wars, Bushell actively supported the King's cause. He mobilised a force of 1,000 miners as a 'lifeguard',

Smelthouse. (Germany, *c.* 1550) (Münster).
(Two furnaces, showing the bellows, driven by grooved axle of waterwheel.
Molten lead being ladled by Smelter from fore-hearth into moulds or cakes.
Assistant re-charges furnace with ore and charcoal)

raised a troop of horse and provided clothing to the estimated value of £36,000.[7] To help keep the King's armies in the field, £100 worth of silver coin from the mint, which by now had been transferred to Shrewsbury, was sent to Charles. After the war, burdened by debts incurred very largely in the King's cause, and hounded by creditors, Bushell led a rather chequered existence. When he died in 1674 his debts amounted to the considerable sum of £120,000.

Though the industry had virtually come to a standstill during the Civil Wars, it was revived after the Restoration. A great deal of opposition was provoked by the resumption of the Mines Royal monopoly and in 1693 Sir Carbery Pryse of Gogerddan, who had in 1690 discovered a rich vein of ore at Esgair Hir, brought a test case against the Crown over the issue of a landowner's right to work minerals found under his own property and secured a favourable verdict. Parliament, ever sensitive to property rights, now proceeded to pass the Mines Royal Act, by which the monopoly position enjoyed by Mines Royal was abolished since landowners were enabled, by the Act, to exploit their own minerals. However, the Crown reserved to itself the right to purchase, within thirty days, and at a fixed price, the ore which had been brought to the surface.

Fires were now re-kindled on cold hearths in Cardiganshire. When Sir Carbery Pryse of Gogerddan died in 1694, Sir Humphrey Mackworth of Neath bought his shares in the Esgair Hir mine for £14,000 on behalf of his Company of Mine Adventurers. This was a joint-stock company, the capital of which was raised by selling bonds, though Mackworth's methods smacked of a lottery. Mackworth, undoubtedly the outstanding figure in the industrial recovery in Wales during the last decade of the seventeenth century, envisaged Neath as a centre for metal-smelting based on coal as a fuel. With this purpose in mind, he had constructed there, at Melincryddan, possibly as early as 1695, a smelting-house for copper and lead. Mackworth had hoped to make a fortune by transporting the lead from the mine at Esgair Hir by sea from Aberdyfi to the quay at Neath Bank, 'whence a canal or waterway was constructed to carry it to a point within a stone's cast of the smelting-works situated so con-

[7] Supra, p. 32.

veniently to the coalpit that the men could run the coal with
wheel-barrows into the furnaces'.

   After initial success, the Company of Mine Adventurers was
to flounder, giving rise to the House of Commons inquiry into
the Company's affairs, which resulted in Mackworth's being
declared guilty of fraudulent behaviour. Several factors accounted for the declining fortunes of the Company. Not least was the
hostility of neighbours, like Sir Edward Mansel and Thomas
Mansel of Baglan and Briton Ferry, which resulted in attacks
being made on Mackworth's work-force with the express
purpose of frightening them away. Some of his workmen were
even threatened with impressment. Coal stocks belonging to the
Company were purloined and vital equipment like tramways
destroyed. William Waller, steward of the lead mines in Cardiganshire, proved to be an incompetent manager, and, consequently, there was a steady deterioration in the relationship
between himself and Mackworth. Over-expansion in Cardiganshire, and the extension of operations into Flintshire in 1707 with
the purchase of the lead and silver works of Daniel Peck when
profits in those mines were falling, were acts of folly. The establishment of a company bank with insufficient reserves, lack of
oversight on the part of the directors, and Mackworth's own

Cardiganshire—The Cwmsymlog Mine of Mines Royal as it appeared in the
late XVIIth century

extravagant style of management, were also not conducive to success. The cumulative effect of all these factors was the collapse of public confidence. Mackworth was removed from the Board of Directors, and it was only by the skin of his teeth that he escaped public prosecution. Thereafter, he devoted himself to the development of his Neath interests. As far as the Company was concerned these setbacks resulted in its virtually ceasing to operate.

In Flintshire the gentry were not slow to grasp their opportunities and the period from the Restoration onwards saw local families like the Myddeltons, Mostyns, Grosvenors, Hanmers and Pennants, prosper. The rich veins of ore in Halkyn mountain yielded a vast wealth, and this was reflected in the increased activity in ports like Flint, Mostyn, Bagillt and Rhuddlan. Some families profited immensely. In 1703 Sir George Wynne inherited a small parcel of land worth £30 a year on Halkyn mountain. Within twenty-five years he was making a profit of £22,000 from the lead mines established there and Leeswood House was built as a visible and lasting monument to his success. London commercial companies, eager for profit, were also quick to exploit the mineral wealth of the area. In 1703-4 the Quaker Lead Company established a smelting-house at Gadlys, on the slopes above Bagillt, on land leased for forty-two years from Thomas Williams of Plas Ucha. There, the reverberatory furnace, designed by Dr Edward Wright, a physician and chemist of Southwark skilled in metallurgy, which used coal exclusively as a heating fuel, was introduced. It freed the industry from its dependence on charcoal, a development which led to a vast expansion of the industry. The statistics for lead exports from Chester speak for themselves. In 1700 900 tons of lead were exported; by 1720 this had increased to 4,000 tons; and by 1740 to 7,000 tons. During the same period 430,604 ounces of silver were sent to the Royal mint.

There was increased activity in the industry in neighbouring Montgomery as well, since in 1692 an exceptionally rich vein of ore was discovered at Llangynog near Oswestry. A smelting-house was established there in 1706; but it was not until William, Marquis of Powis, placed his steward, James Baker, in charge of operations in 1725 that the momentum there was dramatically increased.

COPPER

In 1561 the Company of Mines Royal was formed and was given the right to search for and smelt all ores of gold, silver, copper and quicksilver in the counties of Cumberland, Westmorland, York and Lancaster, the West Country and Wales (Monmouthshire excluded). The company was well-established when, in May 1568, it became a chartered company with monopoly rights. Foreigners could hold shares but the majority of shareholders were to be English.

The year 1583 saw the mining rights of the Society in Cornwall, Devon and Cardiganshire being taken over by Thomas Smith and the decision was made to take the copper ore mined in Cornwall to Neath to be smelted, and for this purpose a smelting house was established at Aberdulais. The choice of Neath as a centre for copper smelting was dictated very largely by the abundance of coal to be found in the area. Since three tons of coal were required to smelt one ton of copper ore, it was obviously more economic to transport the ore to the coal, especially as coal could be carried in the returning ships as ballast.

The works at Neath were entrusted to an enterprising German engineer, Ulrich Frosse, who had already served the Company long and well. Two furnaces were erected in the new smelting house, but they were never fired to their full capacity, mainly because the supply of ores from Cornwall was insufficient and too intermittent. Moreover, Frosse suffered considerably from ill-health and did not relate well to subordinates. Consequently, the venture never prospered and Neath had to wait another century, until the coming of Sir Humphrey Mackworth in the 1690s, before it emerged as a great copper centre.

Mackworth's smelting and refining operations were carried on at Melincryddan, the ore being brought there from Cornwall and Cardiganshire. Mackworth, like Dr Edward Wright at Gadlys in Flintshire, used at Neath the coal-fired reverberatory furnace. But a continuous supply of copper ore was an essential prerequisite for success, and Mackworth was constantly on the look-out for fresh supplies of ore. In 1696 he joined Philip and James Morgan of Narberth in exploiting a rich vein of copper in the St Elfyw district of Pebidiog in Pembrokeshire. After the failure of the Company of Mine Adventurers, he assisted in the establishment in May 1713 of a new joint-stock company known as 'The Mineral Manufacturers at Neath'. The smelthouses and other houses provided by Mackworth for the Mine Adventurers near the Gnoll were taken over by the new company, and Mackworth was placed in charge with the right to appoint the officers. The new company progressed rapidly, and by 1720 it was already engaged in the manufacture of copper, lead, brass and iron.

But Mackworth's interests in copper were not confined to the Neath area. After the break with the Mine Adventurers, he and his sons acquired a lease of copper works at Ynyspenllwch, near Clydach, in the lower Swansea valley, the copper being sent there by road in waggons. This activity was extremely significant in that it foreshadowed the development of the region as the great centre of non-ferrous industry in Britain, and in this expansion the city of Bristol was to play a close and considerable part.

IMPEDIMENTS

Throughout the period under review there were factors at work which exercised an inhibiting effect on the expansion of industry and commerce. A major consideration, undoubtedly, was the shortage of capital. The amount of coinage in circulation was severely limited—farmers were perennially short of ready cash—and there were no banks to provide credit facilities. Welsh farmers and craftsmen, hard pressed to make both ends meet, could hardly be expected to scrape sufficient capital together to invest in industrial undertakings. Furthermore, few only of the greater landowners and merchants were in a position to do so. This situation resulted in doors being thrown wide open for the penetration of English capital, particularly from London, and some, at least, of these adventurers were to make fat profits.

Possibly linked with the general poverty of the country was the rather primitive nature of working conditions in the mines. Basic problems inextricably linked with mines, which during the century were getting deeper and deeper, were those of drainage, the provision of an adequate supply of fresh air, gas and roof falls. Technologically, Wales lagged far behind Germany, the Netherlands, France and Spain. Some progress was certainly made in the closing decades of the century with the construction of tramways, canals and the introduction of the reverberatory furnace, but for the greater part of the century, mining was almost entirely dependent on muscle power rather than machines. It was only when surplus capital and technical know-how were harnessed together in the eighteenth century that revolutionary changes became possible.

Unhelpful also to industrial expansion in Wales was the continuous in-fighting throughout the period between the Crown on the one hand and enterprising landowners on the other, and this problem was not satisfactorily resolved even by the abolition in 1693 of the monopoly enjoyed for so long by the Society of Mines Royal. The Act of 1693 certainly presented speculators with the opportunity to search for gold, silver, copper and lead, but these activities very often brought them into headlong conflict with landowners determined to protect their property rights at all costs, even to the extent of using physical violence. Whole communities at times proved obstructive to industrial advance, protesting vigorously at the felling of timber in their districts to provide the charcoal so necessary at this time as a fuel in the smelting processes. But the denuding of the countryside of trees was not the sole ground for opposition. The fouling of the atmosphere, and the polluting of rivers and streams, were also matters of grave concern.

Infringement of the legal rights of landowners and ecological considerations, though important, were possibly not as relevant as the absence of good roads, canals and railways. Goods had to be carried on packhorses, or in heavy waggons, and this method of transportation, at the best of times slow, and almost impossible in winter when roads were quagmires, severely curtailed the extent of the market region. It was for this reason that the main locations of industrial activity were to be found near navigable rivers and ports. But even transportation by sea was beset with problems. Sailors were at the mercy of wind and tide, and even when these were favourable, there was the danger of being attacked by pirates who infested the sea lanes and could strike terror into the hearts of the stoutest of men. Extremely disturbing was the fact that these pirates often worked hand in glove with the gentry and port authorities, who extended a protecting arm, and in return shared in the profits of this nefarious trade. The seas that pounded the shores of Britain were eventually cleared of these robbers, but in the meantime commerce suffered from their depredations.

A kindred spirit to the pirate, and equally damaging to commerce, was the smuggler. The long Welsh coastline, with its numerous unwatched creeks and coves, provided an ideal setting for this form of illicit trading. A sense of adventure, as well as the desire to maximise profits by avoiding the payment of customs duties, lay behind these smuggling operations; and tea, coffee, brandy, wine, sugar, tobacco, salt and silk were among the commodities smuggled into the country. There was no limit to the ingenuity and skill displayed by smugglers in their attempts to disguise their activities and to evade capture. Thus wine, brandy and coffee were smuggled in baskets covered with herrings. So profitable was this form of 'enterprise' that officials and Justices were involved, which added to the frustration of central administration, deeply concerned as it was with the loss of revenue, since this co-operation made detection and punishment even more difficult.

Finally, Wales at this time still remained very largely 'terra incognita' to the speculative industrialist. There was very little conception of the vast riches which lay undiscovered under the soil. It was only in the second half of the eighteenth century that the Guests, the Bacons and the Crawshays arrived in the Merthyr area, and even as late as 1807, according to Benjamin Malkin, Cwm Rhondda was a wild and romantic place. But the valleys of South Wales soon began to echo to the sounds of a vast industrial activity, and the night skies became lit up from the glow of blast furnaces. Before this development the basic units of manufacture were small and widely scattered, and their workforces very limited, being numbered in dozens rather than their thousands. However, during the seventeenth century considerable advances had been made in coal, lead and copper mining and these developments were to provide the launching pads for the great industrial expansion of the eighteenth and nineteenth centuries to which the expression 'Industrial Revolution' has been applied.

Chapter 9

SOCIETY

Before embarking on a description of society in general in Wales in the seventeenth century, it is necessary to make some attempt to establish the size of the population with which we are dealing. The problems involved in this kind of examination are very considerable because the first official census was not compiled until 1801. Prior to this date, estimates only of population are possible, based on such sources as chantry returns, hearth tax returns, episcopal returns, parish records and subsidy rolls, and the difficulty is compounded by the unreliability, incompleteness and inadequacy of these records in so many instances. In the later Middle Ages, owing to the effects of the Black Death and subsequent plagues, there had been a catastrophic fall in the demographic curve. However, about the middle of the fifteenth century, there was a gradual recovery, and during the Tudor and Stuart periods there would appear to have been quite a substantial increase in population. Between the mid-sixteenth century and 1670 the population of Wales increased from an estimated 226,000 to about 342,000 people, a 52 *per cent* expansion. The greatest growth seems to have taken place in the North Wales shires, for while the six South Wales shires showed a total increase of some 44,541, the population of the six North Wales shires rose by 71,277. This phenomenon can be attributed, perhaps, to the operation of two factors: firstly to the developments that took place there in agriculture, industry and commerce, and secondly to the peaceful penetration of the North Wales border shires by English settlers. It has been estimated that between 1550 and 1670, 700 English families had moved into Flintshire, 680 into Denbighshire, and 570 into Montgomeryshire.[1] However, it is worthy of note that the shire which appeared to have witnessed the greatest single population increase was Glamorgan, as the population there is estimated to have risen from 29,493 to 48,928, a 66 *per cent* increase and this, undoubtedly, is

[1] Vide Leonard Owen, 'The population of Wales in the Sixteenth and Seventeenth Centuries', *Trans. Cymmr.*, 1959.

attributable to the quickening of the economic pulse in that county. [2]

ESTIMATED POPULATION OF WALES IN 16th AND 17th
CENTURIES

Hundreds and towns	1545/63		1670			1801	
	House-holds	Popul-ation	House-holds	Popul-ation	% change	Occu-pied houses	% change
Anglesey	1,954	9,770	3,239	16,175	66	6,679	106
Brecon	4,238	21,190	5,437	27,185	28	6,315	16
Cardigan	3,464	17,320	4,003	20,015	15	8,819	120
Carmarthen	6,875	34,375	7,651	37,255	11	13,449	76
Caernarvon	2,984	14,920	5,245	26,225	76	8,304	53
Denbigh	4,733	22,482	8,594	40,820	82	12,621	47
Flint	2,405	12,570	4,364	22,899	81	7,585	73
Glamorgan	5,530	29,493	9,174	48,928	66	14,225	55
Merioneth	2,094	10,470	3,887	19,435	85	5,787	49
Montgomery	3,450	18,972	6,366	34,907	84	8,802	39
Pembroke	4,225	20,079	6,635	31,535	58	11,869	80
Radnor	2,837	14,185	3,259	16,295	15	3,675	13
Totals	44,789	225,826	67,854	341,674	52	108,130	59

This population was widely dispersed in small communities which, in an economic sense, were virtually self-supporting. They had, of necessity, to provide for their own needs since the geography of the country, and lack of adequate roads, made effective contact between them extremely difficult. Since the departure of the Roman legions, few new roads had been constructed. The ones that did exist were dirt tracks, full of deep ruts

[2] *Supra*, pp. 162-5; 167-70; 171-2; 178-9.

and holes, which became virtually impassable in winter. After undertaking a journey from Gwydir to Chirk Castle in 1656, Richard Wynn declared wryly that he had been extremely fortunate since he had fallen from his horse on three occasions only before reaching journey's end. When the rivers were in flood, bridges could be swept away, and this was exemplified in Denbigh and its neighbourhood in 1706 when, after a violent storm, 30 bridges were destroyed. Such calamitous happenings presented the intrepid traveller with additional hazards; in 1617, for instance, David Kemeys, the squire of Cefnmabli in Monmouthshire, was drowned while adventuring on the alternative means of crossing a river, which was by putting his horse to the water. Town streets were in no better state, since for the most part they were unpaved, and in 1587 Henllan street in Denbigh was described as being in too dangerous a state to be used. When the abominable state of the roads is borne in mind, it is hardly surprising that goods were conveyed mainly along the waterways and the sea-lanes, even though these presented their own problems. However, even though communities were remote, and largely cut off from each other and the outside world, there was quite obviously a certain degree of social and economic intercourse between them. Farmers and their wives frequented the numerous markets and fairs; *porthmyn* took the cattle in noisy droves to the English markets at Smithfield and elsewhere to be sold; judges went on circuit to administer justice; religious reformers left a fiery trail across the length and breadth of the land; beggars pursued their weary and unenviable way from town to town, and especially did the boroughs attract within their walls people from their immediate hinterland in search of work or advancement, but who, more often than not, were to have their fondest dreams shattered. Harvest-labourers from Wales reaped English harvests before returning home to gather their own later and more meagre crops. Particularly was movement of population greatly increased during periods of great hardship and famine when there was a natural drift into areas where food was more plentiful. Primogeniture, the English system of land inheritance by the eldest son, as a result of which all the kittens except one were thrown into the water, saw the younger sons of the Welsh gentry seeking to make their fortunes in other directions. They flocked to the Universities and the Inns of

Court, entered the Church, the legal profession and the world of trade, commerce and banking. The fortunate few secured positions at Court, while others sailed before the mast, even on ships displaying the skull and crossbones, or drew sword for their sovereign on many a bloody battlefield in Flanders.

However, though the population was increasing, the size of families was small, the average being in the region of five persons. Obviously there were families much larger than this, and especially did this apply to the gentry. At the other end of the scale, it was not uncommon to find families of three persons or even fewer. But whatever the size, the family was still regarded by the authorities as the cornerstone of a well-ordered and unified society. The family was society in microcosm, and on the shoulders of the *pater familias* rested the responsibility of ensuring not only that his charges grew up in the fear of God, but that they also displayed due reverence and obedience to the laws of the land and to those who enforced them.

But despite these migratory movements, the vast majority of the Welsh people were born, lived and died within their own parishes. These were their domains, and their lives were encompassed within very narrow horizons. These little worlds comprised communities of people who knew each other intimately, were well-versed in each other's family histories, and were often interrelated, being knit together by ties of kinship or marriage. Since their roots were so deeply embedded in the soil of a particular *bro* or district, Welshmen of the period displayed a deep and abiding love and affection for their *gwlad*, the place of their birth, and this love they carried with them wherever they went, whether it be to Ludlow or London, the Continent or the Americas. Indeed, it was this love that gave birth to that Elizabethan classic, *The Description of Pembrokeshire*, by George Owen of Henllys. Each district had its quite distinctive life-style enshrined in its own peculiar practices, customs, and even dialect. It is hardly surprising that Welshmen did not readily forget the rock from which they had been hewn.

Strangers who entered these communities immediately became the focal point of attention, and the reception accorded them was cool, suspicious and even hostile. Within the boroughs, 'foreigners' or 'censers' were forbidden to trade unless they had been licensed by the corporation to do so; English settlers sometimes had their homes burnt to the ground, as happened in Montgomeryshire where, in 1602, it was maintained that forty of their homes had been destroyed over a period of five years. During the Civil War the Welsh protested vigorously at having to serve under English commanders like Rupert and Gerard; the designs of English industrialists were often frustrated by the opposition of local residents determined to resist the denuding of their countryside of trees to make charcoal; and even as late as 1854, when George Borrow set out on his long-premeditated tour of Wales, his reception at the Farmers' Arms in Brynaman was most unfriendly. Strangers or 'foreigners' were people outside the family circle and as such they were resented.

Insulated as they were from outside influences, the Welsh were naturally conservative in their habits and outlook, and they clung tenaciously to traditional beliefs and practices. This attitude of mind effectively militated against advances being made in agriculture, the occupation which afforded, after all, employment for the vast majority of them. Since they were denied the benefits of satellite photographs of weather conditions over the Atlantic, they had to rely of necessity on the behaviour of animals and birds, the position of the stars and the phases of the moon, and even the aspect of plants and trees. Matters were certainly not helped by the absence of agencies like daily newspapers for the dissemination of information, and the fact that the majority of the people were never afforded the opportunity of a formal education. Even at the commencement of the eighteenth century leading Welsh writers still clung to the Ptolemaic view that the earth was the centre of the universe, and in 1752 there was a marked reluctance among the people to adopt the Gregorian calendar and abandon the old. This ignorance of the physical world about them also applied to the human body, and ailments were attributed to such causes as attacks of the vapours, the influence of evil spirits or even witchcraft.

In such small, widely scattered and closely-knit societies it was also natural, especially considering the absence of modern implements and machinery which have lightened the labours of the farmer today, that there should have been a considerable degree of inter-dependence and co-operation. Particularly was help forthcoming during the busy periods on the land such as

ploughing, sowing and harvesting, and this tradition of community support applied also to the less fortunate members of
society, the ill, the handicapped and the poor. But despite the
cohesiveness which on the whole characterised these communities, they could also be rent by quarrels and strife, occasioned by malice, slander and envy. William Morgan, the vicar of
Llanrhaeadr-ym-Mochnant, and the translator of the Bible into
Welsh in 1588, had constantly been at loggerheads with his
parishioners and had on more than one occasion to appear before
Star Chamber. In 1677 Stephen Hughes maintained that litigation was an indispensable adjunct to a Welshman's existence.
Doubtless, the fractiousness of Welshmen can be attributed very
largely not only to their isolation, but also to the fact that life on
the whole tended to be short, nasty and brutish.

Life, indeed, for so many people, was a vale of tears and few
attained the allotted life-span of three score years and ten. The
average expectation of life could hardly have exceeded thirty-five
years. Though in the absence of modern methods of contra-
ception the birth-rate was high, many children died at birth or
very soon afterwards. Sir Richard Bulkeley III, who died in
1621, had nine children but only one survived to inherit despite
having been born to a wealthy family of gentry, and in the early
sixteenth century the whole course of English history had been
changed by the miscarriages of Henry VIII's Queen, Catherine
of Aragon. There were few periods when people did not suffer
from some ailment or other, and they viewed with dread the
onset of the long winter months. They longed for the coming of
spring and summer, seasons which brought with them warmth
and growth. The manor houses of the gentry, and the long-
houses of the yeomen and the more prosperous farmers, despite
improvements in standards of domestic comfort, could still be
cold, draughty and wet. In his description of the stone houses in
Pembrokeshire, George Owen declared that 'the wall made with
lyme of this Countrey Contynueth for ever moist in hitself, and
thereby maketh all the rooms dankish and apt to Corrupt with
rust and rottinge anything that is kept in the roome, especially if
it be yron, writtinges or bookes . . . for in these buildings you
shall find the verye stones in the wall against any wett weather to
sweat with great dropps of water, and all the walles of the house to
be all weapinge and running with streams of water'. Infinitely

worse, however, were the one-room hovels of the poor, as these were abominable dwellings. Little attention was paid to personal hygiene, since it was rare for people to wash frequently and thoroughly and their bodies consequently, exuded the most objectionable odours. Clothes were never washed, and it was not until the nineteenth century that the washing of one's hair became a regular habit. Doubtless the liberal use of perfume by ladies of fashion, and the taking of snuff by gentlemen of leisure, had an important therapeutic purpose.

The food that they ate was also not conducive to good health, since it consisted mainly of bread made of oat-meal or barley, porridge and flummery, a rather monotonous and insipid diet. A labourer, fortunate enough to have a piece of land attached to his cottage, could grow vegetables and fruit to meet his own domestic needs, but it was rare for the poorer people to eat meat, though doubtless many a table benefited occasionally from the presence of a hare or a pheasant poached on the squire's land, or a fat trout or salmon taken from a neighbouring stream or river. The gentry, on the other hand, kept magnificent tables. The usual practice was two meals a day, dinner at mid-day and supper about six in the evening. Breakfast was not an important meal, and was either dispensed with altogether or, if taken, simply consisted of bread and cheese washed down with a mug of beer. Dinner was the main meal, and tables would be laden with all kinds of meat, roasted and boiled, poultry and fish. Expensive wines from France, Spain and Portugal would also be in evidence as a supplement to the home-made ale and mead. Books on the culinary arts were appearing on the market, and the reader was introduced to such techniques as roasting a hare, the working of tea and eggs, and the preparation of a plain syllabub. The method enjoined for cooking a hare would not appeal to all palates, for the instruction reads as follows: 'Case your hare, but not cut off her eares nor her legs. Then wash her and dry her with a cloth. Then make a pudding and put in her belly and sew it up close. Then truss her as if she were running, then spit her. Then take some claret wine and grated bread, sugar, barberries and butter. Boyle these together for your sauce'.

New beverages that became increasingly popular during the course of the century were tea, coffee and chocolate. The Herbert family of Powis castle, in its desire to put tea to the test, sent to London for instructions on its proper preparation and received the following advice: 'a quart of spring water just boyled and then taken off, to which proportion of Water you must put a spoonfull of Tea and sweeten it to your pallate with Candy Sugar. As soon as the Tea and Sudger is put in you must be sure to keepe the Steame in as much as may bee and soe lett it lye halfe or quarter of an hower in the heate of the fyer but not to boyle after Tea and Sudger put in'.

A satisfying meal might well be rounded off by a pipeful of tobacco, but since the pipes were made of clay, and consequently very brittle, it is hardly surprising that in 1654 Sir Thomas Myddelton should have ordered a gross of them to be delivered to his castle at Chirk.

The wealthy, then, unlike the labouring poor, certainly did not suffer from lack of sustenance. Rather did they partake too generously of rich food and drink with the inevitable result that many a squire suffered almost intolerable agony from the gout, the curse of the well-to-do.

But there were pestilences which decimated the ranks of both *bonedd* and *gwreng*,[3] and foremost among these was the plague. Unwashed bodies, overcrowded dwellings, basic sanitary arrangements, polluted water, an insufficient and unbalanced diet, the primitive state of medical knowledge, all contributed to the frequency and virulence of the visitations, and whole communities could virtually be wiped out overnight. The plague killed all but three of the 314 inhabitants of Presteigne in 1593. The town suffered again in 1638, and on this occasion the plague spread to Machynlleth, Llanidloes and Newtown, and in 1651 the inhabitants of Haverfordwest felt its fury. All that the authorities could do to limit its effects was to attempt to sever all connection with the outside world, and to confine the afflicted to their own homes, or to treat them in a pest house. A visitation of the plague would place a heavy strain on the meagre resources of a small town like Haverfordwest, and in 1652 benevolences were collected in the various hundreds of Pembroke in an attempt to alleviate the distress of the sick.

Doctors fought a very uneven battle against disease and plague since their world was almost totally shrouded in darkness.

---

[3] Upper and lower classes.

and the gloom was unrelieved by many shafts of light. Licensed practitioners were few in number in Wales, and those that did exist were sadly lacking in scientific knowledge. The common palliative for illness was bleeding, and this could be effected either by applying leeches to the body, or by securing the services of the barber-surgeon who would open a vein. On 23 January 1662, at Chirk castle, 'for letting blood on most of the servants', ten-shillings was 'paid Mistress Mary Lloyd of Bers what she paid the barber of Oswestry'. Since the services of doctors were expensive, and their remedies calculated as much to bring about the hasty demise of the patient as to effect his recovery, recourse was made by the poorer people to the *dyn hysbys*,[4] the itinerant quack doctor or even the 'white' witch.[5] These were skilled in the preparation of herbal medicines, and their concoctions would appear to have been more effective and acceptable than the cures offered by the more 'learned' physician.

Though diseases and the plague exacted a heavy toll of life, death, like the Devil, could assume many guises and beckon from many directions. Harvests were heavily dependent on the weather, and a cold spring and a wet and windy summer could play havoc with the crops as well as lead to sickness among animals. One harvest failure was bad enough; a succession of failures spelled disaster. Great suffering followed in the wake of the failure of harvests in 1629, 1645-49, 1656-9, the 1670s and the 1690s. During these periods food was in short supply, prices were high, there was increased unemployment, and widespread malnutrition adding to the likelihood of disease. In such circumstances it was inevitable that people with empty stomachs should raid grain stores and markets, destroy flour mills and threaten social parasites like engrossers and regraters.

But man, and his possessions, could also be threatened by possibly the most dangerous of all the elements, fire. The Great Fire, which wrought such devastation in London in 1666, was only great because of its magnitude. Lesser catastrophes were regular occurrences everywhere, but particularly in areas where dwellings or buildings were made of timber. Homes, invariably

---

[4] Soothsayer.
[5] Even as eminent a doctor as Sir Thomas Brown believed in witches and spirits. Vide Sir Thomas Brown, *Religio Medici*, Ed. W. A. Greenhill, London, 1946, p. 51.

draughty, were especially vulnerable since they were lit by candles, though occasionally they could be set alight by being struck by lightning. Extremely devastating were the effects of fire in the towns, with houses in such close proximity, and town authorities lacking any effective means of controlling a blaze once started. In 1643 a quarter of Wrexham was burnt to the ground, and Builth was almost completely destroyed by fire in 1690. During the Tudor period Oswestry had suffered destruction by fire on three separate occasions. The countryman, also, had every reason to fear the all-consuming flame and farmers could suffer substantial losses when their barns were reduced to ashes.

But every cloud has its silver lining and despite the hardships and dangers of everyday existence, life did have its lighter moments and compensations. The Christian calendar provided the opportunities for people on Sundays, Holy Days and Saints' Days (*Gŵyl Mabsaint*) to relax and rid themselves of their frustrations through drink, play, music and dancing. As towns expanded in the seventeenth century, so did taverns multiply; in 1634 there were 57 inns in Caernarvon, a number which had dramatically increased to 107 by 1672, and there was a similar number in Bangor. These taverns were frequented not only by the labouring poor, but also by gentry, clergymen and travellers. Within their walls could be found warmth and companionship, and in addition to eating and drinking, there was also gambling with cards or by a throw of the dice. Puritan authorities viewed these inns with disfavour since to them they were dens of iniquity. They were places where people could fritter away their substance, get too addicted to the bottle and indulge in riotous behaviour. Other opportunities for drink were provided by marriages, births, baptisms and funerals.

Games were invariably played in the churchyard, before an inn, or in the open fields. Contests of running, leaping, wrestling and throwing heavy stones or iron bars were held on Sundays and other holidays in the summer. Other vigorous games indulged in were *cnapan* and *bando* or *bandy*, which were communal games involving contests between rival parishes. *Cnapan* or football demanded great physical strength and a fierce competitive spirit, and those involved had to be prepared to suffer bleeding noses, bruises and even broken limbs. This element of cruelty was evident also in such spectator sports as cockfighting and bull-baiting. Both gentry and clergy kept fighting cocks, and the pits were to be found in churchyards as well as in the yards of inns. Apart from hunting—and a good hunting dog was a highly prized possession—and hawking, popular pastimes among the gentry and yeomen were tennis, bowls and skittles, and, for calmer moments, particularly during the long winter months, there were in addition to cards and dice, chess and back-gammon.

Leisure was also whiled away with music and dancing, and the ghostly or romantic tale of the *cyfarwydd* (story teller), who took full advantage of the credulity of his audience. After all, this was an age when superstitious practices were rife, and there was still general belief in the supernatural and magical. People, in order to ward off the forces of evil, wore charms on their bodies, and secreted them about their homes, and to them fairies, pixies and spirits were very real. Despite Christian teaching that man's destiny here on earth was determined by a Divine Being, many still doggedly clung to the belief in planetary influences, and that man's fate was decided by chance or fortune. Weddings and Saints' Days were also occasions for merriment and fun, with dancing and singing to the accompaniment of the fiddle and the harp. Dancing was an aspect of every public jollification, and companies of Morris dancers were a feature of the social scene. The practice of maypole dancing, to the music of the pipes, was also spreading across the border from Chester and Shropshire. Everywhere, itinerant bards and minstrels were welcomed, and in the towns Welsh and English strolling players, who frequently used the town hall for the presentation of their art, were patron-ised by borough corporations. The native *anterliwt* was also a popular village festival though the gentry, even those who pat-ronised the bards, never thought it worthy of being taken under their wing. However, throughout the century, Puritans den-ounced vigorously these forms of frivolity, since to them they were relics of paganism and popery, and they furthermore corrupted the morals of the people and dissipated their energies in fruitless activities. Instead the Puritan, with his strict moral code, wished to inculcate the virtues of godliness and humility, seriousness and self-discipline. To a people seeking relief from the daily grind of a hum-drum existence, this was difficult med-

The convivial atmosphere of an inn.

Bedroom of a substantial yeoman farmer.

'Friendly' rivalry between parishes—a game of football.

A cock fight.

icine to swallow, and it is hardly surprising that the Puritan message received few encores.

THE STRUCTURE OF SOCIETY

Just as it was believed that there was order in the Universe, so was it held that there should be order here on earth; and society in Wales in the seventeenth century, as elsewhere in Western Europe, was stratified, and man's position in that society was divinely ordained. At the apex of the social pyramid in Wales was to be found the squirearchy, since the execution of Essex, and the death of the 2nd Earl of Pembroke in 1601, though he hardly ever resided in Wales, had witnessed the end of the dominant position of the hereditary peers, and the next generation of rich peers were to be entirely non-resident. The base, on the other hand, comprised the landless labourers and indigent poor. In between came the 'middling' sort such as the clergy, merchants, traders, drovers, shopkeepers, lawyers, doctors and teachers. Only slightly removed from these were the farmers, the most numerous group of all, and the craftsmen who, together with the yeomen, formed the backbone of rural society. People were exhorted by magistrate and clergyman alike to be content with their lot in life, to accept what providence had ordained for them, and to be loyal and obedient to those who exercised authority over them. Social mobility was discouraged, but this was an ideal that was never to be attained. Since wealth and chance, which often walked hand in hand, were, in reality, the open sesames to advancement, economic developments, and the opportunities afforded by the upheavals of the Civil Wars and Commonwealth, resulted in the emergence of new families which, having begun to ascend the social ladder, were determined to retain, or even improve upon, their position.

A gentry group had begun to emerge in Wales in the later Middle Ages, but it was the Tudor age that provided it with unprecedented opportunities for expansion. The gentry took full advantage of an extremely fluid land market as monastic, chantry and Crown lands became available for purchase to extend their estates. The Union legislation also helped in the consolidation of estates by legalising the replacement of gavelkind by primogeniture. Furthermore, the introduction of English land law was helpful since it not only legalised mortgage, and the free buying and selling of land, but it also permitted entail, so that the heir to an estate could be prevented from disposing of it at will. To develop mineral resources, and exploit fully the possibilities of sheep and cattle rearing, the gentry also enclosed mountain and common land. The value of arranged marriages was not lost upon them, and there was considerable intermarriage between Welsh gentry families, and between Welsh gentry families and their counterparts across the border. There were, in addition, the official families who took advantage of royal favour to secure lands and offices. By these means a numerous, influential class of landed gentry emerged which was to dominate Wales, politically, down to the nineteenth century, and socially to 1914. It was the First World War that led to the splendour departing from the country houses.

According to the English Elizabethan ideal, a gentleman was well-educated, did not work with his hands, and could live like a gentleman. A number of the Welsh gentry could not live up to this concept, since many did work on their estates. Few of the gentry in Wales could compete with their wealthier neighbours in England. Certainly Sir Richard Bulkeley (d. 1621) could have held his head high in their company since he held land, spread over three shires in North Wales, to the annual value of £4,300, but it is significant that when James I offered baronetcies to all those in receipt of an annual income of £1,000, there were only a dozen Welshmen among the 200 so honoured. James Berry, who was Cromwell's Major-General in Wales in the 1650s, declared that it was easier to find there 50 gentlemen of £50 a year than five of £100 and in England even the landowner of £500 was re-garded as belonging to the smaller gentry. The events of the Civil War and Commonwealth hastened the decline of some families in Wales since the Welsh gentry, for the most part, backed the wrong horse. The defeat of the King meant that they had to pay heavily for their delinquency, and some had their estates seques-trated, while others escaped on payment of heavy fines. But while the fortunes of families with royalist sympathies became depressed—some of these had been in decline since the middle of the sixteenth century—other families had taken advantage of the fortunes of war to improve themselves economically and socially. During the Interregnum these new men were to be found at the upper levels of society, and many remained there after 1660. It was the wealthier landlord who prospered after the Restoration. Since he was in possession of a larger rent-roll, he was better able to survive the vicissitudes of the Civil Wars and Commonwealth, as his wealth could be used to employ the finest lawyers to defend him, or buy back what had been lost. Surpluses could be invested in the funds, to buy the hand of a wealthy heiress—and this was a major factor in the building up of large estates in Glamorgan—or secure a fine position at Court. While the small squire with fewer acres languished, falling victim to heavy debts, high taxation, mortgage repayments, family feuds, drink and the gaming table, the great Leviathans, like the Mansels of Margam, the Morgans of Tredegar, the Myddeltons of Chirk and the Wynns of Wynnstay, with their superior economic power, went from strength to strength, and the century after 1660 undoubtedly constituted a golden age for them. The wealthiest in their ranks enjoyed incomes in excess of £2,000 a year and in Glamorgan, between 1640 and 1710, there were at least eighteen estates with incomes of £1,000 and more. Many of the old familiar family names, like those of Glyncywarch and Nannau in Merionethshire, disappeared for ever and new names, foreign to the Principality, appeared. Within the counties, where earlier power had been spread across a fairly wide spectrum, politics came increasingly under the control of one house, or of a small group of closely interrelated ones.

According to Sir Thomas Smith a gentleman had to 'bear the port, charge and countenance of a gentleman'. In other words, he had to adopt the life-style, possess the deportment and be attired like a gentleman. His status and breeding were reflected in the expensive, fashionable clothes that he wore, and these clothes were so highly prized that they were frequently bequeathed to relatives and friends. An inventory taken of Sir John Wynn of Gwydir's clothes in June, 1616, reveals that he was possessed of a very extensive wardrobe. Apart from three black coats and two black riding coats and various other items, he had:

'Item. ii blacke velvett jerkins; two clothe jerkins laced with goulde lace, of the same colour.
Item. One white satten doublett, and blacke satten breeches; one silke grogram coloured suite; and one suite of blacke satten cutt, that came the same time from London.

Item. One blacke satten suite cutt; and one black satten doublett, with a wroughte velvett breeches. Item. One leather doublett, laced with blacke silke lace; one suite of Pteropus laced with silk and golde lace; another suite of Pteropus, laced with greene silke lace.

Item. One blacke silke grogram suite cutt; two blacke frise jerkins.

Item. ii pare of blacke silk stockins; and two pare of black silke garters, laced.

Item. One pare of perle colour silke stockins; one pare of white Siterop stockins; three pare of wosted stockins.

Item. Nine blacke felte hattes, whereof fowre bee mens hattes; and five cipres hatbands.

Item. One guilte rapier and dagger, and one ridinge sworde with a scarfe, with velvet scabbards.

Item. ii pare of Spanishe leather shoes.

Item. ii pare of white boots; one pare of russett boots.

Item. ii pare of damaske spurres, iii pare of guilte spurres'.[6]

The well-attired gentleman, therefore, wore a round soft hat with a feather; a cloak or coat made of cloth but lined with velvet or silk; a waistcoat, doublet or leather jerkin; knee-length trousers, worsted or silk stockings and leather shoes or boots. A scarf and a pair of gloves would add to the sartorial elegance, and, as befitted a person of rank and dignity, a rapier and dagger could hang from the waist.

The lady of the house, not to be outdone, also wore magnificent robes. Her dresses were full length with the shoulders usually bared. The waistline was narrow, and since perfidious nature was not always considerate in this respect, whalebone stays were used to produce the desired effect. The same styles were worn by the children, although little girls were mercifully spared the support of stays. To the Puritan this extravagance in dress was an act of indulgence to be deplored, since his faith enjoined him to wear plain clothes, without any frills.

Status also demanded that they should live in dwellings which were impressive monuments to their wealth and dominant position in local society. The élite among the gentry lived in up-

[6] Thomas Pennant, *Tours in Wales*, Vol. 3, pp. 406-7.

dated medieval strongholds, but the more usual type of house was the two-or three-unit hall house, two-storeyed with a box-frame construction. In Elizabeth's reign, Renaissance ideas led to the evolution of the double-pile plan, and the earliest example in Wales of this type of house appears to have been Newton, Brecon, built in 1582. The gentry were always careful to choose the most desirable sites for their houses and in the seventeenth century tall chimneys, impressive stairways and the general use of glass became prominent features of their dwellings. Rooms were enlarged, ceilings became more highly decorative, and halls and libraries were panelled. Walls were decorated with coats of arms, family portraits and tapestry. Their furniture reflected the most up-to-date fashions, since the wealthier gentry bought choice pieces, in oak and hazel, in Chester, Bristol and London. Their insatiable appetite for silver ware was evidenced by the silver plate, cutlery, goblets, ewers, salt-cellars, basins, and bowls which were to be found on the tables in most mansions, and floors, apart from working areas like kitchens, were boarded and covered with rugs and carpets of Turkish or Persian origin. As befitted men who had received a good education, their libraries were well-stocked, and therein also were to be found rare and expensive volumes.

But whatever the strength of local attachments, many found the attractions of the London scene irresistible. A Welsh dynasty, and the Act of 1536/43, had led, in the sixteenth century, to the migration of Welshmen in increasing numbers to the Court and City, and in the seventeenth century Wales and the Welsh reaped to the full the benefits of union with England. Welshmen contributed significantly to the administrative, political, legal, religious and cultural life of the capital, and they gloried in their British citizenship. The theatres and coffee houses, gambling tables and brothels of London became features of their lives to an extent which their forefathers would never have approved of or even recognised. They copied English ways, adopted the English tongue, ceased to patronise native bards and even dismissed as a tissue of lies the traditions concerning Brutus. However, though by the end of the century the process of anglicisation was complete for most, there were in West Wales gentry families which were still proud of their heritage. At their doors bards found a ready welcome, Welsh still passed their lips, and in the history of their native land they displayed a lively interest and justifiable pride.

The clergy occupied a position in society second only to the squirearchy and they were recruited from a very wide social circle. Most of the upper clergy were drawn from the ranks of the gentry and many held university degrees. As the century progressed, an increasing number of Englishmen were admitted to their ranks. The dissolution of the religious houses in the sixteenth century, the transfer of monastic lands and tithes to lay hands, and the acquisition by the laity of episcopal and capitular estates, had greatly impoverished the Church in Wales, and in the seventeenth century St David's and Llandaff were among the poorest bishoprics in the Kingdom. About a quarter of the livings in St David's were worth less than £10 a year. In the northern bishoprics, the position was considerably better, since they had not suffered to anything like the same extent from the spoliation of the Church. The majority of livings in Bangor and St Asaph were worth between £50 and £100 a year. Curates, drawn invariably from the ranks of native society, many barely literate, received very low stipends, and in order to make both ends meet were compelled to become pluralists, and even to hold school. They were objects of derision because of their poverty, their ragged attire and their undignified behaviour. This beggarly existence drove many to seek consolation in taverns, and they became slaves to Bacchus. Among the nonconformists, also, there were ministers of some social standing. Stephen Hughes of Meidrim (d. 1688) was the son of a Carmarthen mercer, while Rhys Prydderch of Ystradwallter (d. 1699) was a substantial farmer.

The general economic expansion of the seventeenth century increased the numbers of those dedicated to the worship of the golden calf, and particularly did Welshmen seek and find fame and fortune in London. So successful were the business ventures of Sir Thomas Myddelton (d. 1631) that in 1595 he was able to realise his fondest dream, which was the purchase of the castle and lordship of Chirk. A founder member of the East India Company, he was knighted in 1603 and ten years later, in 1613, he became Lord Mayor of the City of London. He was one of the most enterprising and astute of the London merchants who invested in the cargoes of sugar, hides and bullion seized in the

Caribbean. The voyage of Richard Hawkins to the Pacific in 1592-3 was partly financed by him, and he invested also in the last voyage of Drake and Hawkins to the West Indies in 1595-6. As the privateering war with Spain came gradually to an end, he was quick to involve himself in peaceful trade with the West Indies, and his ship, *Vineyard*, made a profitable trading voyage there as early as 1603. He was also an active participant in the colonising ventures of the Virginia Company from 1609 to 1622. Prosperity too came the way of his brother Hugh who, in his youth, had been apprenticed to a London goldsmith, a business which provided him with the foundations of his wealth. His early ventures in coal in the Vale of Clwyd proved a failure. However, in 1617, he leased the Cardiganshire lead mines of the Company of Mines Royal, and from these he was reputed to have made a profit of £2,000 a month. He is chiefly remembered for his New River Scheme which provided London with its first adequate water supply. Successful shopkeepers ran thriving businesses, and inventories of their stock provide some indication of the value and the wide range of goods which they offered for sale on their shelves. Gruffydd Wynne of Caernarvon (d. 1673) had over 600 different items for sale in his shop, while Thomas Williams of Pwllheli, in 1681, had stock to the value of £341.6s.11d. Shopkeepers, also, had interests in land, and Henry Vaughan of Swansea owned corn, 100 sheep, 4 kine, 1 horse, wool, lime and limestone when he died in 1629. Among the business interests Puritanism was strongly entrenched, since worldly success was ascribed to the intervention of divine providence. A desire to do good works, and help one's fellow men, led many entrepreneurs to embark upon charitable ventures. Sir Thomas Myddelton, in conjunction with Rowland Heylin, was responsible for the publication of a popular edition of the Welsh Bible in 1630 known as the 'Beibl Bach', while Sir Humphrey Mackworth established schools for the education of the children of his workforce at Neath and Esgair Hir in Cardiganshire. However, the followers of Mammon were also subject to a great deal of critical comment since forestalling and engrossing were two of the cardinal sins of the day. They were, furthermore, guilty of giving short measure, and well might a bard write in 1696:

'Pwysau bychain a llathen fer
a llyfrau ofer ddigon'.[7]

Substantial men also in Welsh society, and vitally important
as linchpins of the trade between Wales and England, were the
drovers. Drovers had to be thirty years of age and landowners,
and to enable them to follow their trade, they had to receive a
licence annually from a Justice of the Peace. Apart from taking
cattle and sheep to the great English fairs to be sold, they
performed other valuable services as well. They were the
unofficial bankers of the age; they carried rents to absentee
landlords, settled accounts and brought back to Wales the latest
news, gossip and fashions. Fluency in English was essential to
enable them to deal with London buyers, but many were
possessed of considerable literary gifts since, like Edward Morris
of Cerrig y Drudion, they were bards of no mean ability, and in
this capacity participated actively in local *eisteddfodau*.[8]
However, the romantic conception of the drover is very
misleading, since the work was hard and dangerous, and called
for considerable physical strength, fitness and stamina. He had
to pit himself against the elements, and be constantly on guard
against thieves and rustlers. Considering these conditions, it is
hardly surprising that many fell from grace and imbibed too
liberally. Furthermore, there were among them those who were
not above temptation themselves, and many a Welsh farmer had
just cause to curse the dishonest drover who fled to Ireland taking
the farmer's money with him. Twm o'r Nant touched sensitive
nerve ends when he advocated that cheating drovers should all be
hanged: 'O! na byddent hwy gyd yn grogedig'.[9]

The great increase in litigation concerning land in the
seventeenth century, together with the growing tendency for
people to resort to the law rather than to the blade for the

[7] 'Light weight and short measure and suspect books aplenty'.

[8] The *eisteddfod* had its origins in the Middle Ages though the modern
institution dates from 1789. In the seventeenth and eighteenth centuries bards
commonly met in inns, giving rise to the description 'eisteddfod y dafarn' ('the
eisteddfod of the tavern'). Since they were solely poetry sessions, they did not
command a popular following. The poetical output was not of a high literary
standard, and much of it was printed in contemporary almanacks whose publishers were often the sponsors of these *eisteddfodau*.

[9] 'O! that they should all be hanged'.

settlement of disputes, saw lawyers multiply in number. Most were the younger sons of the gentry, and having received a university education at Oxford and Cambridge, they then proceeded to the third university, the Inns of Court, for a legal education. Impressive, to say the least, was the rise to prominence of Sir John Vaughan of Trawscoed. Educated at Worcester School and Christ Church, Oxford, he was called to the Bar in 1630 and became a Bencher in 1664. Though lukewarm in his support of the King during the Civil Wars, he was listed as a delinquent in 1648 and his home, according to his own testimony, 'totally plundered to his greate losse'. During the Interregnum he virtually withdrew from public life, but he surfaced again after the Restoration, and in April 1661 he was returned to Parliament as member for Cardigan County. Within the House of Commons he proved a most eloquent speaker, and he soon became one of the principal leaders of the 'country party'. In May 1668 he was appointed Chief Justice of the Court of Common Pleas and knighted. Lasting fame came his way as a result of his decision in Bushell's Case that juries were not to be fined for returning verdicts contrary to the direction of the judge. His successful career in the law enabled him to extend considerably the Crosswood estate.

Though it was unusual before the Civil Wars for persons of humble origin to enter the law, some still succeeded and David Jenkins of Hensol in Glamorgan affords an excellent example of the parvenu lawyer. He was the son of one Jenkin Richard of the parish of Pendeulwyn, a person of yeoman origin. During the Civil Wars David Jenkins was a firm and consistent supporter of the King, though in the 1630s he had incurred royal displeasure for his criticisms of the methods adopted by Charles to raise money. In 1643 he was appointed a judge of the Court of Great Sessions for the Carmarthen circuit.

But the lawyer did not enjoy an enviable reputation in Welsh society. From all quarters he was accused of being hypocritical, deceitful and guilty of false and perfidious practices. His palms were ever ready to receive silver from the rich man's purse, and the poor could expect little justice or mercy at his hands. One lawyer, John Jones of Gellilyfdy, was so disenchanted with a profession that appeared to be so blatantly dishonest that he decided to turn his back on it.

It was from this lawyer class that many of the stewards, who proliferated during the late Stuart period, were recruited. Landowners were spending an increasing amount of their time in London, on parliamentary business, or just enjoying the social amenities, and so the management of their estates had, of necessity, to be entrusted to agents. Since the steward was responsible for the efficient running of the estate, the collection of rents, and the assembling of freeholders to vote in elections, the office was one of considerable importance and in consequence, well-remunerated. The Myddeltons of Chirk, between 1688 and 1701 paid their steward a wage in the region of £35 to £45 a year. However, these men did not have a good name, since they were accused of being oppressive and extortionate in their dealings with tenants. Twm o'r Nant was prompted to write:

'Rhwng cyfraith stiwardied a balchder gwŷr mawrion,
mae tenant i'w ganfod fel rhwng diawl a'i gynffon'.[10]

Unlike the drovers and lawyers, doctors were not an important element on the Welsh social scene. The ablest among them chose, naturally enough, to practise in London, and Sir Thomas Williams (d. 1712) of Llangasty, Breconshire, was fortunate enough to be appointed physician to both Charles II and his brother James. Others left for the Continent, or even to the Americas, and Thomas Wynne of Caerwys and Edward Jones of Bala were among those who emigrated to Pennsylvania in the 1680s, inspired by William Penn's 'Holy Experiment'. As a result, there were only a few licensed practitioners in Wales, and these were to be found in the market towns. Even by the middle of the eighteenth century there were only five doctors in the whole of Glamorgan. Lacking in scientific knowledge, their cures were extremely crude, and the general distrust of their methods resulted in people either treating themselves with herbal medicines, or resorting to the village parson or even the good witch.

Primitive though the state of medical knowledge might be, new furrows were being ploughed in the educational field as religious reformers and philanthropists embarked on a 'Reformation of Manners' and the salvation of souls through the establish-

[10] 'Between the law of the steward and the pride of the great, the tenant is caught between the devil and his tail'.

ment of schools. By good works here on earth they hoped to lay up treasures for themselves in heaven. Masters in grammar schools were reasonably well-paid and enjoyed social standing; and at Christ College, Brecon, in 1665, the master was paid £13.13*s*.4*d*. a year. However, their assistants were badly remunerated receiving only half of what was paid to the master and at Brecon, in 1665, the usher was in receipt of only £6.6*s*.8*d*. per annum. The Puritan authorities during the Commonwealth period appear to have been more generous in their attitude towards schoolmasters, and in the sixty or so schools established in Wales at this time, by drawing on the sequestered revenues of the church, they were able to pay salaries in the region of £40 a year. This sum exceeded by far the pitiful payments made to teachers in the Charity schools established after the Restoration, and in the schools of the S.P.C.K. they amounted to only £4 or £5 a year, though these could be augmented through the admission of fee-paying pupils. High moral standards were expected of schoolmasters since they were to be of sober life and conversation.

Narrow was the divide between the middle class and the yeomen. Yeoman was a rather elastic expression, since it was used to describe the large as well as the medium farmer, the freeholder as well as the leaseholder. Their status within the community very largely depended on their personal wealth and the impression they created by their style of living. The yeomen were usually substantial freeholders, and to consolidate their independence they diversified their activities. They kept alehouses, bakehouses and smithies; they were weavers, cobblers and tailors. They leased land, lent or invested capital, hired stock to neighbours and were cattle dealers. As befitted their economic situation, they occupied offices of importance in local administration such as those of church wardens, constables and overseers of the poor and highways. They acted as jurors in the Courts of Great Sessions and the Quarter Sessions. Those among them who owned land to the annual value of 40*s*. a year voted for the return of the knight of the shire. Their long-houses, with the *pen-uchaf*[11] for the family and the *pen-isaf*[12] for the livestock, were widely spread over the countryside and were furnished with a

[11] Upper-end.
[12] Lower-end.

fair degree of domestic comfort. They were not without some education, since post-Restoration wills demonstrate that they could read and append their own signatures.

Below the yeomen came the small farmers with between 5 to 50 acres of land on which they kept cattle, sheep, goats and pigs. Their lives consisted very largely of a daily round of arduous and poorly rewarded labour. Self-sufficiency was the keynote of their existence, and they grew their own food and made their own clothes. Since money had to be found to pay the rent, taxes and tithes, though these were still occasionally paid in kind, a bad harvest, or an outbreak of disease among the cattle, could spell disaster. As their lives were lived so near to subsistence level, rights of common such as pasturage, and the gathering of firewood, were of considerable importance to them, and these were rights which they were prepared to protect jealously.

The craftsmen were indispensable to the rural communities. In their ranks were to be found carpenters, weavers, dyers, masons, blacksmiths, tanners, turners, coopers and cobblers. They made the tools, implements, furniture and clothes which enabled the small communities in Wales to be virtually self-sufficient. But even with craftsmen there was considerable dependence on the countryside, and seventeenth century Swansea inventories demonstrate this quite clearly:

Date	Name	Occupation	Stock
1605	John Symonds	Shoemaker	barley, 22 sheep, 1 calf
1606	Edward Bennett	Dyer	3 kine, 2 horses 1 mare, 40 sheep and lambs
1618	Morgan Thomas	Turner	3 kine, 13 sheep
1638	David Symond	Weaver	2 kine, 1 heifer, 8 sheep, barley
1646	Thomas Morgan	Baker	2 mares, 4 kine, 1 cow, 2 heifers, 10 ewes and lambs, 1 yearling beast, barley, oats.

During the Civil Wars and Commonwealth many of the craftsmen were Puritan 'hot gospellers', and from 1660 onwards they became the backbone of Protestant nonconformity in Wales, since the nature of their employment provided them with

the opportunity to read, reflect and deliberate, and their daily
labour was not such as to reduce them to a condition of mental
and physical exhaustion. In this respect it is interesting to note
that in the fifteenth century, the Lollards, the spiritual disciples
of John Wycliffe, and in the eighteenth century, the Methodist
exhorters, were in many cases recruited from their ranks.

The labourers constituted by the late Stuart period about a
third or a quarter of the total population. According to George
Owen, they worked from dawn to dusk in 'continual labour in
tilling the land, burning of lime, digging of coals and other slav-
eries'. They owned no land apart possibly from a little vegetable
plot attached to their cottages on which they grew onions, peas,
beans, leeks and cabbages, a welcome supplement to the staple
foodstuffs which they bought on a generally rising market, and
which included oats, cheese, butter and meat. Their wages were
low and fixed by law, the most important of which was the
Statute of Artificers and Apprenticeship passed in 1563. In
Pembrokeshire, in Elizabeth's day, they were paid 6*d*. a day and
7*d*. at harvest time. By the middle of the eighteenth century,
labourers in Glamorgan were earning 1*s*. a day. Many were paid
in kind rather than in cash, and this practice could lead to
labourers being cheated of their just reward. Furthermore, they
had no guarantee of employment throughout the year. Theirs
was an exceedingly hard existence since not only was labour
arduous on the farms, and in the mines and bloomeries, but also
the food that they ate was deficient in certain nutrients, their
clothes were ragged and their dwelling places, often *tai-unnos*,
and built literally overnight, were just one-room mud hovels
with roofs of thatch. Occasionally, an extra room in the form of a
loft was provided, approached by a ladder. Windows were
simply apertures cut in the wall, and smoke from the peat fire was
allowed to escape through a hole in the roof. The furnishings
were extremely primitive consisting of a few benches or stools, a
crude table, a straw bed, rushes to cover an earth floor and rush
candles to provide light. Yet, despite the hardship and the
poverty, Restoration wills show that in Glamorgan some of the
labourers were in possession of copies of the Bible and Prayer
Book.

The very base of society was occupied by the poor, and wretched was their plight from the cradle to the grave. Without rights,

privileges, work or hope, they passively accepted their lot in this world doubtless consoling themselves with the prospect of better things to come in the next. The Justices attempted to find some form of employment or apprenticeship for the able-bodied, while others, during periods of hostility, were pressed into service in the army and navy. They were objects of both pity and fear since bands of sturdy beggars roamed the countryside and could terrify small communities by their aspect and presence. The Elizabethan authorities attempted to deal with the problem by means of the Poor Law Acts of 1597 and 1601 which were based on invaluable experience in dealing with the poor gained by municipalities like London. The salient feature of this Poor Law legislation, which made each parish responsible for the care of its own poor, was the distinction which was drawn between the destitute who could not work, and the able-bodied who could. The condition of the former was to be relieved by means of voluntary contributions, the collection of a poor rate and the establishment of alms houses, while the latter were to be found work. Though this legislation remained on the Statute Book until the Poor Law Amendment Act of 1834, it did not need to be used in Wales until the second half of the eighteenth century, and in Stuart times Monmouthshire was virtually the only Welsh county to implement it. In a normal parish, in normal times, there was no obvious need to invoke the legislation. Until then the poor were succoured very largely by means of voluntary charity (*cymorth*). They also went from door to door begging for bread and victuals (*cardota*), and attendance at charity schools was adversely affected by this practice. The more substantial farmers would provide a flour chest (*cist flawd*) for the benefit of the poor, and the Church, and dissenting congregations, would also arrange collections for them. But though the plight of many was relieved in these ways, for others the whip, the stocks, and the bed of 'short and musty straw' were only too often the fate that awaited them.

BIBLIOGRAPHY

This bibliography has no pretensions to be exhaustive. Only those books and articles considered to be of particular importance, relevance and interest are included. Other valuable contributions can be found in the *Bibliography of the History of Wales* published by the University of Wales Press, Cardiff, 1962.

General

Davies, R. R., Griffiths, R. A., Jones, I. G., Morgan, K. O. (Eds.), *Welsh Society and Nationhood*, Cardiff, 1984.

Dodd, A. H., *Studies in Stuart Wales*, Cardiff, 1971.

Id., *Life in Wales*, London, 1972.

Evans, E. D., *A History of Wales, 1660-1815*, Cardiff, 1976.

Jenkins, G. H., *Hanes Cymru yn y Cyfnod Modern Cynnar, 1530-1760*, Cardiff, 1983.

Id., *The Foundations of Modern Wales: Wales 1642-1780*, Oxford, 1987.

Jones, G. E., *Modern Wales: A Concise History c. 1485-1979*, Cambridge, 1984.

Parry, Thomas, *Hanes Llenyddiaeth Gymraeg hyd 1900*, Cardiff, 1953. In translation, Bell, H. I., *A History of Welsh Literature*, Oxford, 1955.

Rees, J. F., *Studies in Welsh History*, Cardiff, 1965.

Rees, William, *An Historical Atlas of Wales*, Cardiff, 1966.

Roderick, A. J. (Ed.), *Wales Through the Ages*, Vol. 2, Llandybie, 1960.

Thomas, Hugh, *A History of Wales, 1485-1660*, Cardiff, 1972.

Williams, David, *A History of Modern Wales*, London, 1969.

Williams, Glanmor, (Ed.), *Glamorgan County History*, IV, Cardiff, 1974.

Id., *Grym Tafodau Tân*, Llandysul, 1984.

Id., *Recovery Reorientation and Reformation: Wales c. 1415-1642*, Oxford, 1987.

Williams, W. Llewelyn, *The Making of Modern Wales*, London, 1919.

Y Bywgraffiadur Cymreig hyd 1940, London, 1953. In translation, *The Dictionary of Welsh Biography Down to 1940*, London, 1959.

Politics and Administration

Dodd, A. H., 'Wales's Parliamentary Apprenticeship (1536-1625)', *Trans. Cymmr.*, 1942.

Id., 'Wales and the Scottish Succession', *Trans. Cymmr.*, 1937.

Id., 'Wales in the Parliaments of Charles I', *Trans. Cymmr.*, 1945, 1946-7.

Id., 'The Pattern of Politics in Stuart Wales', *Trans. Cymmr.*, 1948.

Johnson, A. M., 'Wales during the Interregnum', in *Puritans and Revolutionaries*, Eds. Pennington, D. H. and Thomas, K., 1978.

Jones, J. Gwynfor, 'Caernarvonshire Administration: The Activities of the Justices of the Peace, 1603-1660', *W.H.R.* Dec., 1970.

Leach, A. L., *The History of the Civil War (1642-9) in Pembrokeshire*, London, 1937.

Mathew, David, 'Wales and England in the Early Seventeenth Century', *Trans. Cymmr.*, 1955.

Roberts, Glyn, *The Municipal Development of the Borough of Swansea to 1900*, Cardiff, 1940.

Williams Penry, 'The Attack on the Council in the Marches, 1603-1642', *Trans. Cymmr.*, 1961.

Williams, W. R., *The Parliamentary History of Wales*, Brecknock, 1895.

Church and Dissent

Cleary, J. M., 'The Catholic Resistance in Wales, 1568-1678', *Blackfriars*, 38, 1951.

Dodd, A. H., 'New England Influences in Early Welsh Puritanism', *B.B.C.S.*, XVI, 1954.

Id., *The Character of Early Welsh Emigration to the United States*, Cardiff, 1957.

Id., 'The background of the Welsh Quaker migration to Pennsylvania', *J. Mer. H. and R. S.*, III, 2, 1958.

James, J. W., *A Church History of Wales*, Ilfracombe, 1945.

Jenkins, G. H., *Literature, Religion and Society in Wales, 1660-1730*, Cardiff, 1978.

Jones, R. T., *Hanes Annibynwyr Cymru*, Abertawe, 1966.

Nuttall, G. F., *The Welsh Saints, 1640-1660*, Cardiff, 1957.

Rees, Thomas, *History of Protestant Nonconformity in Wales*, London, 1883.

Rees, T. M., *A History of the Quakers in Wales*, Carmarthen, 1925.

Richards, Thomas, *The Puritan Movement in Wales, 1639 to 1653*, London, 1920.

Id., *Religious Developments in Wales, 1654-1662*, London, 1923.

Id., *Wales under the Penal Code, 1662-1687*, London, 1925.

Id., *Wales under the Indulgence, 1672-1675*, London 1928.

Williams, M. Fay, 'Glamorgan Quakers, 1654-1900', *Morgannwg*, V, 1961.

Industry and Trade

Colyer, R., *The Welsh Cattle Drovers*, Cardiff, 1976.

Davies, D. J., *The Economic History of South Wales Prior to 1800*, Cardiff, 1933.

Jenkins, J. G., *The Welsh Woollen Industry*, Cardiff, 1969.

Lewis, E. A. (Ed.), *The Welsh Port Books, 1550-1603*, London, 1927.

Lewis, W. J., *Lead Mining in Wales*, Cardiff, 1967.

Mendenhall, T. C., *The Shrewsbury Drapers and the Welsh Wool Trade in the Sixteenth and Seventeenth Centuries*, Oxford, 1953.

Nef, J. U., *The Rise of the British Coal Industry*, 2 Vols., London, 1932.

Rees, William, *Industry before the Industrial Revolution*, 2 Vols., Cardiff, 1968.

Skeel, C. A. J., 'The Welsh Woollen Industry in the Sixteenth and Seventeenth Centuries', *Arch. Camb.*, 1922.

Id., 'The Cattle Trade between England and Wales from the Fifteenth to the Nineteenth centuries', *Trans. R. Hist. Soc.*, 4th Series, 1926.

Thirsk, Joan (Ed.), *The Agrarian History of England and Wales, 1500-1640*, Cambridge, 1967.

Williams, D. T., *The Economic Development of Swansea and the Swansea District*, Cardiff, 1940.

Williams, M. I., 'Carmarthenshire's Maritime Trade in the Sixteenth and Seventeenth Centuries', *The Carmarthen Antiquary*, 14, 1978.

Society and Education

Beddoe, Deirdre, *Bywyd Cymdeithasol yng Nghymru yn yr Ail Ganrif ar Bymtheg*, Caerdydd, 1975.

Carter, Harold, *The Towns of Wales*, Cardiff, 1965.

Charles, B. G., *George Owen of Henllys*, Aberystwyth, 1973.

Clement, Mary, *The S.P.C.K. and Wales, 1699-1740*, London, 1954.

Jones, M. G., *The Charity School Movement*, Cambridge, 1938.

Lloyd, Howell A., *The Gentry of South-West Wales, 1540-1640*, Cardiff, 1968.

Owen, George, *The Description of Pembrokeshire*, Ed. Henry Owen, 3 Vols., 1892-1906.

Owen, Leonard, 'The Population of Wales in the Sixteenth and Seventeenth Centuries', *Trans. Cymmr.*, 1959.

Owen, T. M., *Welsh Folk Customs*, 2nd Ed., Cardiff, 1968.

Shankland, T., 'Sir John Philipps and the Charity School Movement', *Trans. Cymmr.*, 1904-5.

Smith, Peter, *Houses of the Welsh Countryside*, London, 1975.

Thomas, W. S. K., 'Tudor and Jacobean Swansea: The Social Scene', *Morgannwg*, V, 1961.

Williams, David, 'A Note on the Population of Wales', *B. B. C. S.*, IV, 1937.

INDEX